Berit Mila
in the Reform Context

Berit Mila
in the Reform Context

EDITED BY

Lewis M. Barth

Berit Mila Board of Reform Judaism

Berit Mila Board of Reform Judaism
a joint program of the
Institutions of Reform Judaism

Central Conference of American Rabbis
Hebrew Union College-Jewish Institute of Religion
Union of American Hebrew Congregations

Manufactured in the United States of America

Library of Congress Cataloging-in-Publication Data

Berit mila in the Reform context / edited by Lewis M. Barth.
     p.   cm.
    Includes bibliographical references and index.
    ISBN 0-8216-5082-3
    1. Berit mila. 2. Reform Judaism. I. Barth, Lewis M.
II. Berit Mila Board of Reform Judaism.
  BM705.B455   1990
  296.4'422--dc20   90-30020
                                       CIP

To Dr. David F. James
Founding Chair of the Berit Mila Board of Reform Judaism
For his vision, commitment and friendship

Contents

Acknowledgments

It is a pleasant task to express appreciation to the sponsoring institutions of the *Berit Mila* Program and to the many individuals who have contributed to helping make this textbook possible. The *Berit Mila* Program is a joint project of the Central Conference of American Rabbis, the Hebrew Union College-Jewish Institute of Religion and the Union of American Hebrew Congregations. My thanks to past presidents of the C.C.A.R., Rabbis Gunther Plaut and Jack Stern, and to Rabbis Joseph Glaser, Elliot Stevens and Stanley Dreyfus for their continuing encouragement. The Presidents of the H.U.C.-J.I.R. and the U.A.H.C., Rabbis Alfred Gottschalk and Alexander Schindler, have supported this project from the beginning. Special thanks to Rabbis Uri Herscher and Daniel Syme, of the College and the Union respectively, for helping to make the project possible and offering assistance every step of the way. Rabbis Lee Bycel and Lawrence Raphael, Deans of the Los Angeles and New York Campuses of the College, respectively, and Rabbis Richard Address, Morris Hershman, Paul Menitoff, Lennard Thal and Bernard Zlotowitz, Directors of the U.A.H.C. regional offices in Philadephia, San Francisco, Boston, Los Angeles and New York, have given of their time and effort to make the program work. Rabbis Howard Bogot and Gary Bretton-Granatoor and their staff of the U.A.H.C. Department of Education, are our partners in the administrative aspects of the program, and continually work on its behalf. Ms. Lydia Kukoff, Director of the U.A.H.C. Outreach Program, Rabbi Nina Mizrahi, Associate Director of Outreach in New York, and Mrs. Irene Saiger in Los Angeles have helped build the program which follows up the work of our *mohalim/ot* in reaching out to the unaffiliated.

In addition, I want to express appreciation to Rabbis Wolli

Kaelter of Long Beach, Martin Ryback of the Los Angeles Board of
Rabbis and Levi Meier, Jewish Chaplain of Cedars-Sinai Hospital of
Los Angeles, for their strong initial encouragement and continuing
interest in this project.

The recent *berit mila* training courses were the result of
significant efforts by a number of individuals: Rabbis Lawrence
Raphael, Susan Lemmle and Marcie Zimmerman in New York, and
Rabbi Rifat Sonsino in Boston. It is a pleasure now to add Rabbi
James Mirel and Dr. Stephen Chentow of Seattle, Rabbi Ron Kaplan
of Philadelphia, Rabbi Paul Citrin of Albuquerque, and Rabbi
Morris Hershman of San Francisco to this list of co-ordinators,
without whom the development of the program would not have been
possible.

This textbook is the result of the commitment of the members of
the H.U.C.-J.I.R. faculty and rabbinic colleagues who taught in the
first years of the program in Los Angeles, New York and Boston.
Their enthusiasm, scholarship and devotion gave intellectual shape
to this book as the product of the actual classroom experience of
teaching doctors to become *mohalim/ot*. I especially want to thank
my colleagues at H.U.C.-J.I.R., Los Angeles, for their pioneering
efforts in creating the first course for the training of *mohalim/ot* in
the history of Reform Judaism.

Many individuals made suggestions for stylistic improvement or
changes in content. Dr. Stan Stead of the U.C.L.A. Medical School
was most helpful in reviewing medical aspects of the book. The
staff members of the Hebrew Union College Skirball Museum went
out of their way to provide most of the illustrative material and have
been continually helpful; Mrs. Judith Maslin, Museum Director,
Congregation Keneseth Israel of Elkins Park, Pennsylvania, shared
additional photos; the Director of the Peggy Guggenheim Gallery,
Venice, Italy, was most gracious in permitting us to use Jackson
Pollack's "Circumcision." The Jewish Publication Society and Indiana University Press graciously allowed us to include poetry published in several of their books. Stanley Chyet contributed his consummate skill in proofreading and correcting numerous errors;
many drafts of the textbooks were typed with speed and dedication
by Marian Thomas; Zari Weiss deserves special praise and appreciation for the numerous hours she spent in preparing the final copy to
go to the printer.

All of us connected with the *Berit Mila* Program are deeply grateful to Mr. Steven Shragis for his exceptional generosity in printing this book.

Finally, and naturally, the *Berit Mila* Program would not have been possible without the devotion and dedication of the outstanding individuals who have committed themselves to become *mohalim/ot* and have now been certified by the *Berit Mila* Board of Reform Judaism. This textbook is dedicated to Drs. David James and Deborah Cohen, real pioneers, and to their classmates and colleagues who have chosen to serve the Jewish People.

List of Illustrations

List of Tables

Introduction

Lewis M. Barth

This textbook is intended for doctors and other licensed practitioners who are interested in becoming certified as Reform *mohalim/ot*. It has been developed out of several years of experience teaching the course, "An Introduction to *Berit Mila*." Many of the physicians enrolled in the course have subsequently been certified by the *Berit Mila* Board of Reform Judaism. Our immediate goal has been to provide a training manual for physicians and other licensed practitioners studying with their rabbis or, occasionally, on their own. The textbook will introduce the student to the practical issues of conducting a *berit mila* ceremony and to the wealth of religious, historical and legal material dealing with this ancient ceremony. Through careful study of the material presented and the issues raised, a physician who meets the other requirements for certification established by the *Berit Mila* Board of Reform Judaism should be prepared to sit for the examination required of all candidates.

We have a broader goal as well. Many of us involved in the *Berit Mila* Program have become aware that its ramifications extend significantly beyond the training of *mohalim/ot* to serve the non-Orthodox Jewish community. In preparing the course, in beginning this textbook, and in grappling with the richness of sources in Jewish tradition about *berit mila,* we have experienced in a very concrete way the uniqueness of Reform Judaism in dealing with a central Jewish religious act. We hope that *Berit Mila in the Reform Context* will express what may be called "the Reform hermeneutic"; that is to say, the way Reform Jews experience, understand, practice and explain their religion.

The ceremony of *berit mila* is a perfect test case for this Reform hermeneutic. Reform is broad enough to encompass a rather traditional liturgical view which sees *berit mila* as a *mitzvah,* understood as "a request from God to be taken very seriously" (Levy), as well as to learn from insights gleaned from critical explorations of the development of this rite throughout Jewish history and in Jewish literature (see Section, *Berit Mila* Through the Ages). It is one of the most ancient of all Jewish practices. According to tradition, it originated with God's command to Abraham; according to biblical scholarship, it was a brilliant religious innovation and creation of the priestly authors of the Pentateuch (Gevirtz).

The origin of the practice of circumcision is, in fact, unknown. Attitudes toward circumcision have varied sharply from antiquity to the modern period. We have become aware of the curious fact that all explanations of circumcision, and of the *berit mila* ceremony as well, are ex-post facto. That fact, however, neither diminishes its significance, nor fully explains the staying power of this religious ritual. *Berit mila* may represent an act of sacrifice (Chyet/Mirsky), or of identity formation (Ellenson and Phillips). It touches the impulse to create artistically (Aron/Grossman), provides an ideal teaching moment (Zeldin), and opens up complex issues of personal and religious feeling (Cutter). It certainly has stimulated extensive exegesis of selected biblical texts for polemical purposes (Barth and Signer). Halachic material dealing with *berit mila* is extensive, and related to major Jewish legal conceptions of Sabbath observance, medical practice and concern for human welfare (Zlotowitz). In addition to the complexities of *halacha,* legal definitions of Jewish identity come into sharp conflict with sociological and community definitions of "Who is a Jew?" in the modern world (Finley). From a modern historical perspective, the forces shaping the rise of Reform Judaism have impacted on the manner in which Jews viewed their own religious practices, from a coolness or even negativity toward such practices as *berit mila,* to the contemporary embracing of a variety of traditional observances (Ragins and Meyer). It is central to the Reform Jew's struggle to understand the meaning of the Covenant in the modern world (Borowitz). The medical literature on circumcision is vast, and all of the skill of the physician or *mohel/et* is required in the performance of a public operation which is a religious ceremony (Goldenberg).

In creating the course, "An Introduction to *Berit Mila*," we were faced with the recurring question: "What do we expect a Jewishly well educated layperson to know of Judaism?" From our perspective, the same Reform hermeneutic which allows for personal autonomy in religious viewpoint and practice, wherever such autonomy leads, roots observance in the richness of Jewish tradition, and is grounded in the most serious study of Jewish sources. The rabbis and scholars teaching the course quickly discovered that the physicians who desired to become *mohalim/ot* were hungry for Jewish knowledge, exceedingly teachable, and eventually transformed by the experience from being "laypersons" to being religious co-workers. They needed to know as much as it was possible to teach them, from the tradition as well as from the Reform perspective— about Judaism and about *berit mila*.

Prospective *mohalim/ot* also need to recognize the special concerns regarding circumcision which are found in contemporary society. Within the last decade, the practice of circumcision, whether for medical, cosmetic or religious reasons, has come under increasing attack. Over ten years ago, the American Academy of Pediatrics stopped recommending circumcision as a routine medical procedure (see Appendix B). However, recently the Academy has begun to revise its position. Advocates of holistic medicine have argued against circumcision as a violation of nature. With the general concern in American society regarding child-abuse, there has been a resurfacing of terminology such as "mutilation" and "castration" to describe it. This highly charged rhetorical description has its roots in ancient Greek and Roman attitudes toward circumcision. Most recently, theological expression among some feminist thinkers has targeted circumcision as a visible sign of the establishment of patriarchy, of male dominance and denigration of women—excluded by the very nature of the act from the Covenant.

The seriousness of these contrary voices needs to be heard and responded to within the framework of Reform Jewish thought and practice. Medical perspectives do change, and there has been some indication recently of a shift back to encouraging routine circumcision. Nevertheless, it must be underscored that from a Jewish perspective *berit mila* is a religious act. Modern Jews may perhaps find it quaint that rabbis of the Talmudic Period described circumcision in cosmetic terms, as the removal of a physical imperfection to make the body perfect. More to the point are the many attempts within Reform Judaism and other forms of contemporary non-orthodox Judaism to create significant Covenant ceremonies for female infants in a religiously egalitarian environment.

Finally, *mohalim/ot* must have an understanding of the special needs of intermarried families who have made a decision to raise their children as Jews. Within the context of Reform Judaism, there is no disagreement on the status of a convert—that person is a Jew. In addition, with the Patrilineal Descent Resolution of the Central Conference of American Rabbis, the Reform Movement recognizes the Jewish identity of the child of either a Jewish mother or father, as long as that identity is confirmed by public acts of Jewish commitment. Often the *mohel/et* is the intermarried family's initial contact with the organized Jewish religious community. The *berit mila* in this situation is the first concrete act confirming the child's Jewish identity. The *mohel/et* needs to know of the various outreach programs developed within Reform Judaism in order to help the intermarried family continue in their commitment to raise their child Jewishly.

The textbook found here went through several "experimental" stages. The editor and the contributors have been united in their willingness to receive reactions and suggestions for change and improvement from those using it.

Each chapter is authored by a separate contributor, all but one of whom has actually taught in the course. In addition, the bibliography contains extensive references for further reading. The textbook also has a glossary of terms which we expect a Reform *mohel/et* to know. The glossary has been compiled from the materials taught in the course and the resources of Jewish tradition. It also contains medical terms which are commonly used by physicians concerning various aspects of circumcision. Many rabbis and physicians reviewed the glossary and made excellent suggestions for the modification of definitions.

The textbook is divided into sections, and there has been a serious attempt to integrate the material into a unified whole. Nevertheless, some repetition remains, unavoidable in a multi-authored document, but especially useful in an educational tool. Our experience with the initial "Experimental Edition" suggests that some prefer to teach and study the book going systematically from beginning to end, while others will prefer to explore the historical sections first.

At the urging of those who have completed the course, a second volume is now in preparation, which will include the complete religious texts which we have used in the classroom setting and which are discussed by our authors here. For example, the source book will contain, in addition to full *berit mila* liturgies, Rabbi Bernard Zlotowitz' translation of significant sections of "Laws of *Mila*" from the *Shulchan Aruch,* as well as contemporary Reform responsa dealing with modern halachic issues from a liberal religious perspective, and much more. To meet practical religious needs, the second volume will also provide model brochures by Drs. Deborah Cohen and Gerald Weiss and Rabbi Norman M. Cohen and others, which answer questions about religious and medical aspects of circumcision.

The publication of *Berit Mila in the Reform Context* is the fulfillment of the first stage of the *Berit Mila* Program. All of those who had a hand in shaping the program and the book feel a sense of pride that we have come this far so quickly. It was only a few years ago that Dr. Deborah Cohen, of Los Angeles, called the Hebrew Union College requesting to be trained as a *mohelet;* only a few years since Dr. David James, of New York, began to urge the Union of American Hebrew Congregations to start a program to train *mohalim/ot;* only a few short years since the *Berit Mila* Board of Reform Judaism was established by these instititions, in conjunction with the Central Conference of American Rabbis.

This book is a beginning step in meeting a religious need and filling a void. We have come to understand the crises faced by many communities and many young parents: the lack of any *mohalim/ot* in some parts of the United States, and the inability of Reform Jews to find *mohalim/ot* who can respond to their religious needs at a very crucial life-cycle moment. By the time we go to press, over sixty-four *mohalim/ot* will have received certification through our program. We hope they will soon be joined by others. We pray that this collection will present a model, offer a paradigm of adult religious instruction, and help to transform those who learn to those who serve.

Berit Mila
in the Reform Context

The Liturgy of *Berit Mila*

Richard N. Levy

PART I

THE SERVICE

The house, so hectic for the past week, is immaculate now, as family and friends arrive with toys and gifts, and parents shuttle between their infant and the guests, anxious, expectant, joyful at this new person who has so changed their lives. Older sisters or brothers, ambivalent at the attention, try to decide whether the day will be better for them if they act grown-up or babyish; grandparents, great-grandparents, try to strike a balance between handling their own anxieties, calming and assisting the new parents, ogling the new baby and attending to their other grandchildren. A new generation has come not only into this house, but into the life of the Jewish people. The Covenant in which God promised Abraham that the Jewish People would live forever is being renewed again. A time of joy for this family is also an event in the history of Israel.

Everyone is awaiting the arrival of the *mohel,* or if a woman, the *mohelet.* Traditionally the *mohel* has been a rabbi, learned in Jewish tradition, skilled in the surgical procedures of *mila,* circumcision, by having done so many of them in the ancient Jewish way of welcoming baby boys into the Covenant between God and the Jewish People. In the Reform context, the *mohel/et* will probably be a surgeon, skilled in the surgical procedures of circumcision, who has made a commitment through study and practice to turn this surgical

Illustration 1

"The Circumcision of the Portuguese Jews," engraving by Bernard Picart from *The Ceremonies and Religious Customs of the Various Nations of the Known World*, Amsterdam, 18th C. From the collection of the Hebrew Union College Skirball Museum, (66.345), Lelo Carter, photographer.

knowledge to the service of God and the Jewish People. As the *mohel/et* approaches the house of joy (or, as is sometimes done, the social hall of the synagogue or a hospital room), he or she is well aware that much more is in store than a routine surgical procedure which will ensure that this boy will not look different from other boys: the *mohel/et* is about to enact a religious rite, becoming the agent through which this family can observe God's command to welcome their newborn son into the Covenant through the act of circumcision, *berit mila.*

Before approaching the house, the *mohel/et* will have done some preparation. The *mohel/et* may well have met in person with the family before the baby was born, or shortly afterward, discussing the meaning of the service and its significance to the family. If a child is to be welcomed into the Covenant between God and the Jewish People, the parents need to know what the Covenant is, what their responsibilities are in helping the child fulfill his responsibilities under the Covenant. If they have been unable to meet with their rabbi, the *mohel/et* may be the one to begin this discussion with them, particularly since it is appropriate that the parents make some statement at the *berit* as to what the service means to them, and how they hope to assist their child to be a good and serious Jew. The *mohel/et* serves as a fine model of the importance of infusing one's work and one's life with Jewish awareness; the parents will be models for their children every day.

MATERIALS

Having arrived at the place where the *berit* will be done, the *mohel/et* will meet with the parents, and make sure that the following have been set out [medical equipment is discussed in Section VI]:

1. Two chairs are placed next to each other: an elegant one representing the *kisei shel Eili-yahu,* the Throne of Elijah (see Part II) and another upon which the *sandak* will sit. These will probably be chairs that the family will have used for other purposes all year around, but which today will be transformed into vessels for the doing of God's will. This is part of the meaning of the event: an organ which represents the most physical part of the human being is being transformed into a spiritual vessel

for the service of God; a "routine surgical procedure" is being transformed into a religious celebration; and a physician, two parents, old and honored relatives become priests at an altar, in keeping with the Reform belief that all of us are to act out our calling as "a realm of priests and a holy people" (Exod. 19:6).

2. Candles may be lit. This is perhaps a reminder of times when *mila* was forbidden to Jews, and the candles served as silent witnesses to Israel's faithfulness even in times of persecution, advising those in the know: a *berit mila* was taking place in the house. Candles are also a reminder of the Proverbs verse, "A *mitzvah* is a lamp and *Torah* is light" (Prov. 6:23).

3. A table should be prepared near the chairs with the materials the *mohel/et* requires as well as a cup of wine. As will be discussed in the next section, the table represents the altar upon which the covenantal renewal is being celebrated.

4. The baby should be dressed in an elaborate gown as a demonstration of the beauty with which the family wishes to surround their observance of the *mitzvah* of *mila* (see *hidur mitzvah* below, Part II, B).

THE SERVICE

(The order of this service is based on the CCAR book of home service, *Gates of the House*, to which page numbers refer.[1] Additional comments and rituals are noted within parenthesis ( ), traditional practice by asterisk "*".)

1. It is a custom to conduct a *berit mila* in the morning, if possible right after the *shacharit* (morning) service, as an example of the family's enthusiasm to perform this *mitzvah* as early as possible.

    (Arising early in the morning to do the will of God was a quality ascribed to the patriarchs and to the righteous.)

    *If participants in the morning service wore *talit* and *te-filin* during the service, they should all continue wearing them for the *berit;* if not, the parents, the *mohel/et* and the *sandak* may wear them. Reform practice countenances the wearing of *talit* and *te-filin* by men and women.

2. It is desirable, but not required, to have at least a *minyan-*

(which in Reform comprises ten Jewish men and/or women over the age of thirteen).

3. A man chosen as *kvatter* and a woman chosen as *kvatterin* (godfather and godmother) carry the child in on a pillow.

4. As the baby is brought in, all rise (perhaps in observance of 2 Kings 23:3 when all rose up in honor of the Covenant celebrated by King Josiah), and joyously proclaim, בָּרוּךְ הַבָּא , *baruch ha-ba!* ("May he who comes be blessed", p. 111).

> (The Hebrew word *ha-ba* is variously understood as a *gematria* for the eighth day, and as an abbreviation of *hine ba Eili-yahu*, "Here comes Elijah.")

5. "The rite of circumcision" (p. 111) is read by the *mohel/et* or parent, as a reminder of the historical and spiritual significance of the event.

6. The parents demonstrate their readiness to fulfill God's command to enter their child into the Covenant by saying the words, "Joyfully do we present our son for circumcision," adding the biblical texts: "Lord, You established . . . (Ps. 78:5-6), "You are forever mindful . . ." (Ps. 105:8-10), and "O give thanks to the Lord . . ." (Ps. 107:1); (pp. 111–112).

> *Traditionally the father, or in liberal circles both parents, say *hineni muchan.* . . , "I am ready to fulfill the *mitzvah* of circumcising my (our) son, as the blessed Creator commanded us in the *Torah:* 'Every male throughout your generation shall be circumcised at the age of eight days' " (Gen. 17:12).

> *The child may be placed by the *mohel/et* on the *kisei shel Eili-yahu* (Elijah's Throne) accompanied by the reading of paragraph, *zeh ha-kisei.* . . , "This is the Throne of Elijah." All present may joint in a silent prayer that Elijah will bless the child.

7. The *mohel/et* takes the baby from Elijah's chair and places him on a sturdy table.

> *Traditionally the baby is placed on the lap of the *sandak,* or on a board on his lap, or on a table over the knees of the *sandak* sitting at the table. (The term *sandak* probably derives from the Greek *sunteknos,* "helper," and is a role traditionally taken by a grandparent, a rabbi, or some other person [in Reform tradition, either male or female], whose character represents qualities the parents would like to flow from the lap (i.e., the loins, seat of potency and fruitfulness) of the *sandak* to the baby. The

sandak's lap represents an altar to God upon which the *berit* will be offered.)

*The father and mother may then issue a statement naming the *mohel/et* their agent in doing the *mitzvah* of *mila,* and may hand the knife to the *mohel/et*, who then recites the *beracha* in number 8, below.

8. When the baby has been placed on the table or on the lap where the *mila* will be performed, the *mohel/et* or the parents dedicate the surgical act of circumcision to the service of God with this *beracha* (blessing) (p. 112):   בָּרוּךְ אַתָּה, יְיָ אֱלֹהֵינוּ,
מֶלֶךְ הָעוֹלָם, אֲשֶׁר קִדְּשָׁנוּ בְּמִצְוֹתָיו וְצִוָּנוּ עַל הַמִּילָה.
    "Blessed is the Lord our God, Ruler of the universe, by whose *mitzvot* we are hallowed, who has given us the *mitzvah* of circumcision."

9. The foreskin is removed.

10. The parents complete the *mila* with the *beracha* pledging themselves to bring the child into Abraham's Covenant (p. 112):   בָּרוּךְ אַתָּה, יְיָ אֱלֹהֵינוּ, מֶלֶךְ הָעוֹלָם,
אֲשֶׁר קִדְּשָׁנוּ בְּמִצְוֹתָיו וְצִוָּנוּ לְהַכְנִיסוֹ בִּבְרִיתוֹ שֶׁל אַבְרָהָם אָבִינוּ.
    "Blessed is the Lord our God, Ruler of the Universe, by whose *mitzvot* we are hallowed, who commands us to bring our sons into the Covenant of Abraham." All respond with the hope that, as they have witnessed his entrance into the Covenant, they may also witness his entrance into *Torah* study, *chuppa,* and the practice of good deeds.
    כְּשֵׁם שֶׁנִּכְנַס לַבְּרִית כֵּן יִכָּנֵס לְתוֹרָה, לְחֻפָּה, וּלְמַעֲשִׂים טוֹבִים.

11. The *mohel/et* (or other leader) concludes with the blessing over wine, always used to celebrate joyous occasions.
    בָּרוּךְ אַתָּה, יְיָ אֱלֹהֵינוּ, מֶלֶךְ הָעוֹלָם, בּוֹרֵא פְּרִי הַגָּפֶן.
    "Blessed is the Lord our God, Ruler of the universe, Creator of the fruit of the vine."

* This may be followed by the prayer praising God for sanctifying the first baby (Isaac) circumcised on the eighth day.

12. Now a prayer is offered by the *mohel/et* or another leader of the service, in which the name of the child is announced, just as Abraham received his name in conjunction with the command to circumcise ("Our God and God of our people. . . ," pp. 112–113).

(The family rabbi, the *mohel/et*, or the parents themselves, may wish, either at this point or before the service, to speak about the individuals for whom the baby is being named, as well as some traditional descriptions of the original bearers of the Hebrew name in the Bible or rabbinic literature.[2] Parents may also wish to read their own covenant with their son, pledging themselves to strive for certain goals in raising him as a good, Jewish, human being.)

13. The *mohel/et* then drinks the wine and gives the infant a few drops by letting him suck on a handkerchief soaked in wine. The mother and father also drink.

> * The *mohel/et* may recite the prayer for God's acceptance of this *berit mila* as a symbolic performance of all 613 *mitzvot,* as well as a *mi-she-berach* blessing for the baby's health and for the hope that his parents will indeed bring him to *Torah, chuppa,* and the practice of good deeds.[3]

14. The *birkat kohanim,* the concluding blessing once offered by the priest (Num. 6:24-26) may be invoked (p. 113);

יְבָרֶכְךָ יְיָ וְיִשְׁמְרֶךָ

יָאֵר יְיָ פָּנָיו אֵלֶיךָ וִיחֻנֶּךָ

יִשָּׂא יְיָ פָּנָיו אֵלֶיךָ וְיָשֵׂם לְךָ שָׁלוֹם.

"The Lord bless you and keep you;
The Lord look kindly upon you and be gracious to you;
The Lord bestow favor upon you and give you peace. Amen."

An alphabetical acrostic chosen from the letters of the child's name in Ps. 119, may also be read.

> * Guests may join the *mohel/et* or leader in a chorus of *"Siman tov u-mazal tov,"* traditionally offered at the conclusion of joyous events.

15. The *kvatter/kvatterin* returns the baby to the crib; the *mohel/et* should look in on the child.

16. The *se-udat mitzvah* (*mitzvah* feast) follows, with *motsi* (the blessing over the bread) and *birkat hamazon* (grace after the meal) (pp. 6–18).[4]

PART II

THE SIGNIFICANCE OF THE SERVICE

Berit mila means "the Covenant of circumcision"—the Covenant sealed through circumcision. The name raises a number of questions:

1. What is a Covenant—to which Covenant does *berit mila* refer?
2. Why is circumcision a symbol of the Covenant?
3. Why is circumcision a *mitzvah* (a commandment)?
4. How does this surgical act become a *mitzvah?*
5. What is the role of the blood in *berit mila?*

These questions lead us to three major themes which help the *mohel/et*—who is a medical practitioner—transform a surgical process into a religious act. The themes are represented by three Hebrew words: *berit* (Covenant); *mitzvah* (commandment); *dam* (blood).

A.   *Berit* (Covenant)
   In Genesis 15:1-7, God shows Abraham the stars and tells him that as uncountable as they are, so numerous will be his progeny. That prophecy has come true: the Jewish People, with all that it has suffered, is as indestructible, as permanent, as the stars in heaven. Each *berit mila*, then, serves to bear witness that as one more child is being added to the firmament of Israel, God is keeping the promise. Covenant is thus a pact, a treaty between powers, a promise whose fulfillment is part of the very being of each of the parties. God says in Exodus 6:7: "I will be God to you, and you will be people to me"—through the Covenant, both God and Israel express their inner natures. In Genesis 15, Abraham celebrates the promise (the Covenant) by cutting up *(koret)* pieces of animals and birds to suggest, as does the word for oath *(she-vuah,* from *sheva,* seven), a symbolic statement by the offerer, "May I be cut up in (seven or more) pieces if I fail to keep my part of the oath." This expression

occurs frequently: the Hebrew phrase for "making a covenant" is literally, "cutting a covenant," *koret berit.*

In Exodus 19:3-6, Israel is given obligations as its side of the Covenant. Our responsibility is to obey the *Torah* and its *mitzvot,* God's commandments, as a result of which we will become God's treasured people and an *am kadosh,* a holy people—a people manifesting the holiness of God.

Genesis 17:1-14 describes one of the *mitzvot* through which Israel, from Abraham on, is to demonstrate the existence of *berit:* through *mila,* the removal of the foreskin called *orla.* This removal is an *ot,* a sign, of the Covenant with Israel; Shabbat is also an *ot.* It is as though removal of the *orla* revealed the sign of the Covenant beneath it, as Shabbat reveals the equally invisible sign of the day of rest. Another example of an *ot* is the rainbow, which is a sign of the Covenant with humanity. That God has given Israel invisible signs is perhaps an indication that God wishes us to develop great spiritual perceptivity.

Also included in this covenantal passage is the account of God's giving a new name to Abraham, and later to Sarah. Naming is itself an act of creation, as was God's naming of day and night, heaven and earth.

B. *Mitzvah* (Commandment)

Berit mila transforms the surgical procedure of circumcision into a *mitzvah,* a response to a command of God. In the same way, *mitzvot* transformed a band of straggling slaves into a holy nation, a people of God. Two things are necessary for this transformation: a *beracha* and *kavana.*

A *beracha* (blessing) begins with the word *baruch* ("blessed" or "praised," or in its root meaning, "powerful"). This word invokes the awesome, powerful presence of God, and transports us to Sinai, where we first heard the *mitzvah* presented to us as a People and we responded, *na-aseh ve-nishma,* "we shall do and we shall hearken" (Exod. 24:7).

Kavana means the intention to do a *mitzvah,* the consciousness that we are responding to a request by God. It is not just our hands that do the circumcision, not just our mouths that say the *beracha,* but our minds and souls fill the act and the words with the desire to do a command of God. If the parents are unable to do the *mila* themselves, the *mohet/et,* the circumciser, becomes their agent. The *mohel/et's kavana* needs to be pure to fulfill the *mitzvah* incumbent on the parent.

(Indeed, the *mohel/et's* act extends beyond this particular *mitzvah*. As the closing prayer in the *Ha-madrikh* text reads, the circumciser desires to fulfill all 613 *mitzvot* of the *Torah*, a number derived from the *gematria* (numerical value) of the word *Torah*, which Moses commanded us, plus the two commands given directly by God, the first two of the Decalogue.)

Associated with *mila* as a *mitzvah* is the quality of *hidur mitzvah*, the beautification of the *mitzvah*, responding to God's request not in the most minimal way, but with as much adornment as possible—dressing the baby in a lovely gown, using an elegant chair for Elijah, etc.[5]

C.   *Dam* (Blood)

The most intimate relationship with God has traditionally been regarded as the material offering, usually called the sacrifice. Sacrifices were common to most ancient peoples, and a number of contemporary ones as well. What differentiated Jewish sacrifice from other rites was that offerings were brought not to a partial deity but to the single source of power and form in the universe, the One God. For centuries these sacrifices were brought to sacred shrines around the land of Israel, but from the time of the prophet Jeremiah, in the seventh century B.C.E., animals and produce could be brought only to the single sanctuary in Jerusalem, the Holy Temple. Even though the Temple has lain in ruins since the year 70 of this era, Jews have traditionally believed that the bringing of material offerings to God in the Holy of Holies was the most intimate manner in which Jews could approach God. Though Jews differ in their view of the role that the Temple will play in the future, we have retained reminiscences of these sacrifices in many aspects of our religious lives—including *berit mila*. The custom of washing before eating bread, or salting bread, or using two loaves on Shabbat and holidays, are all attempts to reveal ways in which our ordinary table symbolizes the table that used to stand at the sacrificial altar in the Temple. The celebratory meal that follows the *berit* is another example of this: it is called a *se-udat mitzvah*, a meal eaten as part of the *mitzvah* of *mila*, as many offerings in the

Temple were eaten by the offerers as well as being shared with the priests.

Worshippers would place their hands on the head of the animal, or on the grains they were bringing. In effect they were saying: "God, please accept this offering as though it were me." They would then consign their offering to the flames through which the corporeal creature, representing the offerer, was changed into smoke that mingled with the invisible, incorporeal realm of God. In the process of offering, the blood of the animal was allowed to flow freely around the altar, so that this fluid through which life flowed might return to God, the source of life.

Mystical commentaries on *berit mila* indicate that part of the *kavana* of participants in the service should be that they are preparing an offering to God. The offering is in two parts: the foreskin itself, *orla,* and the blood. As other uses of the term in the Bible indicate, the *orla* belongs to God. The biblical prophets speak of circumcising the foreskin of the heart—offering the *orla,* our hard-heartedness, to God, so that God can enter in. The *Torah* uses the word *orla* to refer also to the first three years of fruit on fruit trees, which is not to be eaten, but returns into the godly cycle. Similarly the *orla* of the penis "belongs" to God and is to be returned to God.

Like other offerings, the blood also belongs to God. Part of the traditional *berit mila* services includes a citation from Ezekiel 16:6, *be-damayich chay-yi,* "in your blood, live," or, more literally, "through your blood, live." The *Mechilta* (an ancient *midrash*) applies this verse to the two acts through which Israel merited redemption from Egypt: putting the blood of the lamb on the doorpost, and *dam berit,* "the blood of the Covenant." In a *korban* (offering, or sacrifice), blood flows only from an animal that has been killed; when blood flows from a living human being as *dam berit,* it symbolizes the individual's own survival, in this world and the next, and as well the survival of the Jewish People, evidence of God's faithfulness to the promise to Abraham. It reminds us that the life that flows in our veins finds its source in God.

PART III

Berit SERVICES FOR GIRLS

Genesis 17:15 suggests that Sarah is given her permanent name by God in the same covenantal utterance in which Abraham is told to circumcise Isaac on the eighth day. The naming of girls is an appropriate way to celebrate their entrance into the Covenant. Just as with boys, the *berit* of girls can appropriately be observed on the eighth day of life. As the person who officiates over the boy's entrance into the *berit,* the *mohel/et* may also wish to preside over the girl's entrance, even though no surgical procedures are involved.

Gates of the House offers a service called "The Covenant of Life" (pp. 114–117).[6]

It is possible to use the basic text of the traditional *berit mila* service and celebrate *dam berit* for a girl by looking upon the tiny flow in the baby's early days as an earnest of the flow that marks the onset of her own menstruation, and to dedicate the flow to the Covenant. One way of doing this is through the old folk rite practiced by many mothers when their daughters began to menstruate, tapping the baby's cheek. One interpretation of this custom suggested that it represented an attempt to bring blood back to her cheeks, making the blood to flow again, as another evidence of *dam berit.*

An alternative symbol, one suggested in the *Second Jewish Catalog,*[7] is immersion of the baby, or part of her, in water. Converts who affiliate with the Reform Movement are increasingly enacting the rite of immersion, *tevila,* as a symbol of their "new birth" into the Jewish People. The medieval commentator Meiri understands a passage in the *Talmud,* to mean that Sarah celebrated her new name by immersing herself (Yeb. 46a). It is an appropriate adaptation to immerse the baby carefully in water, or to immerse only her feet, as a reminder of the *mitzvah* of the hospitality performed by Sarah and Abraham in Genesis 18:4. A basin may sit in the middle of the floor, and cups of water may be given to each guest, who may pour their cup into the basin, offering a blessing to the child at the same time. The baby or her feet may then be immersed in this water that has flowed from the blessings of all those beloved friends and family. The company might sing a song like *u-she-avtem mayim be-sasson mi-maai-ney ha-ye-shu-ah* ("Pour forth water in joy from the wells of salvation," Isa. 12:3).

As at a *berit* for a boy, parents may wish to speak about the people for whom the child is being named, and do some research on the biblical or rabbinic origins of the Hebrew name. These may all be inserted at appropriate places into the services in *Gates of the House*.

The service is over. As you leave the joyful celebrants, the ever-present beeper sounds. You smile; for the past two hours you realized you have been responding to a call from another place.

NOTES

1. Chaim Stern, ed., *Gates of the House* (New York, 1977).
2. Alfred J. Kolatch, *The Complete Dictionary of English and Hebrew First Names* (Middle Village, New York, 1984).
3. Hyman E. Goldin, *Hamadrikh: The Rabbi's Guide* (New York, 1939), p. 36.
4. A special introductory section of *birkat hamazon*, especially for a *berit mila*, may be found in Rabbi Eugene J. Cohen, *Guide to Ritual Circumcision and Redemption of the First-Born Son*. Also, traditional aspects of the *berit mila* not found in *Gates of the House* may be found in Cohen, *Guide to Ritual Circumcision. . .* , pp. 38–43, pp. 55–51; Goldin, *Hamadrikh*, pp. 33–37; or Abraham Chill, *The Minhagim: The Customs and Ceremonies of Judaism, Their Origins and Rationale*, 3rd corr. printing (New York, 1980, c1979), pp. 291–307.
5. For a fuller description of the way in which the Reform Movement has viewed *mitzvot*, as a concept and as a series of prescriptions for life, see Simeon J. Maslin, ed., *Gates of Mitzvah: A Guide to the Jewish Life Cycle*, especially pp. 2–5, 97–115 (New York, 1979).
6. *The Second Jewish Catalog* offers an even larger selection; see "Oh Boy, It's a Girl!!!," edited by Daniel Margolis and Patty Margolis, in *The Second Jewish Catalog*, ed. Sharon and Michael Strassfield, 1st ed. (Philadelphia, 1976), pp. 30–36. The desirability of a central rite around which the service is built guides some of the suggestions in the *Catalog*.
7. Ibid.

Enhancing the Ritual of *Berit Mila* Through the Use of Ceremonial Art

Isa Aron and Grace Cohen Grossman

INTRODUCTION

The *mitzvah* of *berit mila* is rather straightforward, and can be fulfilled in a matter of minutes. However, as with most Jewish rituals, a multiplicity of customs, developed in different times and places, has transformed the enactment of this *mitzvah* from a simple, perfunctory ceremony into a celebration of major significance. These customs include: various naming traditions; special clothing worn by the infant; particular foods served at the *se-udat mitzvah;* and the singing of special songs. This phenomenon of creating customs specific to a particular community continues today. In recent years, especially among Reform Jews, there has been growing concern not just with the obligatory, technical aspects of the *mitzvah,* but with its personal significance as well. In this context, the aesthetics of the *berit mila* ceremony become very important: poetry, music and the sharing of personal statements enhance the simple traditional ceremony and make it a memorable event.

The notion of augmenting through art the performance of a *mitzvah* was termed by the rabbis *hidur mitzvah,* a concept which originates in the rabbinic commentary on the verse "This is my God and I will glorify Him" (Exod. 15:2). The talmudic interpretation of this verse stresses the aesthetic of the objects used in the performance of ritual: "Make a beautiful *sukkah* in His honor, a beautiful *lulav,* a beautiful *shofar,* beautiful fringes and a beautiful Scroll of the Law, and wrap it about with beautiful silks" (Shab. 133b).

This chapter deals with the ways in which the *mitzvah* of *berit mila* can be enhanced by the use of a variety of special ritual objects. Though traditionally Jews were not involved in the visual and plastic arts to the degree to which they were involved in music and literature, there have always been Jewish artists and artisans. Wherever Jews lived, they crafted (or, in places where Jewish artisans were restricted, commissioned) ceremonial objects which added an extra dimension to their participation in and appreciation of Jewish ritual. Unfortunately, only a fraction of these objects have survived. The natural deterioration of certain materials claimed some; successive waves of immigration and flight destroyed many more. The objects preserved in Judaica collections provide but a glimpse of the cumulative artistic production of Jews throughout history.

In the past decade, an unprecedented number of artists, both in the United States and in Israel, have turned their talents towards the creation of Jewish art in general, and Jewish ceremonial art, in particular. This spurt of Jewish creativity has been described as embodying a second Jewish concept, that of *teshuva,* or "return." Jewish artists and artisans have focused on Jewish themes as a vehicle for exploring their own roots, and of finding their own path back to the tradition. Concurrent with the renascence in the production of Jewish art has been a renewal of interest in collecting and viewing Jewish art, an interest which has led to the establishment of dozens of new Judaic museums and galleries throughout North America, Europe and Israel.

The first part of this article is devoted to the visual images and motifs common to Jewish ceremonial objects. The second part contains an explanation of the various ritual objects associated with the ceremony of *berit mila.* The final section focuses on a particular ritual object, the *wimpel,* and provides instructions for making one's own *wimpel.*

DECODING JEWISH RITUAL OBJECTS

Prior to our discussion of art associated with *berit mila* and the *wimpel,* which is the one of the most fascinating, accessible and replicable of Jewish ceremonial objects, we would like to offer a guide to looking at Jewish ritual art in general. This guide can enrich one's understanding and appreciation of any Jewish ceremonial object; it is offered here as a specific aid in preparing a *berit mila* ceremony and in the design of a baby's *wimpel.*

The designs or motifs found on Jewish ceremonial art can be divided into four categories: 1) designs which have specific Jewish references, such as the *menorah;* 2) designs which have more universal appeal, such as flowers or birds; 3) designs which offer clues as to the origin of the ceremonial object, and/or the nationality of its owner, such as an identifiable architectural element; 4) designs which have a more personal significance, for example, a family crest. Of course, the categories are not mutually exclusive, and some symbols and images fit into more than one category. For example, a motif which has universal meaning can also have strong personal significance. Because in most cases we know little or nothing about the creator of the object, or its original owner, the process of interpretation will always be somewhat speculative. With these limitations in mind, we offer this typology as a useful way of deepening one's encounter with ceremonial art.

1. *Jewish Symbols.* Many people are aware that lions, crowns and the *menorah* are used as Jewish symbols; but few people know their origin, or their specific reference. Even knowledgeable Jews are often unaware that the most important Jewish iconography dates back to the Tabernacle which accompanied the Israelites in the desert, and, subsequently, the Temple in Jerusalem.

Illustration 2 is an engraving, likely from eighteenth century France, of the items in the Temple, as described in 1 Kings 7:21-51 and 2 Chronicles 2-5. At the entrance were two tall pillars, named *Jachin* (sic) and *Boaz.* Inside were an altar, the shewbread table (a table with twelves loaves of bread, representing the twelve tribes of Israel), and the sacrificial altar. This area also contained the *menorah,* the seven-branched candelabrum, which, over time, became a symbol of Judaism itself. Within the Holy of Holies, which was entered only by the High Priest on Yom Kippur, stood the Ark of the Covenant, which contained the Tablets of the Law, or the Ten Commandments. The Ark was shielded by two cherubim. According to Exodus 25:20, the cherubim were winged creatures. The *Midrash* suggests that they had bodies of lions and human faces. In depicting the Temple, artists portrayed the cherubim in

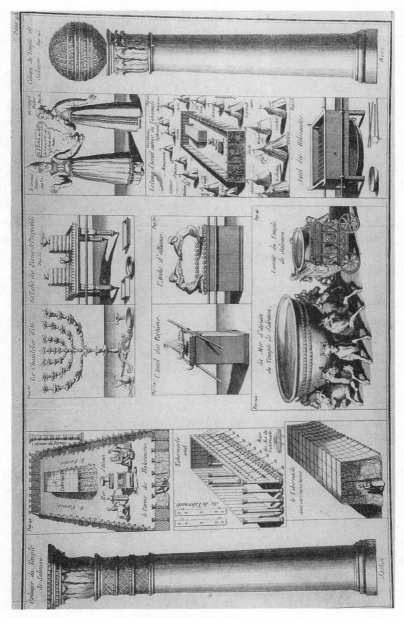

Illustration 2

"Implements of the Temple," engraving, France? 18th C? From the collection of the Hebrew Union College Skirball Museum, (66.1734), Lelo Carter, photographer.

various ways, sometimes drawing lion-like creatures, sometimes drawing winged human-like creatures. In this particular engraving, the cherubim appear more human.

The items enumerated above form the basic iconography of Jewish ceremonial art, and are found on numerous objects from different eras and different parts of the world. Some, such as the *shofar,* the pillars, and the *luchot,* the tablets, as the Ten Commandments are known in Hebrew, are common; others, such as the altar and the shewbread table, are more rare. Representations of the cherubim are very inventive, as mentioned above. References to the High Priest are sometimes found in the form of a mitre (akin to a Bishop's mitre), censer, and hands stretched out as for the Priestly Blessing. Images of the Temple facade or structure, as imagined throughout history and rendered in a wide variety of architectural styles, or even composite views of Jerusalem, are used for similar symbolic association.

Aside from the motifs which refer to the Temple, there are two additional Jewish symbols which appear with regularity: First is the *keter Torah,* crown of the Torah, inspired by the saying, "There are three crowns: the crown of learning *(Torah),* the crown of priesthood, and the crown of royalty; but the crown of a good name excels them all" (Pirkei Avot 4:17). The second symbol, the six-pointed Star of David, which has become the Jewish symbol par excellence in this century, is the only symbol which has no biblical or talmudic referent. A widely used geometric motif in many cultures, this star was first used as a specifically Jewish symbol in Prague in 1629, as part of an emblem given to the Jewish community by Ferdinand II in gratitude for that community's assistance in his battle against Swedish invaders. The six-pointed star was used as the emblem on the flag developed by the Zionist Movement and thus became a major symbol of the Jewish People.

2. *Universal Symbols or Motifs.* Aside from designs with specific Jewish reference, ceremonial objects often incorporate floral and animal motifs, especially birds and lions. The lion is the symbol of the tribe of Judah, from which, according to legend, the Messiah will be descended. Though flora and fauna are, of course, cited regularly in the Bible and in rabbinic aphorisms (such as the famous saying from Pirkei Avot 5:20: "Be bold as a leopard, light as an eagle . . ."), it seems just as likely that often the artists who created

ceremonial objects incorporated these images without any specific intent or meaning.

Contemporary Jews are surprised to find that another set of symbols which is common to many cultures, the signs of the zodiac, is also frequently utilized in Jewish ceremonial art. These symbols may have been used because of their association with the lunar calendar; alternately, their use may simply reflect artistic convention. Likewise, the presence of a unicorn, griffin, or dragon, for example, may signify nothing more than the fact that such imagery was in vogue at the time of the object's creation.

3. *National or Cultural Symbols.* Sometimes an image found on a ceremonial object has a clear association to a particular nationality or culture. Examples are the double-headed eagle, a symbol of the Austro-Hungarian empire, and the American flag. In these cases it would seem that the object's creator intended to clearly mark it as the product of a particular place. On other objects, the allusion to a particular place is more subtle. *Chanukiot* (another Hebrew term for *Chanuka* menorahs), for example, often include architectural elements such as the onion shaped domes of Russia or the keyhole arches of the Middle East. Familiarity with some basic architectural elements, such as a neo-classical facade or a Rose window of a cathedral, can give a hint as to an object's country of origin.

4. *Personal Symbols.* On the ceremonial objects of prominent or wealthy families we sometimes find symbols which are entirely personal or familial. Some examples of this are: the crest of the Rothschild family displayed on that family's *chanukiah;* a deer labeled with the Hebrew names *Shmuel* on a *chanukiah* belonging to one Samuel Hirsch ("deer" in Yiddish); a Masonic symbol on the same *chanukiah* which suggests that its owner was a Mason; a picture of the patriarch Abraham on the *ketuba* (wedding contract) of a groom by the same name. Folk art objects such as embroidered *chala* covers sometimes also bear the names or initials of their creator.

CEREMONIAL ART OF THE *Berit Mila* CEREMONY

Surveying the Judaica collections of the major Jewish museums, one finds relatively few objects associated with the ceremony of *berit mila*. These include the "Chair of Elijah," the circumcision

Illustration 3

Chair of Elijah, Rheda, Westphalia, 1803. From the collection of the Hebrew Union College Skirball Museum, (15.32), John Reed Forsman, photographer.

Illustration 4

"Circumcision Implements," engraving by Bernard Picart, France, 18th C.
From the collection of the Hebrew Union College Skirball Museum,
(66.2611), Lelo Carter, photographer.

implements, a double cup set, and a manual for *mohalim*. While most ritual objects directly related to the *berit mila* ceremony come from previous eras and different countries, there is no reason why similar objects could not be made today.

The prophet Elijah is described in Malachi 3:1 as the "messenger of the Covenant." The term covenant, in this phrase, has traditionally been interpreted as the Covenant of circumcision (as in Genesis 17:10); hence the custom of providing a chair for Elijah at the *berit* ceremony.[1] The "Chair of Elijah" is often a bench with two seats, as depicted in Illustration 3. Some of the chairs are quite ornate; others are simple. The Hebrew inscription on the bench in Illustration 3 contains: the name Yehuda Mata, who was either the maker or the donor; the verse "on the eighth day the flesh of his foreskin shall be circumcised" (Lev. 12:3); and the declaration of the *mohel* as he briefly places the infant on the seat, "This is the Chair of Elijah, may his memory be for a blessing." The *sandak* is seated adjacent to the place for Elijah.

Throughout the years a variety of implements have been used in performing the circumcision. These include knives, shields used as clamps, bowls for the foreskin, pincers, scissors, and flacons for substances used as coagulants (see Illustration 4). Sometimes, a round leather tube was used to restrain the baby. Most circumcision implements found in museum collections today are made of silver, and some of them are decorated. A unique eighteenth century German knife (shown in Illustration 5) bears a picture of a circumcision ceremony, including a figure who seems to be the Prophet Elijah.

Another ritual object commonly associated with *berit mila* is a double cup set; one cup is used as a *kos shel beracha* (Cup for Blessing) and the other, as a *kos shel metsitsa* (Cup for Collection of Blood) (see Illustration 6).

A most interesting object is the "*mohel* book," a small, thin volume containing the liturgy of the *berit* ceremony, as well as some instructions for the *mohel*. Some *mohalim* used this type of book to keep a record of the circumcisions they performed. Many books contain illustrations of the ceremony. An eighteenth century example was printed in Amsterdam and illustrated by Gabriel Voel of Almen. The opening pages contain two images referring to Jacob Hirsch, the man to whom the book was dedicated: a little deer (*hirsh* in Yiddish), and the biblical scene of Jacob's dream (see Illustration 7).

Illustration 5

Circumcision Knife (handle), Germany, 18th Century. From the collection of the Hebrew Union College Skirball Museum, (15.1), Erich Hockley, photographer.

Illustration 6

Double Circumcision Cups and Case, Germany, late 17th Century. From the collection of the Hebrew Union College Skirball Museum, (15.34), Lelo Carter, photographer.

Other images include a baby being brought to his circumcision ceremony (see Illustration 8) and several vignettes of the *akeida,* the binding of Isaac.

Finally, it is worthwhile to mention two types of objects not tied specifically to the *berit mila* ceremony, but connected to childbirth in general. The first of these is the amulet, which was used to protect both the child and the mother against the evils of the demonic Lilith. According to Jewish legend, Lilith was Adam's first wife, alluded to in the verse "And God created man in His own image, in the image of God He created him; male and female created He them" (Gen. 1:27). When Lilith's demand for equality was denied, and Eve was created as a "helpmate" for Adam, Lilith became the antagonist to pregnant women and children. Amulets have, over the years, taken many forms, sometimes worn by pregnant and birthing women, and sometimes hung on the baby's cradle or on the wall. Some amulets are inscribed on metal, while others are written or printed on paper or parchment. Like all Hebrew amulets, the inscriptions include biblical verses and invoke God's protection.

The second ceremonial object, found among Ashkenazi Jews, is the *pidyon haben* plate, a platter used at the ceremony of the Redemption of the First Born, held when a first-born male is thirty days old. It is unclear whether the infant or the *shekalim* for redemption were placed on the platter, which seems too small for the first purpose and too large for the latter. A common motif for the *pidyon haben* plate is a scene from the *akeida* (see Illustration 9). Some plates include, in addition to the *akeida,* the *mazalot,* the signs of the zodiac.

THE *Wimpel*

A *wimpel* is a fabric *Torah* binder which, because of its folk origin, and because of its role in several different life-cycle events, has captured the imagination and affection of many contemporary American Jews. The custom of making *wimpels* originated among the Ashkenazi Jews of Southern Germany in the sixteenth century. The *wimpel* is made from inexpensive and readily available materials, and creating one can be an easy, yet very special, individual or group effort.

The *wimpels* currently found in museum collections began their life as swaddling cloths for baby boys during the *berit mila*

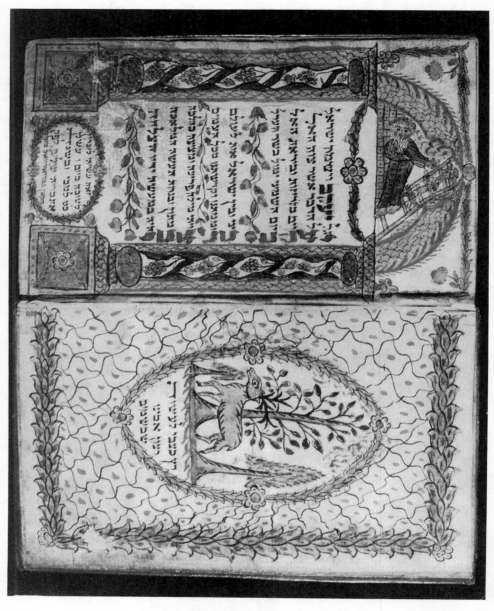

Illustration 7

"Jacob's Ladder" and deer (from the Yiddish *Hirsch* and Hebrew *Zvi*),
Illustrations referring to Jacob Hirsch, the man to whom the book is
dedicated; Book for *Mohel*, Amsterdam; Printed 1745; illustrated 1786 1806.
From the collection of the Hebrew Union College Frances-Henry Library;
John Reed Forsman, photographer.

Illustration 8

"Baruch Haba" The welcoming greeting for the baby in an illustration of a contemporary *berit mila* ceremony; Book for *Mohel*, Amsterdam; Printed 1745; illustrated 1786, 1806. From the collection of the Hebrew Union College Frances-Henry Library; John Reed Forsman, photographer.

Illustration 9

Pidyon haben Plate, Poland, late 19th Century. From the collection of the Hebrew Union College Skirball Museum, (15.36), John Reed Forsman, photographer.

ceremony. After the ceremony, the linen cloth (occasionally silk for very wealthy families) was washed and cut lengthwise into four sections, which were then sewn end-to-end. The result was a banner approximately seven inches wide and ten feet long. On this banner the mother, grandmother, or, at times, a professional artist embroidered or painted the following information (in Hebrew): the boy's name; his father's name, his date of birth, according to the Jewish calendar; and the following phrase from the *berit* ceremony:

כְּשֵׁם שֶׁנִּכְנַס לַבְּרִית כֵּן יִכָּנֵס לְתוֹרָה, לְחֻפָּה, וּלְמַעֲשִׂים טוֹבִים.

"May he grow to a life of *Torah, chuppa* (the wedding canopy) and good deeds."

Many *wimpels* are simple, but others have very elaborate decorations. A magnificent embroidered *wimpel* for Eliakum, son of Joel of Halberstadt, made in 1731, contains images from all four of the categories enumerated above: fanciful animals; a tiny baby wrapped in swaddling clothes; the child's zodiac sign; an open *Torah* scroll; and a couple dressed in clothing of the period standing under an extremely ornate *chuppa* (see Illustration 10).

Upon the baby's first visit to the synagogue, the timing of which varied according to the community, the *wimpel* was presented to the synagogue, and kept there as a birth record. On the Shabbat of the boy's *bar mitzvah,* and again on the Shabbat before his marriage, it was wrapped around the entire length of the *Torah.*

A folk custom so appealing was bound to catch on in the United States, where *wimpels* have been made for girls as well as boys, and are more likely to be kept at home than in the synagogue. A *wimpel* made in 1980 for Rebecca Bloch, daughter of Nancy Berman, the Director of the Hebrew Union College Skirball Museum, was made by Ms. Berman's co-workers at the Museum, each of whom took responsibility for illustration of one word. The word Bloch, for example, is surrounded by pictures of baby blocks; Rebecca, by a likeness of the biblical Rebecca at the well; the year, which was the year of the Egyptian-Israeli peace accord, is illustrated by flags of the two nations, and by a picture of a handshake; and the wedding canopy is an American flag. Of course, the *wimpel* abounds in traditional Jewish symbols as well: pillars, the Temple facade, rampant lions, a crown, the Ten Commandments and a Tree of Life (see Illustration 11).

The act of creating a *wimpel* can be a wonderful way for parents, family and friends to extend and preserve the joy experienced at the

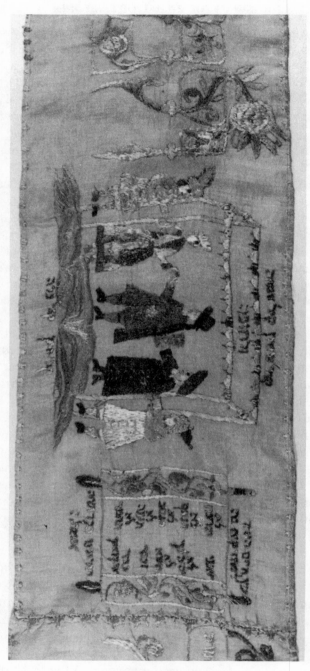

Illustration 10

Torah Binder (*Wimpel*), (detail) Germany, 1731. From the collection of the Hebrew Union College Skirball Museum, (56.1), Lelo Carter, photographer.

time of the *berit* ceremony, and to create, at the same time, an enduring Jewish heirloom.

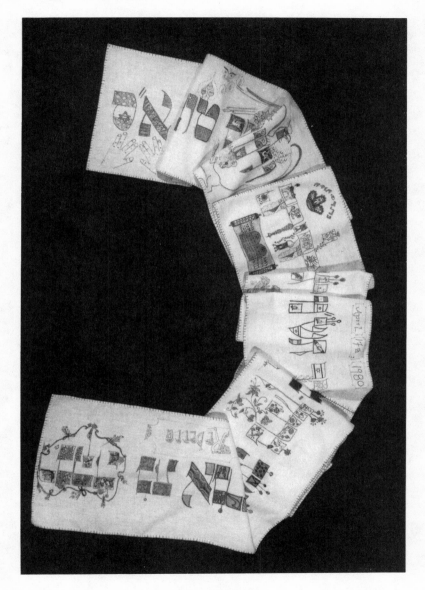

Illustration 11

Torah Binder (*Wimpel*), for Rebecca Berman Block, Los Angeles, California 1980. Lelo Carter, photographer.

NOTES

1. [The earliest literary reference to the Chair of Elijah appears in the eighth century C.E. *midrash, Pirke de Rabbi Eliezer* chap. 29. See *Pirke de Rabbi Eliezer,* trans. Gerald Friedlander (London, 1916), p. 214 and notes 1-4; —ed.]

Berit Mila
as Educational Experience

Michael Zeldin

INTRODUCTION

The ceremony of *berit mila* can be a deeply religious experience;
it can be an emotionally charged moment; it can even be an occasion which cements family ties. But it can also present a profound
educational opportunity. It can be a "teaching moment," a time in
which parents and grandparents are open and willing to learn about
Judaism and develop their sense of connectedness with the Jewish
People.

Yet the ceremony is so short, so packed with emotion, and so
filled with medical and ritual responsibilities to be discharged. How
can it possibly be a moment of education as well? Can the *mohel/et*
be expected to turn the living room or hospital room into a classroom? Doesn't the *mohel/et* have enough to worry about already,
being a doctor and religious functionary, without also becoming an
educator? It may be difficult to officiate and educate simultaneously,
but the true and lasting significance of the *berit mila* ceremony for
the family may depend directly on the degree to which the experiences surrounding *berit mila* can be designed to have an educational
impact. To explore the educational possibilities inherent in *berit
mila*, we begin by looking at some insights from the field of education that may be useful in enhancing the *berit mila* experience. We
then turn to a Jewish ceremony which is explicitly designed to be
educational—the Passover *seder*—in order to draw out implications

for planning an educationally enriched *berit mila*.

FOUR VIEWS OF EDUCATION

When people think of education, they generally think of the facts and generalizations, the concepts and ideas, that are communicated from teacher to learner. The purpose of education, according to this view, is the transmission of a cultural heritage from one generation to the next. Whether the cultural heritage is the American democratic system, the adherence to the scientific method, or the traditions of Judaism, the teacher's task is to impart as much information as possible to students as effectively as possible.

But this is not the only view of education which is widely accepted in the general educational community or among Jewish educators. Another view holds that education aims at changing the behavior of the learner. The success of any educational effort can be determined by measuring the degree to which learners have developed new skills or abilities and the degree to which new competencies have become part of their repertoire of behaviors. The teacher's responsibility is to determine in advance what new behaviors students ought to learn, and then provide instruction, modeling and opportunities for students to practice. For a religious heritage such as Judaism which is so dependent on action, in both the ritual and ethical realms, a competency-based view of education may be as appropriate as an information-oriented approach.

A third view of education focuses on the personal development of the learner rather than on the acquisition of information or skills. The function of education, according to this view, is to help learners maximize their human potential so that they can become fulfilled human beings and active contributors to the betterment of society. The individual learner thus takes center stage in any educational experience, and the role of the teacher is to encourage students' spiritual, ethical, emotional and intellectual growth by following individual interests and concerns. Judaism's emphasis on the dignity and worth of each human being and its concern for a Messianic future make the personal development view of education quite suitable for Jewish education.

Finally, a fourth perspective emphasizes that the true impact of an educational experience may result from the process of education itself. This view suggests that education serves to socialize learners into the values and norms of a social group. Medical school, for example, not only teaches medicine—it also teaches future doctors how to see themselves and their relationships to others, and how to act as doctors. Jewish education can teach not only *about* Judaism, it can stimulate people to see themselves as part of the Jewish community. The teacher's role in this view is to attend to the *process* of organizing educational experiences, not to limit planning to the *content* of learning.

Berit mila then, as an educational experience, can be appropriately based on any or all of these conceptions of education. The ceremony and surrounding experiences can include cultural transmission, the development of competencies, personal growth and socialization. The *mohel/et* can assume teaching responsibilities in all four modes: The *mohel/et* can convey information about *berit mila* and about Judaism in general, encourage the family to learn prayers for the ceremony, help parents and grandparents reflect on their sense of their own Jewishness, and assist them in seeing themselves as connected to the Jewish People. In order to accomplish these ends—all of which can be seen as vital elements in adding significance to the *berit mila—mohalim/ot* must see themselves as teachers and must keep in mind that one of their purposes is to educate.

THE *Mohel/et* AS TEACHER

In order to be successful in the role of teacher the *mohel/et* may want to consider several educational principles that can enhance the effectiveness of any teaching experience. While three such principles are described below, they certainly do not exhaust the educational ideas which can guide the *mohel/et*. They are, however, particularly useful in accomplishing the educational ends described above.

The first principle is the notion of the "teachable moment." This principle suggests that at certain times learners are especially receptive to particular types of learning. Five minutes of teaching at such moments may be more effective than hours of planned lessons at another time. With children, for example, it may be much more effective to teach a group of students about democratic decision making when they are arguing about how to plan an event than to lecture, discuss, provide readings and plan learning activities for another time. Such opportunities may arise as a result of the personal experiences of learners, the developmental stages they are approaching, interests they have expressed, or experiences they have shared. Good teachers utilize teachable moments when they arise and keep their eyes and ears open for such moments. They keep in mind their educational purposes at all times not only in the classroom but also on the playground and in casual conversations with students. In fact, whenever they have contact with students they are on the lookout for opportunities to teach.

In a number of ways, *berit mila* provides a perfect "teachable moment." Parents and grandparents have just shared the exhilarating experience of birth. The emotional "high" of witnessing the creation of new life, the hopes and dreams that are pinned on the new child, and the heightened awareness of relatives no longer alive to share in the experience, all make the family ready for a "teachable moment." Rabbi Edwin Friedman, a practicing family therapist, suggests that all life cycle events should be seen as rites of passage involving significant changes in the life of the family. In describing *bar* and *bat mitzvah,* for example, he points out that the rite of passage signifies changes in roles for *all* members of the family, not just the thirteen year-old. It is not the ceremony of *bar* or *bat mitzvah* itself that is important in this regard, he argues, but the weeks and months surrounding it. As the family is changing, it is particularly open and receptive to input that would help the family members learn and cope with the new situation and new roles that are emerging. If Friedman is correct about the openness of families at *bar* and *bat mitzvah,* what he says is probably even more true around the time of the birth of a child. If *mohalim/ot* are to take advantage of the receptiveness of the family, they must constantly keep in mind the educational purposes of their contact with the family. They must remain focused on the potential of the *berit mila* to educate the family: to inform them, to help them learn Jewish skills, to encourage their personal Jewish growth, and to socialize them into the Jewish community.

A second educational principle of paramount importance is that learners must take an active role in the learning process if they are to benefit significantly from the educational experience. A learner who sits passively and becomes a mere spectator is unlikely to learn. Absorbing information requires that the learner not only hear what the teacher says but also process the information—either by linking it to familiar knowledge, applying it to a particular problem, engaging in analysis, or using it in some creative way. Developing new skills requires practice, personal growth involves significant introspection, and socialization requires active attempts to forge links with others. The teacher, then, must plan opportunities for learners to become active in the process of learning. The *mohel/et* can provide for active learning by encouraging family members to take part in the ceremony and to prepare for it through study and discussion.

The third educational principle is that teachers are most effective when they meet students "where they are" and challenge them to stretch beyond their current capacities. The theorist most influential in this regard is Jean Piaget, the Swiss psychologist who developed the view that growth and development in children's thinking follows an orderly sequence of stages. Building on Piaget's stage theory, educators have reasoned that presenting material at or below the learner's current stage would not stimulate growth but presenting material too far above the learner would be frustrating. In order to enhance growth, teachers should present materials one stage beyond a student's current stage. By presenting new material, new ideas or new insights that are just beyond the learner's current knowledge but not out of the learner's grasp, the teacher can maximize the potential for growth.

Another way to meet students "where they are" lies in the manner in which new material is organized. To a subject matter expert, information makes the most sense when it is organized in a logical and coherent fashion. However, logical organization may not be the best for novice learners; learners learn best when the material is organized "psychologically." What this means is moving from the familiar to the unfamiliar, from the concrete to the abstract, from the personal to the impersonal.

Mohalim/ot who are preparing to make *berit mila* an educational experience may therefore wish to take notice of the family's current state of Jewish knowledge and commitment in order to challenge them to stretch beyond where they are. *Mohalim/ot* may also want to consider how to arrange the *berit mila* in such a way that it is "psychologically" organized from the learner's point of view. This may require drawing on the family's current familiarity with Jewish ritual, the use of concrete symbols, and beginning with their own personal experiences of Judaism.

These three educational principles, then, capitalizing on the "teachable moment," encouraging active involvement in the learning process, and meeting learners "where they are," can guide the *mohel/et* in preparing educational opportunities presented by *berit mila*. With these principles in mind, the *mohel/et* can remain attuned to some of the ways in which teachers effectively accomplish their purposes—of informing, teaching skills, enhancing growth and/or socializing.

AN EDUCATIONAL RITUAL: THE *Seder* AS MODEL

The question still remains, however, how to plan the ceremony of *berit mila* so that it can be maximally educational. Obviously, the medical and ceremonial aspects of *berit mila* are uppermost in the minds of the *mohel/et* and the family. How is it possible to accomplish educational purposes utilizing educational principles while focusing on the performance of a ritual? Jewish tradition provides the perfect model for accomplishing ritual and education simultaneously—the Passover *seder*. A brief analysis of the seder from an educational perspective—looking at the issues of rationale, content, method and approach to learners—will provide some simple guidelines for planning the *berit mila* ceremony as both ritual and educational experience.

Rationale. Why do we have a *seder?* On one level, the intention of the *seder* is to tell a story. The custom of the *seder* is a response to the biblical verse, "And you shall tell your children on that day saying, 'It is because of what the Lord did for me when I went free from Egypt.'" (Exod. 13:8). The *seder* is guided by the *Hagada,* which means "telling," and the major part of the *seder* is devoted to the *magid,* which also means "telling," the actual recitation of the story of the Exodus.

On another level, however, this recounting of the story of the formative moments in the Jewish experience has a greater significance. Its retelling is designed to speak to us in a very powerful way, conveying to us a very particular message: "Identify with the Jewish People!" At the conclusion of the story, after we have heard about the Exodus, and after we have reviewed all of the formative experiences in our People's history in the *"Dayenu"* song, we read these words: "In every generation, each person should feel as though he himself had gone forth from Egypt, as it is written:

'And you shall explain to your child on that day, it is because of what the Lord did for me when I, *myself,* went forth from Egypt.'" (Exod. 13:8). The story we have just read is not to be viewed as an abstract tale of another time and place; we are to see it as our story. We are to become part of it and involve ourselves in it. We are to see the Jewish story as our own personal history. We are to fuse our identity with our People's identity—the Jewish past, present and future.

This too is the purpose of *berit mila.* It is a time for the family to declare: "Our People's past is our past; and our People's future is our future." It is a moment for the family to affirm its identification with the Jewish People, its willingness to share in its fate and to participate in its future. If the *berit mila* is a lesson, the ultimate goal of the lesson plan is to encourage the parents and grandparents of the newborn to connect or re-connect with the Jewish People.

Content.   To accomplish a goal and to convey a message, a lesson plan requires content organized around a theme. The theme of the *seder* is expressed at the beginning of the *magid,* before the retelling of the story commences. Lest anyone miss the major concept expressed by the story, the *Hagada* makes it clear: "Our history moves from slavery toward freedom. Our narration begins with degradation and rises to dignity. Our service opens with the rule of evil and advances toward the kingdom of God." While the story opens on a rather dejected note, it moves towards optimism, towards hope, towards a sense of potential for the future. This optimism is given concrete expression in the welcoming of Elijah, the harbinger of the Messianic Age, near the end of the *seder.*

The theme of *berit mila,* too, is one of hope. What more hopeful moment is there than the birth of a new life, one with unlimited potential, one which will stretch far into the future? In the life of a new child rest all the hopes and dreams of parents and grandparents; all their most precious values are expressed through the life of the child. Just as we welcome Elijah at the seder, so too we reserve a seat for him at the *berit mila.* We concretize the hopeful message of the lesson plan by making sure that the symbol of the ultimate fulfillment of human dreams is present.

Methods.   The seder employs a variety of methods to make sure that the message of the *Hagada* is successfully conveyed. First, the *seder* is designed to arouse curiosity. It begins by marking off the time as special. The frantic preparations are completed and the lighting of the candles signifies the beginning of sacred time. The four questions, to be asked by the youngest child, express four curiosities we may all sense about the *seder*. (There are not, in fact, four distinct questions. One question, "Why is this night different from all other nights?" is followed by four curious examples of differences.) The constant repetition of the number four (four questions, four types of children, four cups of wine) are cause for wondering.

In addition to arousing curiosity, the *seder* is designed to elicit participation by everyone present—through singing, reading, performing rituals and tasting. The *Hagada* includes not only the description of the Exodus, but the interpretations of rabbis centuries later and descriptions of their experiences of participating in the *seder*. Many modern *hagadot* also include modern interpretations and contemporary experiences. The layering of meanings as discovered and expressed by different generations invites—and in fact challenges—readers to find their own meanings and sense of contemporary relevance in the *seder*. Thus the *seder* is participatory both in a physical and an intellectual sense.

The *seder* also includes straightforward teaching, the didactic conveying of information. According to the rabbis, one who has not discussed the meanings of its three main symbols—*pesach,* the paschal lamb; *matsa,* the unleavened bread; and *maror,* the bitter herbs—has not really participated in a *seder*. So the leader of the *seder* holds up each symbol in turn as their meanings are read or discussed.

Finally, the *seder* concludes in a very specific way which is designed to review and reinforce its major theme. At the very end, those gathered around the table read or sing, "Next year in Jerusalem." This statement symbolizes Jewish hopefulness for a brighter collective future for the Jewish People and for humanity. The Jerusalem we wish for is a spiritual one, not the physical Jerusalem, and by recalling it at the end of the *seder*, we once again emphasize that our hope is for a better tomorrow and our responsibility is to try to make the future a reality.

The *berit mila* ceremony can be planned to take advantage of the educational methods which make the *seder* successful. The *seder* piques curiosity in part by setting off the *seder* experience as different and special. The moments of the *berit mila* ceremony similarly can be set aside, perhaps by the lighting of candles. Certainly "*baruch ha-ba,*" "Blessed is he who enters," the traditional opening of the *berit mila*, serves to set aside the ceremony as a special moment in time.

Just in case anyone at a *seder* failed to notice how different the setting is from other dinners, early in the ceremony the four questions point out the differences. It makes sense to introduce an element of curiosity early in the *berit mila* ceremony as well, perhaps by pointing out some of the unique aspects of the ritual, or perhaps by raising the question—but not answering it right away—of how rituals make the *berit mila* different from an ordinary hospital circumcision.

Family and friends present at the *berit mila* can be involved actively in the ceremony, just as they are at the *seder* table. They can participate in the recitation of blessings, for example the *Shehechiyanu* and the blessing over wine, both of which are familiar to many Jews. They can taste wine along with the child. And they can be invited to find their own meanings in the ritual of circumcision and in the ceremony itself. Parents and grandparents in particular can be invited to explain, as part of the ceremony, why they find the *berit mila* significant for them as individuals and as a family.

The conveying of information, as occurs during the *seder*, can be accomplished in many ways during the *berit mila*. Before the ceremony, the *mohel/et* can explain some of the customs and rituals of *berit mila* as well as their origins and their contemporary significance. After the circumcision, the parents can speak about the name they have chosen for their child. They can explain the meaning of the name, its significance in the family's history, and why they have chosen the name.

And the closing of the *seder*, emphasizing hopefulness, can be imitated in the *berit mila* ceremony by using the closing formula of the ceremony as closure to the educational experience. Near the end of the ceremony, we read the lines, "May this little one grow and become big. As he has entered into the Covenant, so may he live a life of *Torah,* committed to the Jewish People, a life of *chuppa,* establishing a fine home, and a life of *ma-asim tovim* (good deeds), dedicated to leaving the world better for his having lived in it." It would be appropriate at this time to invite family and friends to share their hopes and dreams for the child as Jew and as human being, ending the ceremony on a note of hopefulness and re-emphasizing the importance of connection to the Jewish People.

Approach to learners. The approach to learners which the *Hagada* takes is stated quite explicitly just before the telling of the story, in the section on the "Four Children." Four kinds of children are described, and parents are instructed to tell each of them the story of Passover in a different way. The *Hagada* thus recognizes that each person is a different kind of learner and each has a different connection to the Jewish People. In order to reach each of the different types of People, a different approach is needed.

The wise child asks, "What are the precepts, laws, and obser- vances which the Lord our God commanded us?" The wise person is the one who really wants to know, the one who is already con- nected to the Jewish People and now seeks information. The *Hagada* suggests teaching this person about the laws and customs of the *seder* in great detail. The family that approaches *berit mila* as the wise child approaches the *seder* is already connected to Judaism. This family is now ready to add substance to commitment, and *mohalim/ot* can educate effectively by teaching some of the details about circumcision they have learned in their studies of Judaism and *berit mila*. Following the example of the *Hagada,* we might say that for this family it is substantive information about Jewish practice that will strengthen their ties to the Jewish People.

The wicked child is quite different. The wicked child asks, "What is this observance to *you?*" The *Hagada* continues, "Since he says 'to *you*' and not 'to us,' he rejects essentials of our faith: the unity of God and the community of Israel." To this child the *Hagada* sug- gests that we respond, "It is because of what the Lord did for *me* when *I* went forth from Egypt—'for *me*,' that is, and not 'for *you*.' " For the wicked child, the best pedagogy, if indeed there is any pedagogy at all that can be effective, is to speak in very personal terms, emphasizing one's own positive involvement in the Jewish experience. Many families approach *berit mila* from a perspective similar to that of the wicked child. Only reluctantly have they decided to have a ritual circumcision for their child, often respond- ing more to outside pressure than their own inner conviction. To these families, a personal approach may be best. *Mohalim/ot* can explain their own attraction to Jewish life and their own commit- ment to the Jewish People. In particular, doctors can explain why they have chosen to become *mohalim/ot*, functionaries who turn an ordinary medical procedure into a significant religious one. The power of personal example may stimulate the family to seek ties to the Jewish People.

The third child is the simple child who asks, "What is this?" To this child, the *Hagada* suggests we answer, "With a mighty arm God freed us from Egypt, from the house of bondage." The simple child is overwhelmed; so much is happening, so much is different. He or she has no idea what it is all about, so we are directed to give a simple, straightforward answer. This is the same kind of answer we give our children when they ask, "Where do babies come from?"—the simplest answer, factual but not overburdened with details. The details that fascinate the wise child are beyond the grasp of the child so overwhelmed by newness. Most families are at least somewhat like the simple child, dazzled by the newness of the baby. Particularly first-time parents may find the whole experience of birth overwhelming. The goal of the *mohel/et* is to help establish connections between the family and their Jewishness in the simplest terms possible. A simple explanation of the fact that *berit mila* is the first sign of the child's connection to the Jewish People may suffice.

The challenge of the fourth child may be the greatest of all. This child is unable to ask any questions at all. The *Hagada* tells us, "You must begin yourself, as it is written, 'This is because of what the Lord did for me when I went free from Egypt.'" This child is unaware that anything special or important is taking place. To reach this child, the parent is directed to take the initiative, and to start out in the most basic way possible. The family who approaches *berit mila* without a sense of the significance of the event can be approached personally by the *mohel/et*. *Mohalim/ot* can take the initiative by explaining their own first steps towards recognizing the importance of their Jewishness. The personal example of the *mohel/et* may be the most powerful teacher.

With all four types of families, *mohalim/ot* can use a variety of techniques to enrich the *berit mila* ceremony. Since they may not have enough contact with families before the ceremony to know for sure what type of connection family members have to Judaism, *mohalim/ot* may want to combine various approaches in the ceremony. This may include details about the ceremony, descriptions of their own personal Jewish growth, a simple explanation of how *berit mila* ties them and their child to Judaism, and personal modeling of their Jewishness. They can use the methods of arousing curiosity, involving all those present, conveying information and concluding with hopes for the future to turn the *berit mila* into a ceremony that is both ritual and educational. By doing so, *mohalim/ ot* can add meaning to the ceremony for all those present, can capitalize on the hopefulness which typically accompanies the birth of a new child, and can help the families strengthen their Jewish identities and forge stronger connections to the Jewish People. These, after all, are among the most important purposes of *berit mila*.

Berit Mila as Religious Poetic Metaphor

William Cutter

Covenants have unique meaning for physicians. The trust between doctors and patients involves a kind of covenant growing from the basic needs of clients who face a professional armed with mysterious procedures and some influences over life and death. Doctors must communicate a feeling that they can be trusted with the precious life which is being handed over. Their methods make for special authority and may even create confidence in their power. But the methods can also frighten people and can distance them into confusion and distrust.

These comments are designed to urge us to see the *berit mila* experience as a symbol for an agreement that should inform this fragile relationship at all times. It is appropriate that some doctors might choose to participate in the Jewish ceremony which most symbolizes covenantal relationships: the *berit mila*. Armed with circumcision kits, and with the Jewish sensibilities that elevate the surgical contexts to a religious level, *mohalim/ot* take on an additional burden that is more subtle and more elusive than many of the problems faced by a student in medical school. That burden is: How can spirit and body fuse in this medical service, and how can medical technique be part of worship?

In this chapter, spiritual concerns will be linked to the inspired educational ideas of Michael Zeldin. As a way to get to the spiritual questions, I have chosen selections from modern Hebrew poetry which reflect on covenants and on the elements within covenants which have preoccupied *mohalim* throughout the generations.

Covenant is our subject in yet another way. All educational experiences and all ceremonies are grounded in a kind of agreement. People must agree as to what words and gestures mean, before communication begins. This rather obvious notion is actually more beguiling than may first appear, and all manner of literature has been written about the complexity of such covenants. For example, T. Carmi, the contemporary Israeli poet, wrote puckishly of the way in which art itself encourages a mistrust: "Everyone is a poet/ meaning one thing and saying another; saying one thing/and meaning . . ."[1] Poets join doctors and teachers, it seems, in being objects of mistrust. But the poem suggests something further by its open-ended line: it suggests that meaning goes on and on beyond the specific and obvious sense. On the one hand, there is always the danger of saying one thing while meaning another; on the other hand, there exists the hope of developing many meanings out of one sentence.

Teachers, rabbis and doctors are connected in yet another and more vital way. There is a short sermon from the Hasidic rabbi of the early eighteenth century, Nachman of Bratslav, which always surprises me for its insistence that rabbi and doctor are related:

> Everyone needs to seek a proper teacher, who can explain the higher intelligence, that is the apprehension of God. And one needs for this task a very, very great rabbi, who can explain such intelligence by way of our lower intelligence, so the little people can understand [the great thing]. And the littler one is, and the further from God, the more one needs an even greater rabbi. It was this way when Israel was at its lowest *madrega* [level, step], that is, in Egypt. Sunk in the forty gates of impurity, they needed the greatest teacher ever, Moses. For the smaller and further one is, the greater the teacher who is needed. . . . The sicker a patient is, the greater the doctor he needs; . . . and the more the sick person is aware of his illness, the more he is aware of the quality of the doctor he needs.[2]

Some modern thinkers have even argued that the role of the priest, rabbi and minister has been taken over by the role of the physician because of that very technical information which doctors must have. A French philosopher points out that in our technological time the obscurities of our civilization are no longer the property of the religious people who once held the keys to secret and special information, but they are in the hands of the people who understand better the technical mysteries of the universe.[3] Equally so, doctors and teachers may be alike because their clients are needy.

In addition to the secret and mysterious skills which doctors possess, they share with rabbis a secret and special language. Doctors may be more justified in keeping their professional secrets; but to some extent, doctors can gain from that sharing, too. Doctors and rabbis have a tendency to talk about important things in an arcane and professional way. But when rabbis decide to share some of that special language with their people, an entirely new kind of participation takes place. It is appropriate that physicians enhance their priestly function by combining their technical know-how with the religious values of an ancient tradition. Although that tradition remains secret to many people, and full of surprises, it is teachable; and a part of what we set out to do on the occasion of a *berit mila* ceremony is to educate the participants to the notion of *berit,* and bring them to the special language of the Jewish People. Doctors, in other words, may be encouraged to shed some of their secrets in the interest of taking on one rabbinic function as the bearer of information that is to be shared. Indeed, the secrets and the surprises can be marshalled to add to the "teachability" of Jewish ideas on this occasion, and to bringing more people to the secret pleasures of the Covenant. There is nothing more improbable and few things more important than professionals and clients acknowledging their shared destinies. This poem by Dan Pagis sees the issue as an encounter between a young boy and a portrait painter:

THE PORTRAIT

The little boy
keeps fidgeting,
it's hard for me to catch the line
of his profile.
I draw one line
and his wrinkles multiply,
dip my brush
and his lips curl, his hair whitens,
his skin, turned blue, peels from his bones. He's gone.
The old man is gone, And I,
whither shall I go?[4]

Imagine the evening before you perform the *berit mila* service. The parents are tired and anxious as the child has just moved into their home. Their happiness is confused. The grandparents may be pressing a little bit for this or that element in the ceremony; questions about the buffet table overwhelm spiritual attention. If the grandparents are not living, their absence is felt as an overpowering presence. The baby is not quite settled in; and, if the baby is a boy, he is about to undergo surgery. Everyone may be on edge. But it may actually be a good teaching moment, because—being on edge—everyone is also alert. Such alertness can be changed from a diversion into a sharpened atmosphere and a readiness to learn something new. One needs only some sense of what we might want to teach, and how we might best teach it. The contemporary poet, Natan Zach, urges this kind of tautness in our thinking about what to say:

THE PROBLEM
The problem, of course, is to form a shape
like a diamond, but also like a wide bed
where you can stretch out your limbs
without banging your head on the wall
and like a taut string
with no dusty corners.
What we're destined to say
we say with dubious fluency;
what one wants to say
is often said between the lines;
but what one strives to say
remains unsaid, as if destined.[5]

Michael Zeldin proposes that good teaching moves from the concrete to the abstract. Good teachers have those instincts, and good priests do as well. There are ritual events in the lives of people which then serve as touchstones for communication about the more abstract things like values, ideals and beliefs. One poem I love creates a whole world from one twig. It too, comes from T. Carmi:

In The Cafe

What are you doing,
a child asks.

He aims a twig at me
and says

I'm shooting.
I show him your name.

I aim your name
at my heart

(after all, he's a little boy)
and say nothing.[6]

The three concrete parts of the *berit mila* ceremony, the three hopes for the child, serve as concrete opportunities to explore abstract ideas, and many personal meanings. They ought to be utilized in every ceremony. We note that the child will grow into a life of *Torah* (meaning study), *chuppa* (meaning marriage), and *ma'asim tovim* (meaning good acts).

But even before we consider study, marriage and good deeds, we might want to reflect on one of the first things parents think about when a baby is born: What will be the baby's name? Earlier in this century, the poet Zelda offered some thought on the importance of naming. Zelda, herself an observant Jew, had nonetheless a sense of the irony of naming, and an awareness of the way in which life's events add to our names:

Every man has a name
which God gave him,
and which his mother and father gave him
Everyone has a name
Given by his height, and the way of his smile,
and which the weaver gave.[7]

The poem continues to speak of names a person has, given by mountains, stars, neighbors, enemies, work and other aspects of his or her life and death.

Perhaps the words of this poem also cause us to reflect about the role of spiritual leaders in helping the parents of baby girls enter the Covenant. What shall we do with the idea that every "man" has a name? Shall we re-translate that idea into "every person" has a name? If so, why? And if not, why not? There is no instance today in which an educator does not have to ask the question: "What shall I do about women in this case?" It is the kind of question that our tradition is used to asking; but it is a tougher question for *Torah* study as time goes on. Yet it is native to *Torah*, with its constant demands to interpret anew. I like to think that it is the tradition of reading and interpreting the *Torah* that keeps us moving forward; and which will give us ways of addressing women. And so I personally revere, perhaps most of all, the centrality of *Torah* in the ceremony of circumcision.

Torah is partially about the obligation of language, which is the native stuff of poetry. *Torah* represents the effort to try to understand the world through communication with others; to try to heal through communication; to believe that words have a great deal to do with the health of individuals and society. Rabbis see the importance of words especially at times of death, when families are so eager to have us "say the right thing" about the deceased. But we should be no less aware of words at the time of birth.

Torah was never earned easily. For the classic modern Hebrew poet, Bialik, the House of Study was sometimes a burden: "They have all been carried away by a new spirit," his *Talmud* student laments, "dragged to the light of enlightenment, leaving me a tender dove under the wings of God's presence."[8] Yet Bialik, and most Hebrew poets after him, enlivened the old words of *Torah* by locating them within modern poems set in contemporary life in its many manifestations: on the kibbutz, in the city, and even in the privacy of the lovers' room. In modern Israeli poetry, we find instance after instance in which old thoughts live in new contexts; in which old words come alive on the streets of Israel's cities. As the Israeli novelist, Aharon Meged, mused: "Hebrew had to come into the house like a noble aristocratic princess, adorned with jewels and clad in purple, and do all the domestic work, soil her hands, break her back cooking . . ."[9] And it appears that poetry has been the vehicle for making the words of *Torah* function in its contemporary meanings.

Note this poem from Abraham Shlonsky, the great poet and translator of Israel's Third *Aliya* (1920s to early 1930s): "Dress me, pious mother, in a glorious coat of many colors, and with dawn lead me to toil. My land is wrapped in *talit*—light, houses stand out like boxes of *tefilin.*''[10] The ancient covenantal words have been recast into the vocabulary of farmer. The poem challenges us to find the new meanings which these old words carry into our technical and industrial culture.

The *berit mila* ceremony, then, is a time for reminding everyone that the present is made up of the past, and that the classic which has informed Jewish tradition must continue to live through combining the old words with the new.

And here is where you, the *mohel/et*, have an obligation to do some thinking about language, thinking which is frankly too big a project for new parents and for which they need you to solve their problems. What, indeed, do all these Jewish words mean in their new context? Do you mean something other than what is said? Or put in the words of another poet: What do they mean in their silences? Whatever you decide about Jewish language and its words like "faith," "covenants," and "God," one thing is going to matter a great deal—and that is the meaning of the name of the child. It too may mean many things: It may only have a sound the parents like; or it may be in memory of someone beloved in the family (more likely it will recall several and varied things about those ancestors). But it can also associate to an historical figure from the *Torah*, and whatever connections exist, it is the task of the *mohel/et* to make them live. The child's name can become one of the ways of rereading *Torah*. That is, we can reflect on the biblical story when we think of names like David, Benjamin or Samuel.

Let us also talk about marriage since that is the event that brought this life into being in the first place. What kind of marriage shall we recall at this time? Shall it be the traditional Jewish connection between the marriage ceremony and the giving of the *Torah*? Shall it be the view that the love poem, "The Song of Songs," symbolizes the love between God and Israel? Or shall it be the love with which you love the person who shared in the creation of this baby? I want to share a poem by the Israeli poet, Yehuda Amichai, which he calls "Ideal Love" and which recalls some of the irony as well as some of the lust of our love, which connects us to childhood:

To start a love like this: with a cannon shot like Ramadan.
That's a religion! Or with the blowing of a ram's horn,

as at the High Holidays, to exorcise sins.
That's a religion! That's a love!
Souls to the front!
To the firing line of eyes.
No hiding back in the white neck.
Emotions, out of the fat belly, forward!
Emotions, out for close combat!
But let's keep the route to childhood open—
even the most victorious army leaves
a line of retreat open.[11]

From the loud openings of love to the quiet and persistent business of producing a child, to the ambivalence of being a parent, Amichai captures so much of love in this brief Hebrew verse. But love is even more complicated in the Jewish tradition, and even more harsh in its implications. The book of Hosea is the classic prophetic book of God's unconditional love for Israel, and of Israel's constant tendency to break the Covenant. The tale of Hosea is often a surprise to people—especially in light of the fact that it is the book read on the Sabbath between the High Holidays. Hosea—in an act mimicking Israel's behavior—marries a prostitute, and keeps taking her back into his life. God, in this analogy, is compared to the cuckolded husband—faithful to Israel in spite of her infidelities. The relationship between God and Israel, and Hosea and the faithless wife has some echoes of our relationship to our children. Our covenants with them are also one-way covenants.

No matter what they do as "their part of the bargain," we are still their parents. This responsibility facing the new parents is an essential part of the anxiety of child rearing which the *mohel/et* is helping them launch. What is even more fascinating about this association is that traditional Jews who put on *tefilin* in the morning, do so to the words of Hosea: "Behold I espouse you . . ." (Hos. 2:21). That is, as a Jewish person is wrapping the leather straps on his arm, he is quoting the lines which recall the infidelity of the Jewish People, at the same time that one recalls the total fidelity of God. This is one of those complex messages of covenant. How difficult to maintain; yet how essential! And when maintained, then the lover can echo the sentiment from Song of Songs which links our loves to our faith in God: *"Dodi li, va'ani lo"*, "I am my beloved's, and my beloved is mine" (Song of Songs 6:3).

There is so much written about good acts, that I hesitate to add some small pieces of poetry which talk about helping people. But I think perhaps that the most vivid imagery about helping people comes from the Holocaust, and from all of those people who stretched their lives and their ethics beyond anything ever known in history. In any event, that is a suggestion about how you might talk about good deeds. From the extremist case we can make analogies down to the simpler questions of life. But I would like to urge that every family that participates in *berit mila* ceremonies with you be encouraged to share an act of good deeds at just this occasion—a symbol that their lives and the life their new baby will lead will be signalled by giving of themselves. A donation to a favorite cause should mark every covenant occasion, and should be used to remind us never to forget:

INSTRUCTIONS FOR CROSSING THE BORDER
by Dan Pagis

Imaginary man, going. Here is your passport.
You are not allowed to remember.
You have to match the description:
your eyes are already blue.
Don't escape with the sparks
inside the smokestack:
you are a man, you sit in the train.
Sit comfortably.

You've got a decent coat now,
a repaired body, a new name
'ready in your throat.
Go, you are not allowed to forget.[12]

I want to end my comments with an important poem about family—one which points us to the future. Now that our parents have named their child, and now that they have uttered the wish for *Torah* and good deeds, they are faced with the reality of rearing a live being. Soon, the particular day of the particular *berit mila* ceremony will be remembered in broad outline only. The parents can only remember that they can only point their child in the right direction. Israeli poet David Avidan jokes, in "Fire the Babysitter":

> Leaving kids alone is no problem
> a child is something pretty reliable
> like a cassette
> The more you press it the more it shrieks
> It won't spoil it'll
> Work under all conditions it's
> Open to countless possibilities
> There's no reason for it to stop
> Working before your very eyes unless
> It's deliberately tampered with.[13]

I have stretched the meaning of the word covenant—*berit*—to include the many aspects of human relationships: past and present, romantic love and spiritual love, the straightforward and the ironic. My purpose has been to enlarge the sense of the word *berit* and to do so through poetry, whose very nature is to stretch our understanding of language. But there is something more important, even, about having shared some thoughts and some poems with doctors and *mohalim/ot*.

If one is going to achieve what Michael Zeldin suggests—that is, to use the *berit mila* ceremony as one of those primary teaching moments in the life of the Jew, then one has to think of the relations between ritual and learning. We must organize our teaching and prepare ourselves spiritually to do this task. It is essential to enter a mood by reading a poem, or by having a discussion with a spouse or friend. I do not know the formula for combining one's technical and physician role with that of the teacher-priest, but I do know that it is an unbeatable combination. Some things represent information that comes right out of the event: This is Jacob's name, and it means . . . This is the wine we drink for *kiddush*, and it means . . . But many of the things that help me organize myself to undertake the awesome tasks of ritual and teaching come at strange times, and I can't even recognize a pattern. When someone dies, I spend much time with the families, and find my way into their lives and into the connections between my values and theirs. The same is true of my involvement in someone's marriage. It should be all the more so with the birth of the child. Where do all my values, all my technical skills, and all my poetry meet the family's concerns?

Do let me recommend the notion of a "prism," a screen for thinking about this newborn baby. As one gets to know the family, it is important to bring that prism to bear on what the family is and what the baby's name is. For the selection of such a focus, sometimes finding the right poem can be just the thing. The "Song of Songs" remains a rich reminder of how love and faith come together; it helps us recall that "God's love is sweeter than wine." (Song of Songs 1:2).

NOTES

1.   T. Carmi, "Everyone Speaks Poetry," in *Davar Echad*, [trans. here by William Cutter] (Tel Aviv: Am Oved, 1970).

2.   *The Sermons of Nachman*, I, 30:2 (Brooklyn: Hadisei Bratzlav, 1976).

3.   Foucault, *L'archeologie de Savoir* (New York: Pantheon Books, 1981).

4.   Dan Pagis, "The Portrait," *Points of Departure,* trans. Stephen Mitchell (Philadelphia: Jewish Publication Society, 1981).

5.   Natan Zach, "The Problem," in *Israeli Poetry: A Contemporary Anthology,* trans. Warren Bargad and Stanley Chyet (Bloomington: Indiana University Press, 1985).

6.   T. Carmi, "In the Cafe," *At the Stone of Losses,* trans. Grace Schulman (Philadelphia: Jewish Publication Society, 1983).

7.   The full Hebrew poem is found in: Zelda, *"Le Khol Ish Yesh Shem,"* in *Shirei Zelda* (Tel Aviv: HaKibbutz HaMe'uhad, 1985). [trans. here William Cutter. After the first instance of "every man", W. C. has substituted "everyone".—ed.]

8.   Hayyim Nachman Bialik, "Alone."

9.   T. Carmi, in his Introduction to *The Penguin Book of Modern Hebrew Verse,* ed. T. Carmi (New York: Viking Press, 1981).

10.   Abraham Shlonsky, "Toil," in *The Modern Hebrew Poem Itself, from the Beginnings to the Present,* ed. Stanley Burnshaw, T. Carmi, and Ezra Spicehandler (New York: Schocken Books, 1966).

11.   Yehuda Amichai, "Ideal Love," in *Love Poems,* trans. Harold Schimmel (New York: Harper & Row, 1981).

12.   Dan Pagis, "Instructions for Crossing the Border," in *Points of Departure,* trans. Stephen Mitchell (Philadelphia: Jewish Publication Society, 1981).

13.   David Avidan, "Fire the Babysitter," in *Israeli Poetry: A Contemporary Anthology,* trans. Warren Bargad and Stanley Chyet (Bloomington: Indiana University Press, 1985).

Reflections on Circumcision as Sacrifice

Stanley F. Chyet and Norman B. Mirsky

The subject of circumcision draws us into the territory of myth—myth understood not as something fabricated, but as a sort of psychic sub-text in human affairs. Myth suggests the fears and hopes—hence the values—human beings have lived with for eons and continue to live with in our own day. The particular province of myth most hospitable to the rites of circumcision is sacrifice—a great force in biblical Judaism and in myriad other manifestations of religious life all over the world.

Why is sacrifice so central to the biblical view of the cosmos? The Israelites appropriated many ideas and practices from the peoples among whom they lived. In a good many instances, it is clear that the Israelite tendency was to ethicize these practices: Shabbat, for example, may have been derived from the Mesopotamian *shabbatu,* a day when work was suspended for fear of the evil spirits thought to be abroad in the land on that day. What among the Babylonians had been, so to say, the Demon of Days apparently became among the Jews the Queen of Days, a foretaste of heavenly bliss. Observances like *Sukkot, Pesach* and *Shavuot* have a pre-biblical heritage as agricultural festivals celebrating the harvest and praising sacrificially the gods of the harvest. This aspect was not entirely banished in the Jewish appropriation, but the Jewish version testifies to an intensified ethicism: in the post-biblical period, the books of Ecclesiastes, Song of Songs, and Ruth were associated with these observances and lent them, as did the liturgy of Rabbinic

Illustration 12

Jackson Pollock, *Circumcision*, 1946 Oil on canvas, 142.3 × 168 cm. The Peggy Guggenheim Collection, Venice; The Solomon R. Guggenheim Foundation, New York. David Heald, photographer.

Judaism, a profoundly ethical character. But the notion of sacrifice, however ethicized or rationalized in Jewish tradition, retains centrality. No longer operative is the *Avoda,* the daily sacrificial system of Biblical Judaism, but now, or since the destruction of the Temple and the suspension of the *Avoda* in the first century C.E., the daily prayers are regarded rabbinically as a form of sacrifice: If fruit and lambs cannot be sacrificed to God thrice daily, one's time can be sacrificed to God in the form of prayer; indeed, the worship services even bear the names of the sacrifices in the *Avoda* system— *shacharit* (morning), *minchah* (afternoon), *ma-ariv* (evening) and *musaf* (the additional sacrifice). The classical *siddur* requires that every daily *shacharit* service include a reading of the *Akeidat Yitschak* (Genesis 22), recounting Abraham's readiness to offer his son up on the altar—and, in later centuries, constituting a sort of rebuttal to the Christian saga of Jesus as the Agnus Dei, the Lamb of God: it is not happenstance that Jews pray for vicarious atonement through the Patriarchs Abraham, Isaac and Jacob.

Sacrifice, apparently, is an emphatic, basic impulse of the human psyche. Even before the threat of nuclear annihilation, the world was a perilous place—when in human history and pre-history has it not been? Human beings must do what they can to win the favor of the divine powers—at the least, to mitigate their enmity—and it is sacrifice, of what is precious to the individual and the collectivity, that has always been seen to achieve this aim. It is nothing silly, to be dismissed as primitive rubbish or superstition; it is a basic need for security, for divine (which is not remote from parental) favor. It is the more intensified by the certainty that the need to propitiate these authorities arouses resentment in those who must make acts of propitiation—the consequent guilt of the propitiators must be neutralized, masked, denied, and it surely intensifies the force of the sacrificial experience. Such a scene is not alien to biblical literature: Mention has already been made of the *akeida;* there is also the episode of Jephtha's daughter (Judges 11). Perhaps the most mysterious, the most dismaying sacrificial scene in the *Torah* (Exod. 4:24-26) is an episode which the celebrated Israeli writer Hazaz used as the basis for his extraordinary short story "Chatan Damim." It is through sacrifice that salvation comes; circumcision, in this context at least, is manifestly a salvationary rite, performed by the father on his son to save his—the father's—life, to win him—the father—the divine favor.

In addressing this issue of circumcision as salvationary sacrifice, one is struck by the overdetermination of the reasons offered for the sacrifice. Overdetermination means that any one of several motives would explain the phenomenon. For example, in his *Violence and the Sacred*,[1] René Girard argues about sacrifice in general, that what sacrifice does is to sacralize the human impulse to violence and, by so sacralizing the impulse, confines it to a specific time and place and to a specific set of actors (priests, et al., specific victims), restricting the impulse by providing it with necessary but infrequent and costly outlets. If we were to apply his insight to circumcision, it could certainly be argued that by surrounding the act with multitudinous legalisms and by attempting to restrict its performance, when possible, to a specific individual (the father, but most often the *mohel*), the rabbis might even have elevated the act to sacrificial status. This would have taken place after the destruction of the Temple, the very time when normal sacrificial outlets for violence had been diminished. This is certainly a hypothesis worthy of consideration and of further exploration.

Another hypothesis, which ought to be given attention, is one suggested by the writings of the folklorist Alan Dundes, particularly his essay "Wet and Dry, the Evil Eye: An Essay in Indo-European and Semitic Worldview."[2] In seeking an explanation for the universality of the phenomenon of the evil eye among the Indo-Europeans and Semites, Dundes calls attention to the fact that, in addition to flowing from envy by the less fortunate (sicker, poorer) or the projection of envy onto the less fortunate by the more fortunate (wealthier, healthier persons), the evil eye phenomenon is part of a complex which goes beyond manifesting itself in cultural specifics (e.g., who can give one, who can remove one, what objects, rituals and formulae are to be used to give or remove the Evil Eye). There are certain general beliefs and attributes associated with the evil eye complex that transcend cultural, religious or ethnic particularities. One of these universals is the belief that in each society and in the world at large there are only limited goods and this limitation is most obvious when it comes to liquids. Dundes writes:

> Life depends upon liquid. From the concept of the "water of life" to semen, milk, blood, bile, saliva and the like, the consistent principle is that liquid means life while loss of liquid means death. "Wet and Dry" as an oppositional pair means life and death. Liquids are living,

drying is dying!

> There is a finite, limited amount of good—health, wealth, etc.—and because that is so, any gain by one individual can only come at the expense of another . . . If one individual possesses a precious body fluid, *semen,* for instance, this automatically means that some other individual lacks the same fluid.[3] [emphasis added].

Dundes' two points cited above serve to suggest yet another argument for circumcision as sacrifice—that is, an act done not so much to placate a deity, as many propose, or to placate a father, as psychoanalytic writings emphasize, but rather circumcision in its rabbinic formulation, as an attempt to exact from the male child recompense for the loss of semen by the father (and, conceivably, for the loss of amniotic fluid and milk by the mother). The male child, having drained the father of his life-force (semen), must in turn pay the father back by relinquishing his own bodily fluid (blood) in the *berit mila* ritual. (We recognize that the father also relinquishes semen when a female child is born and that there appears to be no corresponding ritual exchange of fluids where girls are involved. Let us offer the possibility that there is a fluid exchange over a protracted time, i.e., semen for blood at menarchy, blood for water at *mikveh*, water for milk at childbirth; however, this cannot be argued here. Let us return to the male realm and concentrate on a new, but in no way all-inclusive, explication of the rabbinic circumcision ritual.)

In analyzing the traditional circumcision ritual, we suggest the possibility of an attempt to rectify the imbalance of life fluids caused by the loss of the ultimate life-force fluid (semen) by the father through the sacrifice of another fluid (blood), which was given directly to the father or his surrogate, the *mohel*, who in turn provided the child with another fluid, wine, this time more symbolic in nature but nevertheless limited in quantity according to the principle of limited good. According to Israel G. Hyman,

> The Ritual Circumcision consists of the following constituents: the excision of the prepuce, the tearing of the mucous membrane to expose the glans, the suction of the wound and the dressing of the wound. The talmudic source for the suction of the wound, known as *Mezizah* is a *Mishnah* in tractate Sabbath (19.2) . . .[4]

Apparently, from the period of the *Mishna* to the late twelfth century C.E., the crucial halachic issue was whether the act of *metsitsa* (sucking) could be performed on the Sabbath, not how the sucking of the blood was to be performed. However, in the twelfth or thirteenth century, the matter of *how* this act was performed became fixed. The blood was orally sucked from the wound. Hyman points out that, according to Jacob haGozer (c. 1215), the one performing the circumcision should "immediately put the member in his mouth and suck the blood with all his strength."[5] Hyman continues,

> Thus, traditionally, *Mezizah* was performed by oral suction. Although for centuries this method was the accepted practice, in the nineteenth and twentieth centuries, controversy raged as to whether this method was indispensable, or whether alternative methods other than *direct oral suction* were permissible. The *literature on the subject is vast...*[6] [emphasis added].

We have italicized the above phrases because they serve to emphasize several issues that are germane to our argument. Most non-Orthodox people who attend *berit mila* performed by an Orthodox *mohel* are unaware that the practice of *metsitsa* takes place (if indeed it does). Furthermore, no Anglo-American prayerbooks and guides for traditional practice which include instruction for the ceremony of *berit mila* also seems to include a reference to *metsitsa*. As Hyman points out in the remainder of his article, due to halachic, polemical and—though he does not overtly state it—aesthetic considerations, one can surmise that when the reformers eliminated the practice, it was for more than strictly hygienic reasons[7]—hence our emphasis on the phrase *"direct oral suction."*

Clearly the nineteenth century brought to the traditional community three problems that had not existed earlier. One was what Hyman sees as central, i.e., "the revolutionary development of medicine which took place in the last century, and even more so, the rise of modern surgery. The aseptic system of surgery became the required procedure for any type of surgery, however minor the operation."[8]

The mere fact that *mohalim* came under the surveillance of those practicing modern medical procedure indicates that the Jews had entered into a world which would give impetus to attempts to reform

Judaism so as to fit contemporary aesthetic standards. Certainly, sucking the blood from a recently lacerated penis with one's bearded mouth could not have conformed to the hygienic, let alone the aesthetic, standards that the reformers sought to introduce.

As Hyman suggests,[9] the mere fact that reforms (*within* traditional Judaism) sought to eliminate the *oral* aspect of *metsitsa* only assured that the anti-reformers would declare it to be an halachic sine qua non.

After reading Dundes' essay, "Wet and Dry, The Evil Eye," one becomes convinced that, whatever the motives of the anti-reformers were, should Dundes' "liquid is life" theory be correct, the anti-reformers consciously or unconsciously sanctified an important element of Indo-European and Semitic folk belief.

Let us recall Dundes' principles quoted above:

> Life depends upon liquid. From the concept of the "water of life" to semen, milk, blood, bile, saliva and the like, the consistent principle is that liquid means life while loss of liquid means death. "Wet and Dry" as an oppositional pair means life and death. Liquids are living, drying is dying!

> There is a finite, limited amount of good—health, wealth, etc.—and because that is so, any gain by one individual can only come at the expense of another . . . If one individual possesses a precious body fluid, *semen,* for instance, this automatically means that some other individual lacks that same fluid.[10]

Again Dundes:

> In the light of the centrality of liquid as a metaphor for life, it makes sense for envy to be expressed in liquid terms. The have-nots envy the haves and desire their various liquids. Whether it is the dead who envy the living (as in vampires who require the blood of the living and who are commonly referred to as "bloodthirsty"), the old who envy the young, or the barren who envy those with children, it is the blood, the sap or vitality of youth, the maternal milk, or masculine semen that is coveted. The notion of limited good means that there is not really enough to go around. Thus, an admiring look or statement (of praise) is understood as a wish for precious fluid. If the looker or declarer receives liquid, then it must be at the expense of the object

or person admired. So the victim's fruit tree withers from a loss of sap or his cow's milk dries up. The point is that the most common effect of the evil eye is a *drying up* process.[11]

Consider now the plight of the Jewish male child, required by God to be deprived of his foreskin on the eighth day of his life, a commandment deeply imbedded in Scripture and, hence, not subject to reinterpretation. The child has, by being conceived, caused his father to lose semen and his mother first to lose amniotic fluid, then milk. The child, since he is male, is the object of flattery to the father, to the mother and to himself. In short, the male child is a prime target for envy—and its Indo-European and Semitic manifestation, the Evil Eye. The word envy, as Dundes shows, is "etymologically derived from the Latin *invidia,* which in turn comes from *in videre,* thus ultimately from 'to see'."[12] Envy or invidia or the Evil Eye, among other ill effects, "threatened to make men impotent."

Thus, the eight day old Jewish male is a source of great danger (his birth making the parents objects of envy) and he is also the object of great danger (from parental enmity for making them the objects of fluid loss and of envy). The knife wielding father and his rabbinic surrogate, the *mohel,* thus have double reason to sacrifice the child: To placate an angry deity—the Projection of the father's own anger at fluid loss and exposure to sterilizing envy—and to protect the child by shedding his blood in fulfillment of the commandment. If the child should die as a result of the violence done to him through the act, then he has died expiating the peril in which he has placed his father and mother and fulfilling a commandment. If he lived, as must have been true most often, he was temporarily free of the perils of the Evil Eye, that is, something had been done to counter the fluid lost and the envy projected.

Here, Girard, Dundes and the rabbinic ceremony of the *berit mila* achieve symmetry. For if Girard is correct in assuming that a ritual sacrifice is a containment of violence, then, given the overdetermined possibilities for wanting or needing to do away with the child, *berit mila* has to be seen as a great festival of violence contained.

Further, if Dundes is correct and both the parents and the child are endangered through fluid loss and envy, then a ritual in which the father's loss of semen and the mother's loss of amniotic fluid and milk are replenished by sucking the blood from the part of the male which gives forth semen is a fair exchange. If, in turn, the child is given wine, the blood of the grape, and the wine is used to anesthetize the child and to slake his thirst (the blood of the grape enters the mouth of the boy whose blood has entered the mouth of the father surrogate), then all are out of danger. The balance is restored.[13] All are out of danger, that is, except the guests who are usually given liquid refreshment and toasted with *l'chayyim!*[14]

NOTES

1. René Girard, *The Violence and the Sacred* (Baltimore, 1986).
2. Alan Dundes, *Interpreting Folklore* (Bloomington, 1980), pp. 93–133.
3. Ibid., pp. 101–102.
4. Israel G. Hyman, "The Halachic Issues of Mezizah," in *Proceedings of the Association of Orthodox Jewish Scientists,* vol. 8–9 (5747-1987), p. 17.
5. Ibid., p. 18.
6. Ibid.
7. Ibid., p. 30.
8. Ibid, p. 19.
9. Ibid., p. 24.
10. Ibid., pp. 101–102.
11. Ibid., pp. 109–110.
12. Ibid., p. 98.
13. See Hyman E. Goldin, *Hamadrikh, The Rabbi's Guide,* rev. ed., (New York, 1939), pp. 30, 35–36: the Hebrew, the English translation of which is omitted in Goldin's edition, prescribes that "after the exposure [of the glans] and the sucking the mohel takes the cup and says the benediction" (p. 35).
14. Dundes, *Interpreting Folklore,* p. 103.

"Who Is a Jew?"

Issues of Jewish Status and Identity and Their Relationship to the Nature of Judaism in the Modern World

David Ellenson

Debate and controversy over the question "Who is a Jew?" have come to occupy a dominant place on the public agenda of the contemporary Jewish community. Within Israel, disputes rage forth annually in the Knesset as to whether persons converted to Judaism under non-Orthodox auspices are to be considered Jews under the Law of Return. In the Diaspora, threats of withdrawal of American Jewish communal support for Israel should the Law be amended so as to exclude such converts are increasingly common. In addition, there exist throughout the world many persons who fulfilled the traditional Jewish legal requirement (i.e., birth from a Jewish mother) for consideration as Jews, but who display neither commitment to nor consciousness of their Jewishness. Conversely, there are others who affirm their identity as Jews, but whose halachic (Jewish legal) status as Jews is, at best, uncertain. Further, in an era where intermarriage is frequent and where the overwhelming majority of conversions are conducted by Reform and Conservative rabbis, the Orthodox maintain a principled refusal to regard such conversions as valid.[1] Finally, recent decisions by the Reform and Reconstructionist Movements in favor of patrilineality (i.e., the notion that descent from a Jewish father, and not just a Jewish mother, may qualify one as a Jew), as well as articles, statements, and responsa by several leading Conservative rabbis in favor of this principle,[2] have given rise to tremendous controversy and discussion.[3]

This paper proposes to explore a variety of historical and sociological factors that have propelled these issues of status and identity to the forefront of modern Jewish communal concerns. In so doing, it hopes to explain how different understandings of these matters emerge within different sectors of the contemporary Jewish community as well as the significance these understandings hold for comprehending the pluralistic nature of modern Judaism.

At the outset, it should be noted that the question "Who is a Jew?" involves matters of both status and identity, and while the meanings of these two terms may overlap, they are two distinct referents that are not necessarily identical. Status, stemming as it does from the Latin word meaning "standing," refers to the condition of a person in the eyes of the law. When employed in regard to a person's relationship to a group, the person's own definition of that relationship may be totally irrelevant. Authorities either external to the group or within the group itself may well make such status designations with absolutely no regard for the individual's own sense of self-definition. For example, there were Christians living in Nazi Germany who were defined as Jews under the Nuremberg Laws of 1935. Similarly, a person born of a Jewish mother who swore allegiance to another religious faith would still be considered Jewish by most traditional Jewish legal authorities. Conversely, despite an individual's own sense of identification and belonging, a group might well deny her legal status as one of their own. Here one need only think of the child of a woman converted to Judaism under Conservative auspices being denied status as a Jew by Orthodox rabbinical authorities. In sum, "status" is essentially a legalistic term.

Identity, in contrast, embraces a more subjective and personalistic component. Its etymological root, derived from the ancient Greek *idios*, means "private" or "individual." When the term "identity," as opposed to "status," is utilized to refer to a person's relationship to a group, it may simply signify the psychological orientation of that individual towards the group. Simply put, it reflects the individual's autonomous understanding of who she is. A person born to a non-Jewish mother who participates in the life of a given Jewish community might well identify herself as a Jew despite having failed to undergo any formal rite of conversion to Judaism. Identity, in this instance, would simply not address the issue of the Jewish legal relationship that obtains between this woman and the Jewish community. It would rather reflect a personal definition of self in reference to a group.[4]

The question "Who is a Jew?" is a complex one precisely because it involves considerations of status and identity. Furthermore, as the examples cited above illustrate, the individual, the group itself, or bodies external to the group who possess authority over it may all be involved, depending upon the particular case, in determining the answer to a given person's status and identity as a Jew. The relevance these distinctions and factors hold for the issue of "Jewishness" is apparent when we reflect upon the nature of Jewish existence in the pre-modern world and contrast it with that of Jewish life in a country like the United States today.

Within the context of a pre-modern feudal political order, status was corporate. Individual citizenship in a nation-state, as a modern western model would have it, was essentially unknown. Furthermore, the Jewish community itself was either politically autonomous or semi-autonomous in governing the lives of its members and it provided these members with a sense of cultural identity. There was thus little or no dissonance between public and private spheres, individual and collective realms, over who was a Jew. The halachic definition of Jewishness, where one is defined as a Jew by virtue of birth to a Jewish mother or conversion into Judaism through the agency of a qualified *beit din* (rabbinical court), is based upon and entirely suitable to a corporate world where pluralism was controlled politically in such matters and where individualism and voluntarism had not yet arisen to the degree they have in the modern world.[5] When an individual was born of a Jewish mother or converted into the community, it was more than a case of religious affiliation. It was a matter of that person's political status and cultural identity. Only in rare instances could a conflict have arisen between the individual and public political bodies as to a person's status and identity as a Jew. Status and identity in the medieval setting were virtually one and the same in almost every case. An individual who defined herself as a Jew could have done so only with the assent of a politically self-governing Jewish community as well as the Gentile authorities who permitted the Jews to enjoy a semi-autonomous political status.

With the advent of "modernity" in the West, the situation began to change. The traditional halachic definition of Jewishness— essentially a status one—was in many ways too narrow to deal with the full parameters of this issue. Modernity largely transformed the matter of Jewishness from a question of status into one of identity. Changes in the political and religious realms reduced the community from its previous position as a political corporation possessing legal authority over its membership into a pluralistic and voluntaristic association. Several varieties of non-Orthodox Judaism as well as secular Zionism arose. This fragmentation not only signaled a diversity of religious viewpoints within the community. It was also marked by a tendency among each of these denominations to arrogate for itself the right to determine who was a Jew. Furthermore, because the political structure and authority of the community was dismantled by the emergence of the modern nation-state, no one denomination within the community could legally impose its definition of Jewishness upon the entire community. In addition, these political and religious changes granted the individual the right to participate in the community and affirm her identity as a Jew or, if she chose, elect not to participate in it. In short, by creating conditions which have made "Jewishness" a matter of option for many individual Jews, modernity has altered the traditional understanding of Jewishness. It is now, in many instances, not a matter of pre-destined fate, but a question of assumed identity.

As Peter Berger, the famed sociologist of religion, has phrased it:

In the situation of the ghetto, . . . it would have been absurd to say that an individual *chose* to be a Jew. To be Jewish was a taken-for-granted given of the individual's existence, ongoingly reaffirmed with ringing certainty by everyone in the individual's milieu . . . There was the theoretical possibility of conversion to Christianity, but the social pressures against this were so strong that it was realized in very few cases. . . . The coming of emancipation changed all this. For more and more individuals it became a viable project to step outside the Jewish community. Suddenly, to be Jewish emerged as one choice among others. . . . The fullest development was reached in America in the twentieth century. Today, within the pluralistic dynamic of American society, there must be very few individuals for whom being Jewish has the quality of a taken-for-granted fact.

Yet those who affirmed an orthodox or even a moderately orthodox version of Jewish identity continued to define the latter as such a fact. Their problem is that they must affirm it in the face of empirical evidence to the contrary. The orthodox precisely defines Jewish identity as destiny, while the social experience of the individual reveals it as an ongoing choice. This dissonance between definition and experience is at the core of every orthodoxy in the modern world. . . . The orthodox defines himself as living in a tradition; it is of the very nature of tradition to be taken for granted; this taken-for-grantedness is continually falsified by the experience of living in a modern society. The orthodox must then present to himself as fate what he knows empirically to be a choice. This is a difficult feat. It goes far to explain the attraction of such movements as that of Lubavitcher Hasidism, which constructs an artificial *shtetl* for its followers. The difference from the old *shtetl* is quite simply this: All the individual has to do to get out of his alleged Jewish destiny is to walk out and take the subway. Outside, waiting, is the emporium of life-styles, identities, and religious preferences that constitute American pluralism.[6]

Berger's observations reveal that what was formerly a matter of fate and destiny has now been transformed into an issue of option and choice. The answer to the query "Who is a Jew?" has evoked a furor in so many Jewish quarters precisely because it speaks to the heart of the struggle that has marked Judaism in the West in its transition from the pre-modern to the modern world. A look at the ferocity of the debate between Orthodox and Reform Jewish leaders surrounding the issue of patrilineality will reveal why this is so. Moreover, the arguments over this issue provide an accurate barometer for measuring how different denominations conceptualize Judaism in the modern setting.

At the 1983 convention of the Central Conference of American Rabbis in Los Angeles, a resolution was passed declaring that "the child of one Jewish parent is under the presumption of Jewish descent" and that "this presumption of the Jewish status of the offspring of any mixed marriage is to be established through appropriate and timely public and formal acts of identification with the Jewish faith and people."[7] While the wording of the resolution has been sharply criticized for its ambiguity,[8] one thing is clear. The framers of the resolution and the CCAR as a whole envision Judaism, in some measure, as a voluntaristic enterprise. The resolution, no matter how interpreted, affirms a modern notion of choice. Jewishness is not automatically accorded the offspring of one Jewish parent.[9] Rather, given the wording of the resolution, "Jewishness" is awarded an individual only when there are "appropriate and timely public and formal acts of identification with the Jewish faith and people." The "birth dogma" of traditional Judaism,[10] whereby an individual born of a Jewish mother is automatically accorded the status of Jew, is seemingly discarded by the intent of the resolution. Berger's contention about the transformed nature of the modern setting, and his observation that Jewish identity is now a matter of choice and not a given, immutable legal status, is not simply acknowledged as a description of contemporary social reality. Rather, it is enshrined as a foundational premise of liberal Judaism and, consequently, Jewish identity.[11]

It is this conceptualization of Judaism as a matter of choice, of the autonomy accorded individuals in determining their religious identity, which provokes the bitter reaction of the Orthodox. As Rabbi Binyamin Walfish, the executive Vice-President of the Orthodox Rabbinical Council of America has written,

> Although the patrilineal descent resolution enacted by the Central Conference of American Rabbis is certainly not the first, or only resolution passed by the Reform rabbinate which breaches *halakhah*, nor is it necessarily the most serious violation of halakhic principle, it has evoked more reaction and comment than prior resolutions since Reform's initial break with halakhah and Jewish tradition. The question is, therefore, what is there about this particular issue which calls forth so much comment and analysis?[12]

Walfish's colleague, Rabbi Walter Wurzburger, the editor of the Orthodox academic journal *Tradition*, echoes those thoughts. He states,

> At first sight it seems strange that acrimony should have developed from what seems only one more in a long series of violations of fundamental halakhic principles. . . . Since its very inception, Reform openly and unabashedly declared its independence from the authority of the *Halakhah*. Why, then, should what amounts merely to another link in the long chain of categorical repudiations of halakhic principles send such shock waves through the Jewish community? Can it really be claimed that the rejection of halakhic criteria for the

determination of Jewish status constitutes a more blatant violation of Jewish law than the sanctioning of *hillul shabbat* . . . , abolition of *kashrut* and *Taharat Hamishpachah,* or the substitution of a civil divorce for the *Get?*

Indeed, Wurzburger continues,

Patrilineal descent is far from being the most serious threat to Jewish unity. It does not even compare with the irreparable damage to Jewish unity that resulted from the Reform policy of sanctioning remarriage without a *Get.* If a woman were to remarry solely on the basis of a civil divorce, her off-spring would be a *Mamzer,* permanently disqualified from marrying any other individual who is not similarly stigmatized. There is no possibility of remedying this unfortunate condition. On the other hand, the consequences of the patrilineal descent resolution are not quite so drastic. Although the offspring of a non-Jewish mother would be regarded as a non-Jew by traditional Jews, there still remains the option of a subsequent conversion to Judaism which would remove obstacles to marrying other Jews . . .[13]

Why then the sharpness of the reaction to the issue of patrilineal descent and the subsequent affirmation of the individual's Jewish identity that flows from it? Wurzburger answers in the following way:

To appreciate fully the revolutionary nature of a patrilineal descent resolution, it is essential to bear in mind that the new Reform policy amounts not merely to a revision of the procedures required to gain admission to the ranks of the Jewish people, but it constitutes the rejection of the biological, ethnic dimension of the covenantal existence of the Jew. It strikes at the very root of Jewish existence. According to the classical conception, Jewish identity is not a matter of a Jew's voluntary choice, but is imposed upon those who qualify by birth for membership in the Jewish people. . . . Jewishness ceases to be acquired simply by birth. It becomes a matter of voluntary self-identification. . . .

The paramount importance assigned to voluntary self-identification as a criterion for children of mixed marriages amounts to a rejection of the ethnic, "tribal" component of Jewish identity. . . . Judaism has always operated with the premise that the accident of birth imposes upon an individual the irrevocable responsibilities and obligations

associated with Jewish identity. Once required, be it by birth or by
conversion, one cannot renounce one's Jewish identity. . . . "Once a
Jew always a Jew."[14]

The Orthodox critique of the Reform position on patrilineality, as
articulated here by Rabbi Wurzburger, reflects a status approach to
the issue of Jewishness. In so doing, it contrasts sharply with the
more voluntaristic stance towards this question adopted by Reform
and reveals an entirely different conceptualization of Judaism in the
present situation. For Orthodoxy, while it may be forced to concede
the empirical correctness of some of Berger's insights about the
nature of the Jewish condition in the modern world, refuses to
accord them normative status. The issue of Jewish status and identity, the question "Who is a Jew?," has been elevated to such a
paramount position on the contemporary Jewish scene because it
reflects the ongoing divisions that divide different Jewish groups'
approaches to Judaism in the current world. The Orthodox continue
to view Judaism and the Jewish community in the traditional way
that it has been conceptualized for over two millennia. In so doing,
the Orthodox reject the "right" of modernity to alter the nature of
the Jewish religion and its community. Reform, in contrast, is
informed by many of the values of the modern world and legitimates
their place in a contemporary approach to Judaism. In sum, Reform
affirms voluntarism and choice as integral parts of modern Judaism.
The battle between Reform and Orthodoxy over Jewish status and
identity, when seen from this perspective, is the reflection of a
deeper controversy over the nature of Judaism itself in the modern
world.

The practical consequences flowing from these differences in
approach to the question of Jewish identity is that Reform, in general, is willing to accept the "Jewishness" of large numbers of individuals whose halachic status as Jews would be denied by the Orthodox. Cases such as this are too numerous to document. Yet, it
should be noted that the considerations involved in this question of
"Jewishness" can sometimes lead in the opposite direction. In Los
Angeles, for instance, where nearly twenty Reform *mohalim/ot* have
been trained and certified during the last few years, a case was
reported in which a Jewish mother who had affirmed a belief in
Jesus as the Messiah desired to have her son ritually circumcised as
a Jew in a *berit mila* ceremony. The Reform *mohel,* feeling that the

mother's decision in the realm of belief obviated her right to hold such a ceremony, declined to perform the ritual circumcision. Subsequently, the mother approached an Orthodox *mohel* who, satisfied that the mother was indeed Jewish, performed the ceremony. Or, to cite another instance, a Reform rabbi was approached to officiate at the marriage of a Jewish man to a woman who, though born of a Jewish mother, was raised as a Christian. When the Reform rabbi refused to officiate at the wedding unless the bride receive formal instruction in Judaism, the couple went to an Orthodox rabbi who agreed to perform the ceremony.

These two examples simply highlight how complex and paradoxical the issue of Jewish status and identity may be in the modern world where no governmental body legally authorized to adjudicate these cases exists. However, the cases also illuminate something of the distinction that often separates the Orthodox from the Reform approach in these matters. For the Orthodox officiants in these cases, Jewishness is ultimately a question of status alone. To be Jewish is to be part of a covenantal community one enters through birth. No action on the individual's part can alter that fact. In contrast, the Reform officiants' decisions in these instances reveal their resolve to reject birth alone as the decisive criterion in assigning Jewish status and identity to an individual.

Before concluding, it is vital to note that this picture of Reform and Orthodox positions towards issues of Jewish status and identity is somewhat overdrawn for the heuristic purpose of defining what is significantly distinctive about each of them. In this sense, it is hoped that the paper has not only succeeded in illuminating the nature of each movement's contemporary stance towards Judaism. Rather, inasmuch as these stances do reflect the distinctive attitude each denomination holds in regard to the nature of Judaism in the modern world, a comprehension of them aids in explaining the extreme hostility and bitterness this matter has engendered on the modern Jewish scene.

Yet, it would be equally misleading not to acknowledge that the social reality surrounding the matter of Jewish status and identity does not entirely conform to the theoretical postures advanced by each of these movements. In many instances within local communities, there is a shared consciousness among both liberal and traditionalistic Jewish leaders that permits them to adopt something of the posture advanced by the other's movement concerning this matter. Thus, most modern Orthodox leaders, while not ready to concede the halachic status of a person converted to Judaism under non-Orthodox rabbinical auspices, will nevertheless facilitate these persons' entry into the Orthodox community should they express such a desire. There is a recognition on the part of these men that such persons, and many others, affirm a sense of Jewish identity and, consequently, share in a Jewish fate.[15]

Conversely, the resolution on patrilineality aside, virtually no Reform leader sees Jewishness simply as a matter of personal choice and affirmation. Indeed, the Reform Movement's 1983 decision on patrilineal status elevated what had been the de facto practice of the Reform Movement for nearly half a century into an official status that children born of non-Jewish mothers and Jewish fathers could now claim de jure. Concern with status is thus hardly alien to Reform. Moreover, questions of wording and logic aside, the intent of the resolution and the way in which it has been interpreted have allowed the offspring of many different types of unions— endogamous Jewish marriages, marriages in which the mother is Jewish—as well as marriages in which the father is Jewish, the right to have their "Jewishness" affirmed by the Reform Jewish community in an overwhelming majority of cases. In short, few Reform leaders are prepared to reject the traditional notion that a person is born into the Jewish community and, as such, shares in a covenantal faith.[16]

This last observation is not meant to obscure the real differences that divide liberal and traditional Jewish camps on these matters. Reform does adopt a socio-psychological posture more in accord with the voluntaristic and pluralistic spirit of the modern world while Orthodoxy continues to affirm a pre-modern approach to Judaism and Jewish existence as a community of destiny and fate. Even if unity in such matters was a *desideratum,* in a country like the United States, where the pre-modern political structure of the community can never be resurrected, it is impossible that this breach could ever be fully healed. And in Israel, the pluralistic nature of Israeli culture makes this unlikely. Nevertheless, these differences, real as they are, should not obscure the fact that the approaches taken to Judaism and Jewishness by adherents and leaders within the various denominations of Judaism in the modern world reflect an admixture of these two world views. As such, they offer a hope that while full-scale consensus over these matters may not be achieved, a total division of the Jewish People into two warring camps may yet be avoided.

(This chapter was originally delivered at the Annual Convention of the Society for the Scientific Study of Religion in Louisville, Kentucky, on October 30, 1987.)

NOTES

1. On this point, see the article by Orthodox Rabbi J. David Bleich, "Parameters and Limits of Communal Unity from the Perspective of Jewish Law," *Journal of Halakha and Contemporary Society* (Fall, 1983), pp. 13–14. For a general survey of contemporary Orthodox attitudes on this issue, see David Ellenson, "Representative Orthodox Responsa on Conversion and Intermarriage in the Contemporary Era," *Jewish Social Studies* (Summer-Fall, 1985), pp. 209–220.

2. For a sample of such Conservative opinions, see Solomon Goldfarb, "Who Is a Jewish Child?," *Conservative Judaism* (Fall, 1976), pp. 3–10; Philip Sigal, "Children of Mixed Marriages, Are They Jewish: A Symposium on Patrilineal Descent," *Judaism* (Winter, 1985), pp. 89–96; Seymour Siegel, *Proceedings of the Rabbinical Assembly*, 1986, Vol. XLVIII, p. 318; Harold Schulweis, *Israel Today* (January 17, 1980), p. 10; and Wolfe Kelman, "Reaching In, Reaching Out: A Comment," *Moment* (March, 1979), p. 24.

3. A sampling of this literature is found in David Ellenson, "The Integrity of Reform Within Kelal Yisrael," *CCAR Yearbook* (1986), Vol. XCVI, pp. 30–31. Also see the many articles contained in the Winter, 1985, issue of *Judaism* cited above.

4. Of course, modernity also creates the obverse situation in which a segment of the community may well refuse to affirm the Jewish identity of a person who may have halachic claim to such status—e.g., a person born of a Jewish mother who is raised in another religion. As the practical locus of the current debate over matters of Jewish status and identity tends to center around the issue of whether the individual's right to affirm her identity and, hence, status as a Jew ought to be confirmed by the group, these obverse cases are not highlighted at this point in the discussion.

5. This is not to assert that individualism was unknown in the pre-modern world. I thank my colleague Michael Signer for sensitizing me to this point.

6. Peter Berger, *The Heretical Imperative* (Garden City, New York, 1979), pp. 29–30.

7. From the Report of the Committee on Patrilineal Descent adopted by the CCAR at its annual convention, March 15, 1983.

8. See Howard Apothaker and Mark Washofsky, "Patrilineality and Presumption," *Journal of Reform Judaism* (Summer, 1984), pp. 39–46; as well as Sol Roth, "Children of Mixed Marriages, Are They Jewish: A Symposium on Patrilineal Descent," pp. 69–70.

9. Indeed, Joseph Edelheit, Chair of the CCAR Committee on Patrilineal Descent which offered the resolution that was passed at the CCAR's 1983 convention, advocates precisely this position in his, "Children of Mixed Marriage: A Non-Lineal Approach," *Journal of Reform Judaism* (Winter, 1983), pp. 37–42.

10. This term is taken from Alvin Reines, "Birth Dogma and Philosophic Religious Faith," *Hebrew Union College Annual* Vol. XLVI, (1975), pp. 297–330.

11. On the notion of choice as a Reform Jewish principle, see, for example, the many works of Eugene Borowitz.

12. Binyamin Walfish, "Children of Mixed Marriages, Are They Jewish: A Symposium on Patrilineal Descent," p. 107.

13. Wurzburger, Ibid., pp. 119–120.

14. Ibid., p. 121.

15. See, for example, Albert Ehrman and C. Abraham Fenster, "Conversion and American Orthodox Judaism," *Jewish Journal of Sociology* (June, 1968), p. 53, for a description of the lenient way in which modern Orthodox rabbis often interpret Jewish law to include persons within the community whose halachic status is doubtful. Also see J. Simcha Cohen, "The Conversion of Children Born to Gentile Mothers and Jewish Fathers," *Tradition* (Winter, 1987), pp. 1–17.

16. I am grateful to Rabbi Patricia Karlin-Newman of UCLA Hillel for helping me to formulate this point.

A Brief Assessment of the Significance of Reform Mohalut in a Social-Historical Context

Bruce A. Phillips

INTRODUCTION

Normally one does not attempt to assess the long-term significance of a program that is only a few years old. Our contemporary vision is limited, and what seems important now could well end up passed over by future historians. My goal in examining the significance of the program to train Reform *mohalim/ot* is to provide a broad perspective on its importance.

The importance of training Reform *mohalim/ot* derives from the conjunction of historical and sociological trends. Historically speaking, I see the *Berit Mila* Program as a continuation of a long term twentieth century trend in the reinfusion of traditional elements into Reform. This program also happens at a time in which the emergence of new socio-demographic trends give added political significance to the place of Reform Judaism in American Life.

THE TREND TOWARD TRADITION

There are really two Reform Judaisms in American Jewish life. The first is called Classical Reform, and the second Neo-Reform.

Classical Reform was born with the German-Jewish immigration of the mid-nineteenth century, which introduced radical changes to Judaism in order to bring it in line with what we call "modernity." Neo-Reform is what became of Classical Reform in the twentieth century after the Eastern European Jewish immigrants from the turn of the century became part of the growing Reform Movement. While I cannot do justice to a history of the Reform Movement, an overview of the transition from Classical Reform to Neo-Reform is helpful for an understanding of the significance of training Reform *mohalim/ot* today.

The Reform Movement began as a bridge between the ghetto and modernity. The Emancipation in Europe brought at least the potential end to the enforced isolation of European Jewry along with an exposure of Jewry to the "modern" intellectual trends of the Enlightenment. The early Reformers sought to make Judaism compatible with the contemporary world. To do so, the early Reformers felt that Judaism must be expunged of those elements which were in conflict with the two most important intellectual movements in the surrounding culture: science and nationalism.

The early Reformers studied Judaism scientifically. They understood Judaism as an historical human phenomenon rather than as the result of a direct divine revelation. Thus they rejected the authority of the *halacha* (Jewish law as codified in the *Talmud* and subsequent legal commentaries). There was no "scientific" basis for a religion based on such mythical revelation. Other elements which stood in direct opposition to modern scientific thinking were also rejected. These include a belief in the Messiah and the resurrection of the dead in the Messianic Age. These were regarded as superstitions. They also rejected the nationalistic elements in Judaism which they perceived as standing in the way of Jews attaining full acceptance as citizens in Western European societies. In American pluralistic society, we categorically reject and condemn the charge of "dual-citizenship." Acceptance into the larger society depended on Jewish conformity. So deep were the scars of emerging from the ghetto that even until recently (basically 1967), American Jews have remained anxious about charges of dual loyalty and have tried to avoid situations which might raise the question.

When these intellectual positions were translated into practice we have the emergence of Reform Judaism as a movement. The new viewpoints and practices were brought to America by the German

Jewish immigrants in the middle of the last century, and the Reform
Movement was crystallized in the last quarter of the century with
the founding of the Union of American Hebrew Congregetions, the
Hebrew Union College and the Central Conference of American
Rabbis.

To the Eastern European Jewish immigrants who began to arrive
in 1881, what we now call Classical Reform (then it was the only
Reform) was a strange and even alienating sight. The service was
conducted largely in English with a prayerbook that was much
shorter than the traditional siddur, and was even missing many familiar prayers; parts of other prayers had been modified or dropped
(for example, those which mention the resurrection of the dead).
The major observance of Shabbat had shifted to Friday night so that
Jewish men could run their businesses on Saturday. The large traditional *talit* had been replaced by a thin scarf-like garment. No head
coverings were worn, and should one unwittingly walk into a
Reform temple with a *yarmulke,* an usher (someone not found in an
Eastern European Orthodox service) would instruct him to remove
it. Men and women sat together and confirmation replaced *bar
mitzvah.*

Although Reform was repugnant to the Eastern European immi-
grant generation, it became increasingly attractive to their children
and grandchildren as they too sought a Judaism appropriate to
modernity.

Most second generation Eastern European Jews found a comfortable home in the Conservative Movement. The more affluent of the
Eastern European Jews, however, were attracted to Reform because
this was the movement of the German Jewish upper class. The ranks
of Eastern European Jews joining Reform synagogues further
increased along with suburbanization. German Jews were first to
move to the suburbs and had established a Reform presence there.
Eastern European Jews were ten times as numerous as Jews of German Jewish stock, and they quickly became the majority of the
Reform Movement well before mid-century.

The Eastern Europeans did not go about purposely bringing traditional elements into the Reform Movement. They had no new ideol-
ogy that they sought to fashion. Rather, they missed certain elements
in what they understood to be the Jewish experience, and brought
them back in. The return of *bar mitzvah* is a good example. From a
strictly philosophical point of view, the German Reformers were

consistent and correct in eliminating this ceremony. If one does not accept the authority of the *mitzvah* system, then why have a ceremony to accept it? But the *bar mitzvah* ceremony is more than an affirmation of a belief system, it is a *rite de passage*. Its anthropological dimensions are more important than its philosophical meaning. Thus the Eastern European Jews in the Reform movement brought back *bar mitzvah,* but also kept the confirmation ceremony.

The Eastern European Jews also brought the Reform Movement in line with their sentiments on Israel and Zionism. Since before the turn of the century, the Reform Movement was on record as opposed to Zionism. Although some of the greatest leaders of the Reform Movement had been Zionists (Stephen S. Wise and Abba Hillel Silver, for example), the movement itself had never changed its official position. Thus, the Reform *Hagada* did not end with the phrase, *le-shana ha-ba'ah birushalayim* ("Next year in Jerusalem!"). Eastern European Jews, however, would end their *seder* with that phrase anyway, in part because it was familiar and in part to affirm their own commitment to Zionism. By the 1980s, the Reform Movement had finally reversed its public stand on Zionism by including "Next Year in Jerusalem" in the *Hagada* and by founding ARZA—the Association of Reform Zionists of America. Even before this, the Hebrew Union College had established a campus in Jerusalem. Other traditional elements had re-entered the Reform Movement as well. The "Presbyterian" looking *Union Prayer Book* was replaced by the *Gates of Prayer* which included more Hebrew, and in appearance, at least, looked like a traditional *siddur*.

I stress the word appearance because the *Gates of Prayer* remained Reform in emphasis and content. Indeed, Reform Judaism at the end of the twentieth century may be characterized as becoming more traditional in style, while becoming more radical in content. Reform, for example, made a major break with Orthodoxy when it voted to ordain women. The confluence of traditional style with radical substance was first made evident to me when I joined the faculty of the Hebrew Union College in 1980. The first student-run service I attended was conducted by a female rabbinic student wearing a *kipa* and a full *talit*. Other than the fact that she was a woman, she could have been a *"yeshiva bucher."*

I see the emergence of the *Berit Mila* Program as part of this trend toward tradition within Reform. Having a *berit mila* ceremony became unfashionable among Reform and Conservative Jews because (a) it was perceived as being unsanitary and not in keeping with the scientific age to perform operations in the home in front of one's friends and family and (b) *berit mila* was seen by many as "barbaric" in that pain would be inflicted on the infant as part of a ceremony. In nineteenth century Germany, many Jews abandoned circumcision because they felt it to be barbaric. In America until recently, the almost universal acceptance of circumcision for health reasons has made this a non-issue. We have the *"mila"* performed surgically in the hospital, without the ceremony of *"berit."*

Why, then, the renewed interest in the *berit mila* ceremony? First, I would suggest that the revolution in how we look at childbirth set the stage. Although few of us actually have home births, the "natural childbirth" movement has encouraged that the hospital setting resemble that of the home delivery. In this context, the *berit mila* ceremony is an extension of direct parental involvement in the birth experience. Further, although some experience the *berit mila* ceremony as barbaric, its experiential nature is compelling.

Where then is the radical substance associated with the Reform *berit mila* ceremony? First, there is the participation of women in the ceremony; second, the inclusion of creative services and readings as part of the ceremony. Third, there is the spin-off ceremony of baby-naming for girls held on the eighth day which stresses the entrance of Jewish females into the *berit* as well. Thus, the *berit mila* ceremony can be seen as the latest innovation in Reform in which traditional elements are re-invigorated in a radical way.

The importance of training *mohalim/ot* to officiate at this ceremony is even more significant when considered in the light of three demographic trends currently taking place in American Jewish life.

DEMOGRAPHIC SIGNIFICANCE OF *Berit Mila*

The first of these demographic trends in American Jewish life is intermarriage. Intermarriage is the essential dilemma of modernity. Jews in America have fought long and hard against discrimination. Quotas at private colleges and universities have all but been entirely eliminated. There are very few neighborhoods or communities in the United States where Jews are unable to buy a house if they can afford one. Jews are even represented in many corporate settings which previously were closed to them. The American Jewish

Committee in Los Angeles is now fighting to have Jews admitted to the most exclusive of the downtown clubs. Although they have yet to succeed, they have reduced the prestige and the influence of these clubs. Government officials, for example, are prohibited from conducting official business there.

American Jews never reckoned on so much success. Jews are accepted everywhere, including within Gentile families. As a result of this acceptance, the rate of mixed-marriage (that is, marriages between Jews and non-Jews) has increased dramatically in only the past decade. In Los Angeles, one out of three Jews under thirty are married to non-Jews and in Denver, the number is three out of five. Further, these mixed-marriage rates are double the rates for Jews between the ages of thirty and thirty-nine in the same cities (see Table 1).

TABLE 1: INTERMARRIAGE BY AGE OF BORN JEW (INDIVIDUAL RATES)

Type of Marriage	18–29	30–39	40–49	50+
Los Angeles				
Two Born Jews	63.3	85.5	89.3	91.2
Born Jew & Convert	4.2	2.6	3.3	0.5
Born Jew & Non-Jew	32.5	12.9	7.3	8.3
TOTAL	100.0	100.0	100.0	100.0
Denver				
Two Born Jews	34.9	60.3	90.1	88.0
Born Jew & Convert	4.7	7.3	1.7	5.3
Born Jew & Non-Jew	60.5	32.3	8.3	6.7
TOTAL	100.0	100.0	100.0	100.0
Phoenix				
Two Born Jews	52.9	71.4	81.5	91.2
Born Jew & Convert	7.1	12.1	5.0	1.5
Born Jew & Non-Jew	40.1	16.6	13.5	7.3
TOTAL	100.0	100.0	100.0	100.0
Houston				
Two Born Jews	53.3	63.3	66.1	89.1
Born Jew & Convert	10.7	9.6	9.3	4.6
Born Jew & Non-Jew	36.0	26.8	13.6	6.3
TOTAL	100.0	100.0	100.0	100.0

NOTE: The rate of intermarriage among *individuals* under thirty is between 1/3 and 2/5—which means that *half or more* of all *couples* being formed are intermarriages.

The real impact of mixed marriage is even more dramatic than the rates above indicate. This is because those Jews who marry each other form one in-married couple, while those other Jews who marry non-Jews form *two* mixed-married couples. Thus, if one third of Jewish individuals under thirty in Los Angeles marry non-Jews (as is the case), then *half* of the marriages among the youngest adult Jews (i.e., under thirty) will be mixed-marriages. In Denver, a sixty percent rate of individual mixed-marriage means that three quarters of all marriages where the Jewish partner is under thirty will include a non-Jewish partner (see Table 2). When these young couples begin to have children, half or more of all Jewish children will have a non-Jewish parent.

The Reform response to the rise in mixed-marriage has been the adoption of patrilineal descent for conferring Jewish status. Sociologically this makes sense since either parent has the potential to influence or decide the religious identity of the child, and in practice the vast majority of Jews simply accept an individual's self-identification as Jewish. Halachically, on the other hand, only the mother can confer Jewish status. Patrilineal descent put the Reform Movement further at odds with Orthodoxy. Orthodox circles have responded by various verbal attacks on Reform and by pulling out of various inter-movement bodies such as the Jewish Welfare Board, which supplies chaplains for the armed services. There have been various threats that have been made that since the adoption of patrilineal descent, all children of Reform offspring will be suspect. Of course, since Reform conversion is not acceptable to the Orthodox, at least some Reform offspring would not have been considered Jews in any case, from an Orthodox perspective. In this context the *Berit Mila* Program gains additional significance. Since the majority of *mohalim* are Orthodox, and since Reform Jewish status has become an issue of contention, the emergence of training of *mohalim/ot* in a Reform context is a logical consequence of patrilineal descent.

TABLE 2: RATES OF COUPLE INTERMARRIAGE

Type of Marriage	Denver	Phoenix	Los Angeles	Houston
Two Born Jews	62.4	65.8	75.5	58.4
Born Jew & Convert	6.6	9.8	4.2	12.9
Born Jew & Non-Jew	30.1	24.3	20.1	29.5
TOTAL	100.0	100.0	100.0	100.0

TABLE 3a: AGE PROFILES

Age	Denver	Phoenix	Los Angeles	Houston
0–4	6.4	6.8	4.3	8.8
5–9	5.6	5.6	6.8	8.5
10–14	5.8	7.4	6.3	8.9
15–17	3.1	4.5	4.3	2.6
18–24	8.4	9.2	9.0	6.0
25–29	13.6	7.5	10.4	8.5
30–34	13.1	11.0	9.2	9.7
35–39	7.9	8.7	8.1	11.9
40–44	6.9	6.5	5.3	9.6
45–49	3.6	4.0	6.8	4.5
50–54	5.9	4.2	6.8	4.3
55–59	4.3	5.4	7.5	3.4
60–64	3.9	5.8	5.3	4.4
65–69	4.4	5.5	4.2	2.8
70–74	3.3	3.5	3.1	2.3
75–79	1.9	1.7	1.9	1.0
80+	1.8	1.3	1.9	1.5
TOTAL	100.0	100.0	100.0	100.0

NOTE: The "Baby Boom" occurred between 1946 and 1964. Thus the Baby Boomers would be the following ages for the studies above:

Los Angeles (1979):	15–33
Phoenix (1983):	19–39
Denver (1981):	17–35
Houston (1986):	21–40

The second trend is what demographers call the "echo of the baby boom." The children of the huge birth cohort of 1946-1964 are now having their own children (see Tables 3a and 3b). This means that there will be many more children being born over the next decade. The emergence of the baby boom echo is probably not surprising to obstetricians and pediatricians who have seen dramatic upswings in patient loads. It is also no longer news for synagogues and Jewish centers which have seen an unanticipated demand for preschool,

TABLE 3b: FAMILY STRUCTURE

Family Structure	Denver	Phoenix	Los Angeles	Houston
Married couple w/kids	24.5	28.1	24.3	35.3
Married couple n/kids	38.6	37.7	33.3	30.3
Single Parent Family	3.9	5.0	4.0	2.5
Single Household	32.9	29.1	38.4	31.8
TOTAL	100.0	100.0	100.0	100.0

daycare and nursery school service. The echo of the baby boom has created a cultural focus on childbirth which may bring about renewed interest in the *berit mila* ceremony.

The third trend is the emergence of the fourth generation (see Table 4). The immigrants are the first generation, the children of immigrants are the second, and the grandchildren of immigrants the third. The fourth generation, like the third, have American-born parents. Unlike the third generation, they also have American-born grandparents. They have no direct link to European Jewish culture within their own families. A third or more of all Jews between eighteen and forty are fourth generation, and as time goes by, this proportion will grow. This will increasingly be the generation that is having children.

The emergence of the fourth generation is important in two ways. First, the fourth generation largely identifies itself as Reform. When asked "How do you think of yourself: as Reform, Conservative, Orthodox, Reconstructionist, 'Just Jewish,' or something else?," half or more of fourth generation Jews (depending on the particular survey) identify as Reform.[1] When these fourth generation Jews have children and join synagogues, they will presumably join Reform synagogues.

TABLE 4: AGE BY GENERATION

Generation	18–29	30–39	40–49	50–59	60+
Denver					
First	5.5	6.2	16.5	19.1	25.7
Second	7.6	8.7	24.4	34.0	60.2
Third	34.3	47.3	49.6	42.0	12.3
Fourth	52.5	37.8	9.4	4.9	1.9
TOTAL	100.0	100.0	100.0	100.0	100.0
Los Angeles					
First	15.0	18.2	21.1	19.7	43.0
Second	4.0	10.0	23.6	60.5	50.1
Third	35.5	44.5	44.3	14.0	5.2
Fourth	45.7	27.3	11.0	5.9	1.7
TOTAL	100.0	100.0	100.0	100.0	100.0
Phoenix					
First	6.2	11.3	8.8	8.3	14.3
Second	6.3	10.8	24.4	44.5	62.1
Third	35.0	46.1	46.2	38.7	17.8
Fourth	52.6	31.7	20.5	8.5	5.8
TOTAL	100.0	100.0	100.0	100.0	100.0

Taken together, these three trends suggest that Reform Judaism could well be estranged from Orthodoxy, and in an uneasy situation with Conservative Judaism, while at the same time more than half of these young couples will be mixed-marrieds. The Jewish status of their children will be rejected by the Orthodox if they are mixed-married or even if the non-Jewish female has converted. It is not clear where the Conservative Movement will stand on the Jewish status of children with Jewish fathers by the year 2000. If they hold to their present stand, then they too could end up estranged from Reform. But if the Reform Movement is able to capitalize on the stated preference of fourth generation Jews, both in-married and mixed-married, and translate identification into affiliation, then through numbers alone may come reconciliation with Orthodox and Conservative Judaism.

The emergence of the *Berit Mila* Program, then, comes at a time when the Reform Movement is striking out on its own in response to the tremendous socio-demographic changes taking place during the last quarter of the twentieth century. Reform *mohalim/ot* will encounter these changes in microcosm through the families with whom they come in contact. Many third and fourth generation Jews will be using the *berit mila* ceremony to explore and strengthen their attachment to the larger Jewish community, even though the legitimacy of their connection may rejected by the other two movements in Jewish life. As a *shaliach,* a representative of the community, the *mohel/et* will be there to welcome them and facilitate that process.

NOTE

1   Bruce D. Phillips, "Denver Jewish Population Study" and "Milwaukee Jewish Population Study," in *American Modernity and Jewish Identity,* ed. Steven M. Cohen (London, 1983).

Circumcision in the Biblical Period

Stanley Gevirtz

CIRCUMCISION IN THE ANCIENT NEAR EAST

The practice of circumcision was widespread, though by no means universal, in the ancient Near East; and it was of considerable antiquity, long antedating even the traditional date of Abraham (mid-second millennium B.C.E.—see below). On a pre-Israelite ivory from Megiddo (level VII A, ca. 1350–1150 B.C.E.), there is depicted a royal personage seated on a throne, before whom stand two women and an armed soldier leading two nude prisoners, each of whom is circumcised.[1] The prophet Jeremiah, toward the end of the seventh century B.C.E., is aware that circumcision was practiced not only by his compatriots and their immediate neighbors, the Edomites, Ammonites, Moabites, and desert Arabs, but by Egyptians as well (Jer. 9:25). Independent of the biblical evidence, the fifth century B.C.E. Greek historian, Herodotus, e.g., relates that,

> They [the Egyptians] are the only people in the world—they and such as have learnt the practice from them—who use circumcision. . . . They practice circumcision for the sake of cleanliness, considering it better to be clean than comely.[2]

Whatever the realities behind these observations of "the father of history," circumcision among the Egyptians may be traced back to at least the last quarter of the third millennium B.C.E. On a stele, dated to the twenty-third century B.C.E., an official of the king of

Lower Egypt (the region of the Nile Delta) records the following:

> I was one beloved of his father, favored of his mother, whom his brothers and sisters loved. When I was circumcised, together with one hundred and twenty men, there was none thereof who hit out, there was none thereof who was hit, there was none thereof who scratched, there was none thereof who was scratched. I was a commoner of repute, who lived on his (own) property, plowed with (his own) span of oxen, and sailed in his (own) ship, and not through that which I had found in the possession of my father, the honored Uha.[3]

The king of Egypt, Senusert I (mid-twentieth century B.C.E.), referring to himself, says, "As a child, when I had not yet lost my foreskin, he (Re-Ha-akhti, the sun-god) appointed me lord of mankind," just as Khnumhotep II, ruler of Beni Hassan (ca. nineteenth century B.C.E.), says of his father, "He governed at a time when he had not yet lost his foreskin; he executed a royal commission . . . as a child not yet circumcised."[4] And there is another literary reference, in the Book of the Dead, that may relate an instance of self-induced circumcision: "From the blood that fell from the phallus of Re, after he had finished cutting himself."[5]

Statues and bas-reliefs also provide unequivocal evidence that circumcision was practiced in Egypt from a very early period in its history. A Sixth Dynasty (2350–2000 B.C.E.) tomb scene, with the legend "Circumcision," shows a youth being circumcised and having the wound treated.[6] And a scene from the Temple of Mut at Karnak, dated to the reign of Thutmoses III (1490–1436 B.C.E.) depicts two young boys—perhaps six to eight years of age—being circumcised.[7] While complete removal of the prepuce, the "foreskin," is indicated by the literary evidence and some statuary, one bas-relief clearly reveals incomplete circumcision, a condition produced by a dorsal incision that exposes the *glans penis,* a form of circumcision that is said to be practiced by the Masai.[8] It is also to be noted that examination of several mummies has revealed the fact, however, that circumcision (whether complete or incomplete) was not performed universally in Egypt. And it may be either one of these facts to which the passage in Joshua 5:2-3,9 alludes when Joshua, about to lead the people of Israel across the Jordan to conquer the Promised Land, is commanded by God:

Make flint knives and circumcise the people of Israel again, the second time. So Joshua made flint knives and circumcised the people at Gibeath-haaraloth. . . . And the Lord said to Joshua, "This day I have rolled away the reproach of Egypt from you."

Just how old the practice of circumcision in the ancient Near East may be is impossible to say. In Egypt, as we have seen, it can be traced back to the Sixth Dynasty (2350-2000 B.C.E.). But the reference in Joshua 5:2-3 to the use—indeed, the requirement—of "flint knives" in the performance of the rite (cf. Exod. 4:25) distinctly implies that the practice may (and probably did) have its origin at a time when flint, rather than metal, was in common use: that is to say, in the Stone Age. Now in the Near East the Bronze Age, successor to the Stone Ages, began ca. 3200 B.C.E., about a thousand years earlier than the Egyptian Sixth Dynasty referred to above. And in North Syria, in the Plain of Antioch, not far from the reputed homeland of the patriarchs (Gen. 24:4,10; Josh. 24:2-3), several mounds were investigated and these revealed evidence of human occupation from ca. 6000-2000 B.C.E. in eleven phases of culture, designated by the excavators alphabetically, A-K. Phase F, beginning at about 3200 B.C.E., appears to have been ushered in by a new ethnic element, a people in possession of a technology superior to that of the people of the preceding phases. The new population utilized a potter's wheel, mud brick architecture, and a knowledge of metallurgy. The succeeding phase, G, ca. 2800 B.C.E., represents an essential continuum of Phase F, but one that witnessed the achievement of new cultural heights. Found here was a cache of six statuettes made of cast metal, with each of them cast in a different mold. The figures, three adult males and three adult females, vary in height from 146 mm. (the shortest female) to 265 mm. (the tallest male). Except for headdresses on the females, and helmets and waistbands on the males (each of whom is bearded), the figures are represented as nude, with their genitalia exposed. A member of the Department of Urology of Billings Hospital in Chicago, Dr. Cornelius W. Vermuelen, has noted that, insofar as on each of the male figures the penis is pendulous, and as the corona of the penis on two of the males is entirely visible, complete circumcision is represented, whereas on the third only partial circumcision.[9] Circumcision, then, was certainly being practiced in North Syria in approximately 2800 B.C.E., or shortly after the advent of the

Bronze Age in the ancient Near East. And it is not unlikely that the practice is older yet.

What we may glean from the evidence examined thus far is that circumcision in the ancient Near East was widely, though not universally, practiced; that its origins may be traced back at least as far as the beginnings of civilization and probably reach further back into into the Stone Ages; that the rite was performed—among the Egyptians, at least—sometime between childhood and adulthood, and was executed in groups. In none of our extra-biblical sources is there any indication that spiritual value attached itself to the performance of the rite, or that it had any specifically religious significance. Undoubtedly it had social value and meaning, and to the extent that religion may have informed this aspect of life, circumcision may have shared in it. But nowhere is it even intimated that deity demanded it, or that it may have constituted a covenantal requirement. And this assessment accords with what is known of the practice among contemporary non-Jewish societies. Muslim boys who undergo the procedure usually do so in childhood, not in infancy, most often in large groups; and though the event is celebrated, it is more a social than a religious one, albeit among some groups it is performed at a shrine sometimes accompanied by sacrifices. But the *Qur'an* does not require it.[10]

CIRCUMCISION IN THE HEBREW BIBLE

For the significance of circumcision in the history of Jewish tradition the single most important text among the biblical sources that refer to the practice is Genesis 17:9-14:

And God said to Abraham, "As for you, you shall keep my Covenant, you and your descendants after you throughout their generations. This is my Covenant which you shall keep, between me and you and your descendants after you: Every male among you shall be circumcised. You shall be circumcised in the flesh of your foreskins, and it shall be a sign of the Covenant between me and you. He that is eight days old among you shall be circumcised; every male throughout your generations, whether born in your house or bought with your money from any foreigner who is not of your offspring. Both he that is born in your house and he that is bought with your money, shall be circumcised. So shall my Covenant be in your flesh an everlasting Covenant. Any uncircumcised male who is not circumcised in the flesh of his foreskin shall be cut off from his people; he has broken my Covenant."

The other passages are directly dependent upon this one; and if they are not by the same priestly author, they unquestionably emanate from the same priestly tradition:

And Abraham circumcised his son Isaac when he was eight days old, as God had commended him. (Gen. 21:4)

and

The Lord said to Moses, "Say to the people of Israel, If a woman conceives, and bears a male child, then she shall be unclean seven days; as at the time of her menstruation, she shall be unclean. *And on the eighth day the flesh of his foreskin shall be circumcised.* Then she shall continue for thirty-three days in the blood of her purifying; she shall not touch any hallowed thing, nor come into the sanctuary, until the days of her purifying be completed. But if she bears a female child, then she shall be unclean two weeks as in her menstruation; and she shall continue in the blood of her purifying the sixty-six days." (Lev. 12:1-5)

The latter reference, here italicized, is self-evidently an interpolation, for it interrupts and is irrelevant to the matter at hand: the series of regulations concerning a woman who has given birth and the length of time of her state of impurity that is dependent upon the sex of the child she has borne. As an interpolation, it must be later than the text into which it was inserted and, indeed, in the opinion of most modern biblical interpreters, it is to be assigned to a very late source. Insofar as Genesis 17: 9-14, Genesis 21:4, and Leviticus 12:3 are of the same priestly tradition, if not by the same author, Genesis 17, which has so thoroughly informed our understanding of circumcision in the biblical period, must also be late. And this is in part confirmed by the reference in God's promise to Abraham that "kings shall come forth from you," for it implies that the author is living during or after the time of kingship in Israel, sometime in the middle of the first millennium B.C.E., about a thousand years after the time that Abraham presumably lived.

The author of Genesis 17 traces the origin of circumcision among his people to God's directive to Abraham, "you shall be circumcised in the flesh of your foreskins and it shall be a sign of the Covenant between me and you. He that is eight days old among you shall be circumcised . . ." Because it is here declared to be a Covenant between God, on the one hand, and Abraham and his descendants, on the other, as well as a sign or stipulation of that Covenant, and because it is here commanded by God, for the author of Genesis 17 circumcision constitutes an eminently religious procedure. Furthermore, because it is required of every male who has attained the age of eight days—meaning that it must be performed on each and every eight-day-old male child (cf. Gen. 21:4)—circumcision has been rendered an individualized event.

These two aspects of circumcision, its religious nature and its individualization, appear to have been the innovation of the author of this late priestly tradition, and they have distinguished Jewish circumcision, *berit mila,* ever since. Whether they may have characterized Israelite circumcision prior to the composition of these passages in the mid-first millennium B.C.E. is uncertain but unlikely, for aside from these three passages, there is nothing in biblical literature to suggest that the Israelite practice of circumcision differed in this regard, in any essential way, from that of Israel's neighbors, and there is no evidence to indicate that the rite was a particularly religious one, or that it was performed at any specific time—much less, on the eighth day. Rather, what evidence we have points to the practice having been performed en masse, at some time between early childhood and adulthood, or, perhaps, puberty. And despite the appeal to Genesis 17:25, wherein it is recorded that Ishmael was thirteen years of age when he was circumcised, there is nothing to suggest that it was an initiation or puberty rite.

When we turn to examine biblical passages other than Genesis 17, Genesis 21:4, and Leviticus 12:3, wherein circumcision is enjoined, and do so without benefit of the priestly perspective afforded by the texts cited, the practice and its significance do not appear to differ intrinsically from what we have been able to determine of these elsewhere in the ancient world. At most it seems to have been regarded as an act of "disgrace" removal. Just why the foreskin should have constituted a disgrace, however, is not explained.

Genesis 34 relates that Hamor's son, Shechem, raped Jacob's daughter, Dinah, and, having fallen in love with her, entreated his father to negotiate their marriage. As an inducement to effect the marriage between his son and Dinah, Hamor offered to her father and brothers an alliance with social and economic advantages, and Shechem indicated his willingness to pay whatever marriage present might be demanded of him (cf. Exod. 22:15-16). The response of Dinah's brothers to Shechem and his father was that marriage with someone who is uncircumcised would constitute a disgrace *(cherpah)*, that only on the condition that all males of their community be circumcised would the brothers consent to the union. The condition is accepted and the operation is performed. But while the Shechemites were still sore, Dinah's brothers, Simeon and Levi, slaughtered them. The relevant points to be noted here are (a) that circumcision requires no religious commitment, no covenant with the God of Israel, and (b) that it is performed en masse and without regard to age.

Mass circumcision, again without concern for age, is explicitly demanded of Israelites in Joshua 5:2-3 (see above). When it is completed, God remarks (v. 9), "This day I have removed the disgrace *(cherpah)* of Egypt from you." (This accords with the attitude expressed by Dinah's brothers that having a foreskin constitutes for the Israelite community a "disgrace.") Immediately following, in verse 10, we are informed that the People of Israel kept the Passover. This is of interest because in the passage to be cited next, circumcision is a prerequisite for partaking of the Passover. Ex. 12:43-45 and 48 legislates that no uncircumcised foreigner may partake of the Passover. Slaves of Israelites may do so only after they have been circumcised. And a sojourning stranger who wishes to share in the Passover may do so only after he and all his males(!) have been circumcised. Apparently, once having been circumcised, he is to be regarded as a native of the land. No oath, no swearing of allegiance to, or acceptance of, Israel's God is involved. Circumcision is the only requirement.

We may then suggest that the term, *cherpah,* translated above as "disgrace," a condition adhering to one who retains his foreskin, may better be rendered "social stigma," a meaning that is common to it (cf. Gen. 30:23; 2 Sam. 13:13; Isa. 54:4; Job 19:5; etc.). And this may explain how the term, *areil,* meaning "uncircumcised" (literally: having foreskin), came to be used as a term of contempt vis-à-vis the Philistines (Jud. 14: 3; 15:18; 1 Sam. 14:6; 17:26, 36; 31:4 [= 1 Ch. 10:41]; 2 Sam. 1:20), and identified with a sense of revulsion (e.g., Ezek. 32:24 ff.).

Thus it is that an author in the priestly tradition could employ the term, *orla,* "uncircumcised" (having foreskin), in its verbal form "to regard as having a foreskin," metaphorically in the slightly extended meaning "to regard as taboo." Leviticus 19:23-25 reads:

> When you enter the land and plant any food tree, you shall regard its fruit as having its foreskin. Three years it shall be to you as having foreskin; it shall not be eaten. In the fourth year all its fruit shall be holy, praise-offering to the Lord. And in the fifth year you may eat its fruit . . .

Other figurative uses of the expression suggest that, in Israelite thought, the foreskin may have been viewed as a hindrance to the proper functioning of the organ. The condition of having a foreskin could thus be extended, metaphorically, to other bodily organs, specifically: of speech, i.e., "the lips" (Exod. 6:12,30), of hearing, i.e., "the ears" (Jer. 6:10) and of the intellect, will, or mind, i.e., "the hearts" (Lev. 26:41; Deut. 10:16; 30:6; Jer. 4:4; 9:25; Ezek. 44:7,9). For, when God directs Moses to tell Pharaoh, King of Egypt, to allow the Israelites to leave his land, Moses protests:

> Behold, the Israelites do not listen to me, how then shall Pharaoh listen, when I am a man of uncircumcised lips? (Exod. 6:12,30)

And Jeremiah, frustrated by the recalcitrance of his contemporaries, says:

> To whom shall I speak and give warning that they may hear? Behold, their ears are uncircumcised, and they are unable to listen. (Jer. 6:10)

While the stubborn or closed mind is figuratively represented as the "uncircumcised heart," which leads Jeremiah to enjoin:

> Circumcise yourselves to the Lord, remove the foreskin of your hearts, O men of Judah and inhabitants of Jerusalem; lest my anger go forth like fire, and burn with none to quench it, because of your evil doings. (Jer. 4:4; cf. Deut. 10:16)

The circumcised heart was considered a prerequisite to Israel's proper relationship with God, and for its life in its own land (Deut.

30:6; cf. Lev. 26:41; see further Ezek. 44:7,9). Finally, mention must be made of a passage whose meaning continues to elude savants, but in which circumcision plays a central role. Exodus 4:24-26 reads:

> At a lodging place on the way, the Lord met him and sought to kill him. Then Zipporah took a flint and cut off her son's foreskin, and touched his feet (with it?), and said, "Surely, you are a bridegroom of blood to me," referring to circumcision.

Set immediately following the Lord's directive to Moses to appear before Pharaoh and present certain ultimatums to him, and immediately preceding the Lord's directive to Aaron to meet Moses in the wilderness, it cannot be that the one whom the Lord sought to kill should be Moses. Moreover, insofar as Moses at this point in the account is the father of two children, the term "bridegroom" is inapplicable to him. In all likelihood, therefore, the object of the Lord's murderous intent was the uncircumcised son. A suggestion has been advanced by Hans Kosmala that the expression *chatan damim* ("bridegroom of blood") is not Hebrew but Midianite (Zipporah was the daughter of a Midianite priest) and meant simply "circumcised" (Arabic *chatana* means "to circumcise"), so that her statement means "you are now circumcised." If this is so, then the import of the passage is that the child's uncircumcised state endangered his life. By circumcising him, touching his feet (with the amputated foreskin?), and reciting the formula, "Surely, you are circumcised to (= by) me," Zipporah appeased the deity and averted the slaying of her son. However the problems of the passage may ultimately be resolved, we may note in it an element of the demonic and the intimation that latent in the taboo that is represented by the foreskin was a danger to life, a danger not otherwise hinted at in our sources.

CONCLUSION

Transformation of the rite of circumcision from that of a mass exercise performed at no specified period of time, though ordinarily during childhood, into that of a ceremony executed specifically on the eighth day of life, represented a radical departure from the norm of ancient Near Eastern practice, as this can be deduced, and served to personalize the event. Making the removal of the foreskin an indispensable component of a covenant between deity and man, rather than merely an elimination of a social stigma or a superstitious taboo, imbued it with a religious significance it seems never to have had before. Viewed from this dual perspective, the priestly author's selection of the eighth day for performance of the rite accords well with the primitive requirement that is embedded in what is generally regarded as the earliest of the biblical law "codes," Exodus 22:28-29:

> . . . The firstborn of your sons you shall give to me. You shall do likewise with your oxen and with your sheep: seven days it shall be with its mother; on the eighth day you shall give it to me.

Whether this apparent identification was a conscious one on the part of the priestly author, it effectively permitted the substitution of *pars pro toto,* and served to elevate the essentially secular ritual of circumcision into a supremely religious act.

NOTES

1. *The Ancient Near East in Pictures Relating to the Old Testament* (Princeton, 1954), p. 111, no. 332; cf. p. 288.
2. Herodotus, *Historiae,* Book II, p. 104f.
3. James B. Pritchard, *Ancient Near Eastern Texts Relating to the Old Testament* (Princeton, 1954), p. 326.
4. *Urkunden des ägyptischen Altertums,* VII, 34; cf. James Henry Breasted, *Ancient Records of Egypt,* I (1906), Inscription 636.
5. *The Book of the Dead,* chapter XVII, 23; cf. Frans Jonckheere, "La circoncision des anciens Égyptiens," *Centaurus* 1 (1951), p. 215.
6. Pritchard, *The Ancient Near East in Pictures,* p. 206, No. 629; cf. *ibid.,* p. 325, and Jonckheere, p. 223.
7. Jonckheere, p. 221.
8. Jonckheere, p. 227.
9. Robert J. Braidwood and Linda S. Braidwood, *Excavations in the Plain of Antioch I: The Earlier Assemblages Phases A-J,* (Chicago, 1960), pp. 302 f. and Plates 56–59; cf. pp. 307–309, fig. 240–242).
10. Julian Morgenstern, *Rites of Birth, Marriage, Death and Kindred Occasions Among the Semites* (Cincinnati and Chicago, 1966), pp. 48–80.

Berit Mila in *Midrash* and *Agada*

Lewis M. Barth

INTRODUCTION

Hundreds of references to *berit* and *berit mila* are found scattered throughout rabbinic literature. Nevertheless, it is curious that neither the *Mishna* nor the *Talmud* contains a complete tractate in which the laws of ritual circumcision comprise the main topic. There is a small collection of laws related to *mila* in mShabbath, chapter 19; the *Gemara* to that passage expands this collection through analysis, interpretation and legal and legendary embellishment. Both documents, however, present this material in connection with the general topic "work prohibited on the Sabbath" rather than as a systematic discussion of *mila*. Similarly, there is no early collection of *agada*, Jewish legendary and theological material, which treats only this subject. Instead, in the *Midrash*, references to *berit mila* are found as comments to biblical verses in which the subject is mentioned or inferred.

A significant collection of material on this topic is found in *Bereshit Rabba (BR)*, a fifth-century Palestinian *Midrash* on the biblical book Genesis. Discussions of various aspects of *mila* appear here as comments on Genesis 17, the primary biblical source of religious observance of circumcision among the Jews (see Gevirtz). The rabbinic exegesis of this crucial chapter represents an attempt to rationalize circumcision for the Jewish world and justify it in the larger context of Greco-Roman and Christian civilization.

The need for justification presumes opposition to the practice. A close examination of *BR,* chapter 46, on Genesis 17, suggests that serious questions arose within the Palestinian Jewish community in Late Antiquity regarding circumcision. In addition, the chapter reveals rabbinic sensitivity to the impact on potential converts of the requirement of circumcision for conversion. Finally, it offers direct and indirect responses to the negative attitude among non-Jews toward this practice and to the concrete manifestations of these attitudes in Roman and Byzantine law.

Various types of argumentation are employed to counter contemporary opposition to circumcision and to deepen Jewish commitment to its observance. Naturally, the rabbis also make an appeal to religious conviction, that is, performance of *berit mila* based on its acceptance as a divine commandment.

THE FORESKIN AS BLEMISH

In the Greco-Roman world, a corollary to the ideal of the perfection of the body was the view that circumcision was a form of mutilation (see Signer). In *BR,* chapter 46, a major rabbinic counterargument is presented which represents the extreme opposite point of view: circumcision is a technique to improve a slightly imperfect creation, to remove an insignificant blemish.

In *BR,* chapter 46, this idea is conveyed through two parables and then expanded in an elaborate exegesis of Genesis 17:1. Typical of rabbinic literature, the parables (chapter 46:1 and 4) are grounded in everyday imagery from the realms of agriculture and royalty:

1) R. Judan said: In the case of a fig, its only defect is its stalk. Remove it and the blemish ceases. Thus, the Holy One Blessed be He said to Abraham, "Your only defect is this foreskin. Remove it and the blemish is cancelled. 'Walk before Me and be perfect'" (Gen. 17:1).

4) "Walk before Me and be perfect" (Gen. 17:1). R. Levi said: This may be compared to a noblewoman to whom the king said, 'Pass before me.' As she passed before him she turned pale. She thought, 'Maybe there is some defect in me.' The king said to her, 'There is no defect in you, but the nail on your little finger is a bit too long. Cut it and the blemish is removed.' Thus, the Holy One Blessed be

He said to Abraham, "Your only defect is this foreskin. Remove it and the blemish is cancelled. 'Walk before Me and be perfect'" (Gen. 17:1).

These two parables represent *mila* as cosmetic surgery designed to make the male body physically perfect. The imaginative play in the parables describes God commanding removal of the foreskin, but for reasons very different from the biblical text. The surface implication, which fits well into rabbinic thinking, is that the male child is born with an imperfection which human action can fix. In addition, in the context of the parables, the word *tamim* (Gen. 17:1), "perfect," clearly refers to physical and not spiritual perfection. The rabbinic response to the Greco-Roman notion of the perfection of the body is a direct counter-claim typically associated with and rooted in Scripture.

There is an additional element embedded in these parables. The terms *pesolet* and *mum,* "defect" and "blemish," have special significance in the ancient sacrificial cult of the Jerusalem Temple. *Pasul,* from the same Hebrew root as *pesolet,* means "unfit"; it is often used in connection with *mum,* "blemish." In rabbinic literature these words frequently describe an animal which has become ritually unfit to be offered on the altar because it has a blemish. The same words apply to a priest with a blemish who is, as a consequence, ritually unfit to offer sacrifices.

In the case of the animal or the priest, the disqualifying blemish is typically physical and often refers to some sort of birth defect or a wound which is later incurred. For example, tradition records the incident of a High Priest who was disqualified from serving on Yom Kippur because a rival bit off his ear.

It is therefore quite remarkable that *mila,* the cutting off of the foreskin, is viewed as categorically different from various forms of mutilation prohibited by Scripture and rabbinic tradition. Circumcision does not inflict a blemish on the body; rather, it removes one.

Rabbinic tradition further emphasizes that removal of the foreskin, an act of cutting the body, does not disqualify a priest from service. This linkage is made in *BR,* chapter 46:5 as follows:

Rabbi Ishmael and Rabbi Akiba both agreed. Rabbi Ishmael said, Abraham was a High Priest. As it is said, "The Lord has sworn and will not relent, 'You are a priest forever, because of the words of Melchizedek'" (Ps. 110:4). And elsewhere it is said, "You shall circumcise the flesh of your foreskin" (Gen. 17:11).

If he would be circumcised at the ear, he would be unfit to offer sacrifice; at the mouth, he would be unfit to offer sacrifice; at the heart, he would be unfit to offer sacrifice. Where could he be circumcised and still be fit to offer sacrifice? One must say, this refers to the *orla* (foreskin) of the body.

Rabbi Akiba said, There are four kinds of *orla*. The term *orla* is related to the ear, as it is said, "To whom shall I speak, Give warning that they may hear? Their ears are blocked *(areila)*" (Jer. 6:10). *Orla* is related to the mouth, "Moses appealed to the Lord, saying, 'See, I am of impeded *(areil)* speech'" (Ex. 6:30). *Orla* is related to the heart, "For all these nations are uncircumcised, but all the House of Israel are uncircumcised of the heart" (Jer. 9:25). But He said to him, "Walk before Me and be perfect."

If he would be circumcised from the ear, he could not be perfect; from the mouth, he could not be perfect; from the heart, he could not be perfect. Where could he be circumcised and still be perfect? One must say, this refers to the *orla* (foreskin) of the body.

The significant elements of this passage are:

1. the designation of Abraham as High Priest.
2. connection of *orla* to various parts of the body based on biblical proof-texts.
3. the clarification that removal of *orla* as foreskin is categorically different and would not disqualify a priest from offering sacrifice.

Each of these elements is worthy of more extensive analysis than can be provided here. Nevertheless, some brief comments are in order. This passage certainly reflects a rabbinic penchant for argument-for-argument's-sake, or simply the rabbinic delight in playing with the biblical text. At the same time it should be noted that the argument and play indirectly acknowledge the negative view of Greco-Roman culture toward circumcision.

From the time of the Emperor Hadrian, c. 135 C.E., Roman law increasingly forbade circumcision and restricted its practice to the Jews. As previously mentioned, it was considered a form of mutilation and linked to castration. Even doctors who performed the operation were liable to severe punishment. Extensive penalties were legislated for Jews who circumcised their slaves or tried to impose circumcision on apostates. This act resulted in the automatic manumission of slaves.

At the same time, biblical and rabbinic tradition contains clear prohibitions against various other forms of mutilation, for example: gashing the skin and tattooing. Through a unique interpretive inversion, circumcision is viewed as an enabling act to beautify the body, having nothing to do with mutilation.

The link to priestly service also underscores the significance of circumcision to the rabbis in the highly charged confrontation between Palestinian Judaism and Imperial Byzantine Christianity. The passage just cited implicitly rejects the dominant Western interpretation of Paul's arguments regarding the figure and role of Abraham. According to that view, Abraham was the spiritual ancestor of Gentile Christians, and the natural father of the Jews. He was justified through faith prior to his having received the commandment regarding circumcision. His spiritual descendants, Gentile Christians, "the uncircumcised," are also justified through their faith and will receive the reward of the promises once given to and now removed from the Jews. There is no need for them to undergo circumcision.

Our text, however, presumes that Abraham is the ancestor of the Jewish People, and allows no distinction between his roles as spiritual and natural father. It also recognizes that the biblical incident involving Melchizedek (Gen. 14:18 ff.)—interpreted to signify the removal of the priesthood from him and its transfer to Abraham—took place before the commandment regarding circumcision (Gen. 17). Abraham already was High Priest; circumcision did not disqualify him from serving in this role.

Rabbinic Judaism viewed the Jewish People as replacing the priesthood and standing in its stead. For Jews, following in the line of Abraham, circumcision becomes a special mark of holiness in service to God, and not a blemish disqualifying them from the priesthood.

PLACE AND TIME FOR *Mila*

The above passage assumes the following question: where on the body is circumcision to take place? Although the question is absurd and an obvious pretext for rabbinic argumentation and playfulness, the various answers allow us to glimpse additional dimensions of the rabbinic treatment of *mila*.

A.   Circumcision and Fertility

Circumcision becomes associated with procreation and fertility. For example, *BR*, chapter 46:2, contains an argument in which two rabbis seek to determine the method of scriptural interpretation Abraham used to determine which place on the body is to be circumcised. Scriptural verses are employed to prove that just as fruit trees have *orla*, so the organ to be circumcised is the one "which produces fruit" (cf. Gen. 17:11 and Lev. 19:23); or, that the sign of the Covenant is to be placed on the organ through which Abraham will multiply his seed (Gen. 17:2). Yet another example is based on Genesis 17:12, "And throughout the generations, every male among you shall be circumcised at the age of eight days." As the verse mentions "male," it is argued that one circumcises the place where you can tell the difference between a male and female. One more example connects circumcision with fertility, although its focus is somewhat different than those just mentioned. The topic of *BR*, chapter 46:2, is Abraham being circumcized at an advanced age. The passage concludes with a parable in which Abraham is compared to a cinnamon tree:

> Rabbi Simon ben Lakish said, 'I'm going to bring cinnamon into this world! Just as the cinnamon tree—as long as you fertilize it and hoe around it—produces fruit, so when his [Abraham's] blood ran cold, after his sexual desire ceased, after his lust ceased.'

B.   Abraham's Advanced Age

Underlying the rabbinic discussion of the advanced age at which Abraham was circumcised is the obvious human discomfort with the story in Genesis 17. For the rabbis, this biblical account presents an opportunity to point out Abraham's faith. Abraham is considered by the rabbis to be the first proselyte. Because he was circumcised at age ninety-nine, he serves as a model to indicate that "the door should never be closed before a convert." In an alternate interpretation, Abraham's age becomes a factor in confirming the holiness of his true descendent—Ishmael was born before Abraham was circumcised, Isaac after.

C.   Historical Associations

BR, chapter 46:2, also recognizes that circumcision was not always practiced among the Jews, that is to say, there were times in the biblical period when it was neglected and needed to be reinstated. Thus the juxtaposition of Genesis 17:26, when Abraham was circumcised, and Joshua 5:5. The full context of the Joshua verse is significant. This biblical narrative links circumcision with the departure from Egypt, military service, entry into the land, removal of the disgrace of Egypt, and celebration of the Passover at Gilgal. Joshua 5:2 describes "a second circumcision of the Israelites," the need for which is then explained in Joshua 5:5:

> "Now, whereas all the people who came out of Egypt had been circumcised, none of the people born after the exodus, during the desert wanderings, had been circumcised."

Although it is not completely clear why the *Midrash* cites this text, the sub-text of neglect of circumcision appears to be a primary motif here and throughout *BR,* chapter 46.

OPPOSITION TO *Mila*

In *BR,* chapter 46:3, we find a highly presumptuous question addressed by Abraham to God: "If *mila* is so special, why wasn't it given to Adam?" The question can be understood in at least two ways. First, if *mila* is so special, why wasn't the commandment to do it given to Adam—so that it would be observed by all human groups? Second, if *mila* is so special, why did God not create males without foreskins in the first place?

Abraham addresses a second question to God, less presumptuous but no less significant from a social and religious perspective:

"Before I was circumcised, people came and joined me. Do You think that since I have been circumcised they are still going to come and join me?" This question can also be understood in at least two ways. In rabbinic legend, Abraham is an effective missionary, bringing the nations under the wings of the *Shechina,* attracting converts. The question may suggest concern that the circumcision requirement will detract from the appeal of Judaism. Alternately, the question may suggest a fear in some segments of the Jewish community of the social stigma attached to those who are circumcised within Roman and Byzantine society.

Although the specific answers to these questions contain differences of nuance and detail, the force of the answers is the same: God tells Abraham, "That's enough!" The midrashic source of this answer is found in a play on one of the names by which God identifies Himself in Genesis 17:1, "I am *El Shaddai.''* *Shaddai* is treated as an abbreviation *(notarikon)* for *she-amar dai,* God is "the One who said, 'Enough.'" God abruptly tells Abraham that he should be satisfied that he is alive in this world. If he is unwilling to be circumcised, the world has gone on long enough. And again, Abraham should be satisfied that God is his God and Patron, neither he nor the world needs anyone else.

These arguments between Abraham and God suggest an inner Jewish opposition to the practice of *mila* in the rabbinic period. Nowhere, of course, does rabbinic literature give us any information about the individuals or groups of Jews who may have had second thoughts about circumcision, nor of their ideological or human concerns. Yet the force of the responses which the *Midrash* attributes to God is direct and unmistakable. God, in His capacity as *El Shaddai,* is "God Almighty." This is the God whose power is expressed in the act of creation by setting limits to the world itself, the same deity whom the world cannot contain. The curt answer to Abraham, "Enough," is also an answer to contemporary or subsequent generations which might challenge this *mitzvah:* observe it because God commanded it!

Some additional *aggadot* are found in *BR,* chapter 46, and the chapter concludes with several halachic comments found also in talmudic literature (see Zlotowitz). It should be clear from the above analysis, that the primary thrust of rabbinic commentary in *Bereshit Rabba* on Genesis 17, is apologetic and polemical: to support and preserve the *mitzvah* of *mila.*

THE GREATNESS OF *Mila*

We conclude with a litany of praises of *mila* found in mNedarim 3:11.

Rabbi Eleazer ben Azariah says: The foreskin [i.e., being uncircumcised] is despicable, for the wicked are shamed with it [i.e. it is a term of derision], as it is said, "For all these nations are uncircumcised (Jer. 9:26)."

Rabbi Ishmael says: Circumcision is great [i.e., an exceedingly important *mitzvah*], because with respect to it thirteen covenants were made [i.e. the word *berit* is mentioned thirteen times in Genesis 17].

Rabbi Jose says: Circumcision is great, because it supersedes even the stringent prohibition [against work] on the Sabbath (see mShab. 19:1).

Rabbi Joshua ben Karha says: Circumcision is great, because on its account [the threat of punishment even] for Moses [neglecting to circumcise his sons] was not delayed so much as an hour (see Exod. 4:24 ff.).

Rabbi Nehemiah says: Circumcision is great, because it overrides [the prohibitions against the cutting off of] leprous spots (see mNeg. 7:5).

Rabbi says: Circumcision is great, because, of all the *mitzvot* which Abraham performed, he was not called "perfect" until he was circumcised, as it is said, "Walk before Me and be perfect" (Gen. 17:1).

Another interpretation: Circumcision is great, because had it not been for it [i.e. circumcision], the Holy One Blessed Be He would not have created the world, as it is said, "Thus says the Lord, had it not been for [the observance of] my Covenant day and night, I would not have made the natural order of heaven and earth" (midrashic rendering of Jer. 33:25)

To See Ourselves as Others See Us:
Circumcision in Pagan Antiquity and the Christian Middle Ages

Michael Signer

INTRODUCTION

One of the most common questions asked by Jews in the modern era is, "What do *they* think?" The response of the non-Jewish world to Judaism and its religious practices is born of Judaism's minority status. If the surrounding culture admires what Jews are doing, the implicit assumption is that matters will fare well for their physical safety. A negative reaction from non-Jews might evoke attempts to explain Judaism in different terms, or, it might lead to a revision of Jewish thought and practice.

It would seem that there may be some aspects of Judaism which would be beyond compromise or revision. Jews might attempt to explain these more clearly to non-Jews. However, with respect to such matters the negative response of non-Jews would not force Jews into compromise.

This essay attempts to explore the commandment of circumcision or *berit mila*, one of those Jewish practices which have evoked negative responses since the ancient world. First, we explore the responses of pagan authors who wrote from 500 B.C.E. through the second century C.E. Then, we turn to the writings of the New Testament. Finally, we come to some Jewish responses from the Middle

Illustration 13

Circumcision Ceremony, woodcut from the Book of Customs, *Sefer Minhagim*, Amsterdam, 18th C. From the collection of the Hebrew Union College Klau Library. Lelo Carter, photographer.

Ages. In each era we shall observe the centrality of *berit mila* to the description of Judaism by the non-Jewish world.

THE CLASSICAL WORLD: HERODOTUS TO TACITUS

The discovery of civilizations in the eastern Mediterranean by the ancient Greeks stimulated considerable curiosity about the peoples who lived in the area. Despite the fact that Greeks had been in contact with Semitic civilizations since the Biblical Period, it was during the sixth century B.C.E. that written records emerge about the customs of these non-Greek speaking peoples.

The earliest description of circumcision by a Greek author is provided by Herodotus, who is known as "the Father of History." In his long account of the Oriental nations he describes the practice of circumcision in the context of other Semitic peoples in this way:

> For it is plain to see that the Colchians are Egyptians; and this that I say I myself noted before I heard it from others. When I began to think of this matter, I inquired of both peoples: and the Colchians remembered the Egyptians better than the Egyptians remembered the Colchians. The Egyptians said that they held the Colchians to be part of Seostris' army. I myself guessed it to be so, partly because they are dark-skinned and wooly-haired; though that indeed goes for nothing, seeing that other peoples, too, are such; but my better proof was that the Colchians and Egyptians and Ethiopians are the only nations that have from the first practiced circumcision. The Phoenicians and the Syrians of Palestine acknowledge of themselves that they learnt the custom of the Egyptians, and the Syrians of the valleys of the Thermodon and the Parthenius, as well as their neighbors the Macrones, say that they learnt it lately from the Colchians. [*Histories* II:104:1-3][1]

The practice of circumcision, according to Herodotus, is a rite held in common by these groups who populate the eastern Mediterranean. However, it should be noted that the Egyptians, Colchians, and Ethiopians were the first to practice circumcision. Only later did the peoples in Syria, Palestine and Lebanon (the Phoenicians) utilize this rite. Herotodus does not identify circumcision with the Jewish People. In his *Histories,* the ceremony is associated with the Egyptians.

To discover how the Greek authors link Jews with the Egyptians we may turn to Strabo (64/3 B.C.E.–21 C.E.), a philosopher, historian and geographer. His work, *Geographica,* described the origins of the Jewish People from the teachings of Moses who was an Egyptian priest. According to Strabo, Moses became "disgusted with Egyptian institutions" and led a group to Jerusalem where he established the Temple. Strabo expressed admiration for the sanctuary which Moses established and his legislation. However, the successors to Moses brought about a decline in moral and spiritual standards.

> His successors for some time kept up the same practices and were truly pious. Then the priesthood was held at first by superstitious and then by tyrannical men. From superstition arose abstention from foods, such as are customary even now, and circumcision and excisions and similar uses.   [*Geographica* 16.2.37][2]

Fram Strabo's point of view, superstitious rites were introduced to control the Jewish population. Circumcision would, therefore, not be part of the Law of Moses. In Strabo's *Geographica,* we observe a shift from Herodotus. Circumcision is not a tribal rite practiced for the purpose of identification. Instead, it is described as a superstitious practice utilized by tyrants to control the Jews. This would be consistent with a Hellenistic approach to legislation which praised abstract laws and just social conditions, but which also condemned mutilation of the body.

Roman poets and satirists identified the practice of circumcision as an indication of Jewish affiliation. They utilized it as a standardized epithet—a stock phrase—for Jews. In Horace's *Satires,* we have the following dialogue:

> Didn't you say there was something you wanted to tell me in private?

> I remember it well, but I'll tell you at a better time. Today is the Sabbath. Do you want to insult the circumcised Jews? [*Satires* 1.9.68-70]

In this dialogue, one can discern an awareness of two practices which set Jews apart: the observance of the Sabbath and circumcision. Fear of making a statement lest the Jews might hear it was also expressed by the Roman orator Cicero.[4]

One might expect that the genre of satire would play upon ethnic characteristics. Petronius, the master of satire, has references to circumcision which poke fun at the Jews. In one example, a master describes his slave as talented, yet "He has two blemishes...He is circumcised and he snores [*Satyricon* 68.8]."[5] The other example describes adventurers trying to escape from their enemies by means of disguise. When one of them suggests blackening their faces to look like African slaves, his friend replies, "Why not? Circumcise us too so that we may seem to be Jews and pierce our ears in imitation of the Arabians." [*Satyricon* 102.41]."[6] These images of Jews may have been part of Petronius' literary agenda of mocking the various ethnic groups which had come to live in Rome.

From the identification of the Jews with circumcision in Horace's satires, we observe that Martial (40 C.E.-104 C.E.) wrote numerous epigrams which extend that stereotype, and play upon circumcision and sexuality. He continues the xenophobia expressed by Horace when he castigates Caelia who favors lovers of any nationality except Romans with the words, "nor do you shun the lovemaking of the circumcised Jews [7.30.51]."[7]

In a much more vindictive statement, which may reflect personal sentiments, Martial excoriates another poet:

> Your excessive envy and disparagement everywhere of my little books I pardon; circumcised poet, you are wise. This too I overlook, that while you cavil at my poems you pillage them; in this too circumcised poet, you are wise. What does torment me is this, that though born actually in Solyma [Jerusalem] you, circumcised poet, attach yourself to my favorite boy. See! you deny it and swear to me by the Thunderer's temple [temple of Jupiter]. I don't believe you; swear circumcised one, by Anchialus [11.94].[8]

The rivalry between poets is a source of both flattery and pride for Martial. He believes that the "circumcised poet" plagiarizes his work. However, the rivalry extends beyond the making of verse into the sexual realm. It would appear that Martial is shocked that the poet born in Jerusalem would steal his lover. Ironically, he demands that the Jewish poet make an oath in Jupiter's temple. Such an oath would have no meaning for a Jew who worshipped the God of Jerusalem. In this epigram, we discover the alienation of the Jew in the sexual and religio-political realm. He is both a "circumcised poet" and one whose oath would be considered unacceptable because of his monotheism.

In the historian Tacitus (56 C.E.–early second century) we observed that all the themes associated with Judaism as an exclusive religion coalesce. One of the major themes in Tacitus was the reform of Roman attitudes and morals. He warned his fellow Romans that their adventures in the eastern Mediterranean had brought about a compromise with their stern ancestral traditions. The absorption of Hellenistic ideas and religious practices was corrupting them. In enumerating the practices which these people brought to Rome he includes a description of the Jews and their religious rites:

> Whatever their origin, these rites are maintained by their antiquity; the other customs of the Jews are base and abominable and owe their persistence to their depravity; for the worst rascals among other peoples, renouncing their ancestral religions, always kept sending tribute and contributing to Jerusalem, thereby increasing the wealth of the Jews; again, the Jews are extremely loyal toward one another, and always ready to show compassion, but toward every other people they feel only hate and enmity. They sit apart at meals and they sleep apart, and although as a race, they are prone to lust, they abstain from intercourse with foreign women; yet among themselves nothing is unlawful. *They adopted circumcision to distinguish themselves from other peoples by this difference. Those who are converted to their ways follow the same practice,* and the earliest lesson they receive is to despise the gods, to disown their country, and to regard their parents, children, and brothers as of little account. However, they take thought to increase their numbers for they regard it as a crime to kill any late-born child, and they believe that the souls of those who are killed in battle or by the executioner are immortal; hence comes their passion for begetting children, and their scorn of death. They bury the body rather than burn it, thus following the Egyptians' custom; they likewise bestow the same care on the dead, and hold the same belief about the world below; but their ideas of heavenly things are quite the opposite. The Egyptians worship many animals and monstrous images; the Jews conceive of one god only, and that with the mind only; they regard as impious those who make from perishable materials representations of gods in man's image; that supreme and eternal being is to them incapable of representation and without end. Therefore they set up no statues in their cities, still less in their temples; this flattery is not paid their kings, nor this honor given to

the Caesars. [*Histories* 5.5.8-9][9]

It is possible to observe the development of pagan knowledge about Jews and Judaism from the time of Herodotus in the sixth century B.C.E. until the beginning of the second century C.E. There is a continuity of identifying Jews with Egyptians, but circumcision is associated with Judaism. Moreover, Jews are contrasted with the Egyptians and other pagans in their worship of one God which has no human representation. However, the Jews maintain themselves as a people apart, an exclusive community. Circumcision is the rite of initiation for proselytes. By extension, their circumcision permits them to engage in all forms of sexual practice with one another, while forbidding them such practices with non-Jews. Tacitus asserts that Jews are "prone to lust." This accusation will haunt the Jewish People through the centuries. What is significant for our purposes is that Jewish sexual practices are linked to the rite of circumcision. In the ancient world, ethnic distinctions might be tolerable, but Jewish community practices which were part of their exclusive Covenant put them in a negative light.

THE NEW TESTAMENT AND CIRCUMCISION

During the same period that classical authors offered their identification of Judaism with circumcision, the communities of Christians were commencing their preaching of the "good news" of the resurrection of Jesus as the proof that he was the Messiah. As these groups of believers in Jesus moved out of Palestine into Egypt, Syria, Greece and Rome, they found an audience among pagans and Jews. Besides these two distinct groups, there was another community on the fringes of the Jewish community who were called "Fearers of the Lord." These "Fearers of the Lord" adopted some of the practices of the Jewish community and vowed their loyalty to the God of the Jerusalem Temple. However, they did not fully convert to Judaism. It appears that circumcision was one of the practices which they did not adopt. There were two groups within the newly formed Church: those who were formerly Jews and those who were formerly pagans and "Fearers of the Lord." The two commandments of circumcision and the dietary laws led to disputations within the Christian community about whether or not its members would be required to observe them. They came to serve as the central symbols for the debate about who could become a member of the Church community.

The oral teachings of the first Christians came to be written down into four interrelated narratives called Gospels by the beginning of the second century C.E. The Gospels focus on the life, death and resurrection of Jesus, each with a unique perspective. Three of the Gospels, Matthew, Mark and Luke, narrate details of the birth and earliest years of Jesus. Only one of them, Luke, relates the birth of both Jesus and his predecessor, John the Baptist. After John the Baptist and Jesus were born, each was circumcised (Luke 1:59-66; 2:21). When John the Baptist was circumcised, there was a miraculous event associated with the giving of his name. On the eighth day after Jesus' birth, "they gave him the name Jesus, the name the angel had given him before his conception." In both cases, circumcision was associated with naming. These ceremonies along with others occur "in order that the Law might be fulfilled." The Lucan gospel emphasizes the continuity of the life of Jesus with Judaism.

However, in the Book of Acts, which narrates the early history of the Church, circumcision becomes a focus of the division between those who entered Christianity from Judaism and those from pagan backgrounds who wanted to become part of the community. Paul and Barnabas, who had been preaching to the pagans, disputed with others from Judea who claimed: Unless you have yourselves circumcised in the tradition of Moses, you cannot be saved (cf. Acts 15:1-2). As a result of these arguments, Paul and Barnabas traveled to Jerusalem where they met with the leaders of the Church. Peter and James, two of the most significant leaders of the Jerusalem community, delivered speeches which asked the assembly not to impose "burdens" on the pagan disciples (Acts 15:8-20). The results of the deliberations by the apostles and elders were that pagan converts would be asked only "to abstain from food sacrificed to idols, from blood, from the meat of strangled animals and from fornication" (Acts:15:24-29). After the Council in Jerusalem, according to the Book of Acts, circumcision would no longer serve as a divisive element within the Church.

In the Epistles (letters) of the Apostle Paul, the questions of Jewish law and circumcision arise on two important occasions. When Paul wrote to the Church of Galatia in Asia Minor, he was disturbed that the community had heard a version of the Gospel "different from the one [he] had already preached" (Gal. 1:8). The Galatians must have been told that only if they practiced the Jewish rites would they be saved. Paul indicates that in Jerusalem he had convinced the leaders of the Church that circumcision should not be required of pagans. The Jerusalem community recognized that he had been commissioned to preach the good news to the uncircumcised, just as Peter had been commissioned to preach it to the circumcised (Gal. 2:7). In another meeting at Antioch (Syria), Paul had confronted Peter directly: "In spite of being a Jew, you live like the pagans and not like the Jews, so you have no right to make the pagans copy Jewish ways" (Gal. 2:14).

In Paul's message to the Galatians, he argues that the Jewish Law and its observances no longer provide a means of salvation. A new access had been opened to God with Jesus. This new access was called "faith." Faith and Law are contrasted by Paul as the old and new ways to God. At first, God made a promise to Abraham which would be continued through his descendants. Observance of the Law was added to guarantee the validity of the promise until Jesus. With the coming of Jesus, "there are no more distinctions between Jew and Greek, slave and free, male and female, but all of you are one in Christ Jesus. Merely by belonging to Christ you are the posterity of Abraham, the heirs he was promised" (Gal. 3:27-29).

In Galatians, the Law is depicted as an onerous burden. For Paul, Christ has set his believers free from the Law. The commandment of circumcision becomes central when Paul admonishes the Church of Galatia, "Everyone who accepts circumcision is obliged to keep the whole Law. But if you do look to the Law to make you justified [saved], then you have separated yourselves from Christ and have fallen from grace. Christians are told by the Spirit to look to faith for those rewards that righteousness hopes for" (Gal. 5:3-5). It is significant that circumcision has been selected out of all the commandments to represent Jewish Law and practice. This choice may have been made because Paul focused on the Abraham story as central to his theology of covenant.

Abraham received covenantal promises from God on three different occasions: when God first called him to leave Ur (Gen. 12); when God appeared to him in a vision (Gen. 15); and when God called upon him to become circumcised (Gen. 17). If Christians were to be heirs of Abraham's Covenant, how could they eliminate part of the narrative? Paul resolves this problem in his Letter to the Romans. His central argument is that God operates independent of any human action in bestowing the reward of salvation. This means that salvation comes through God's grace.

Abraham received the divine promise without any action of his own. According to Paul, the crucial passage is Genesis 15:6, "Abraham believed in God and God counted it to him as righteousness." In this verse, Abraham *believes* and God responds. Paul then asks, "In what circumstances was it so counted? Was he circumcised or not?" The response is that Abraham was not yet circumcised. Only later, in Genesis 17, was Abraham circumcised. The purpose of the circumcision, according to Paul, was to provide a "sign and guarantee" of his prior faith. Abraham thereby becomes the ancestor of all who have faith whether they are circumcised or not. Paul then asserts that Abraham becomes through this faith, "the Father of many nations" (Gen. 17:5). The remainder of Paul's Letter to the Romans describes the relationship of Israel's God to the new community which develops around faith in Jesus. Paul asserts that the promises made to Israel which observes the Law and the promises made to the pagans who become Israel according to their faith in Jesus are balanced.

As the central document of Christianity, the New Testament created images of Judaism and Jewish practice which shaped the way in which later Western Civilization thought about Jews. The dichotomy between flesh and spirit, between law and faith, between covenantal promise and messianic fulfillment created the grounds of argument between Christians and Jews. Because the early Church adopted Hebrew Scriptures as part of its Bible, there was a need to explain the new faith in light of Judaism. Abraham emerges as a central figure in this discussion. His circumcision as a sign of the Covenant becomes important if the Church was to claim him as their ancestor. The ambivalence toward the physical commandment of circumcision was extended by the Church toward the observance of all ceremonial laws.

THE MIDDLE AGES

The Medieval Period provides a shift in our focus. Until this point, we have described how pagans and Christians viewed the Jewish practice of circumcision. In both literatures there is either an ambivalence or a repulsion toward this commandment. Both pagan and Christian literature utilize circumcision as a metonymy or

stereotyped epithet which stands for all of Judaism. Learned literature in the European Middle Ages (700–1500) drew upon pagan and
Christian sources and emphasized the contrast between Christianity
and Judaism to the disadvantage of Judaism. In various locations,
these literary themes had a negative impact on the political status of
the Jews. How did medieval Jewry defend itself against these
literary polemics? In particular, was there any specific response to
statements about circumcision?

During the Middle Ages, Jewish authors wrote a number of
treatises to refute Christian claims about Judaism. Often these
treatises were manuals of questions and appropriate answers supply-
ing their readers with scripts to use in case of a disputation. Many
of these documents were composed as commentaries on biblical passages which were controversial. Some examples from the *Sefer Nizzahon Vetus,* composed in Germany during the thirteenth century,
will demonstrate how Jews ennobled the practice of circumcision.

> And Abraham was ninety-nine years old when he was circumcised.
> [Gen. 17:24] One may ask why God did not command him to be cir-
> cumcised at an earlier age. The answer is that he waited so that the
> people of the world would see and learn from Abraham who,
> although an old man, did not balk at circumcision.[10]

In this passage we detect a response to Paul's chronology of the
Abraham promise in the Letter to the Romans. Abraham's advanced
age was not an indication of a supplement to the promise which God
made earlier in Genesis 15. Rather, it was a confirmation of
Abraham's exalted status. He was the teacher of the "nations of the
world," a euphemism for pagan nations. No matter what age one
might be when coming to the divine Covenant, he should be circumcised. Had Abraham been circumcised as a young man, one might
have thought that he found it easier and less painful to respond to
the divine command. Clearly, Abraham's circumcision was integral
to entering the Covenant.

Christian biblical interpretation often appropriated the stories and
symbols in the Hebrew Bible to the sacraments of the Christian
Church. This method of exegesis, known as "spiritual" or allegorical reading of Scripture, was a practice of the Church since antiquity
and continued into the Middle Ages. For example, the allegorical
reading of the Exodus from Egypt would explain the blood on the

lintel and two doorposts of the house (Exod. 12:22) as representing
the cross. The three markings formed a sign of the cross and that is
why the Jews in Egypt were saved. The Jewish author of the *Sefer
Nizzahon* responded:

> God would judge the Jews innocent when he would see the three
> dabs of blood on the entrance, for they symbolize the blood of
> Abraham's circumcision, of the binding of Isaac when Abraham was
> willing to slaughter his son, and of the paschal lamb.[11]

Here we observe a Jewish symbolic reading of the passage. The first
two drops of blood were symbols of confirmation of Abraham's
actions, the third came from the immediate situation of slaughtering
the paschal lamb. God saved the Israelites from Egypt through the
merit of Abraham's fulfilling the divine commandment of circumcision, and his response to God's demand that he surrender Isaac.
Here again, Abraham's circumcision is depicted as a necessary part
of the history of God's plan for Israel.

Jewish authors became acquainted with Christian literature during
the Middle Ages. They utilized it to demonstrate the lack of truth or
logic in Christian claims to Judaism's covenant with God. In many
cases, the Jews would argue that the Gospels contradicted later
Christian literature. There is a passage in the *Sefer Nizzahon* which
describes the three kings who came to visit Jesus. When Mary commanded that he be circumcised, the kings answered, "We shall not
circumcise him because he is divine." But Mary answered them,
"Once he came from the seed of the Jews out of four loins, he must
be circumcised"[12] The implied argument is that Jesus was a Jew and
lived according to Jewish Law. The kings, representing the pagan
nations, did not truly recognize him or appreciate his ancestry. Only
his mother acknowledged his true identity as a Jew.

Jewish authors refuted Christian attempts to appropriate the Bible.
They also sought to prove the superiority of Judaism over Christianity. Judaism, they claimed, led to a life which was carried out on a
higher ethical level than Christianity. Christians asserted that Jews
were engaged in a carnal religion mired in material and sexual concerns, while monks and nuns separated themselves from the world.[13]
One Jewish author, Rabbi Isaac ben Yediah, who lived in Provence
(Southern France) during the thirteenth century, attempted to refute
this argument utilizing circumcision as the primary metaphor of

Jewish moderation in sexual practice.

He asserted that the uncircumcised man is filled with lust. Women are attracted to him specifically because he is uncircumcised: "He thrusts inside her a long time because of the foreskin, which is a barrier against ejaculation in intercourse." She finds such pleasure in him that they copulate constantly. As a result of this continuing lust, the man wastes away. He is "unable to see the light of the King's [God's] face, because the eyes of his intellect are plastered over by women."

By contrast, the Jewish man has intercourse with his wife and ejaculates quickly because of his circumcision. The woman gains little pleasure from such encounters. "It would have been better for her if he had not known her and not drawn her near, for he arouses her passion to no avail." She has an orgasm only once a year. The advantage to the male is that he can concentrate all of his efforts on the study of *Torah*, rather than "empty his brain" on sexual matters.[14]

Rabbi Isaac balances circumcision and *Torah*. If one is to live consonant with God's wishes he must focus all efforts on *Torah*. Rather than inclining a man toward excessive sexual behavior, circumcision lessens that desire. Circumcision thereby becomes the way to fulfillment of all the other commandments and to the study of *Torah*. Non-Jews are, by contrast, those who are mired in sexuality. It is the lack of circumcision which drives them to physical pursuits and distances them from God.

CONCLUSIONS

In the ancient and medieval world the commandment of circumcision became a central focus. While Jews might have viewed it as only one of the six hundred and thirteen injunctions from God, the non-Jewish world perceived it as one of the major tenets of Judaism. From an historical perspective, we know that circumcision did not make Judaism unattractive. Until the fourth century of the Common Era, Jews actively pursued an open attitude toward receiving converts.

Among the pagans, circumcision evoked responses which ranged from admiration for the antiquity of Jewish practice to xenophobia. In nearly every document, one can discern a sense of curiosity about a religious group which required such a rite of entry. The negative attitude in pagan writings derives largely from a sense that the Jews are different *and* exclusive. Circumcision is the predominant sign of their aloof nature.

Christian writings focus almost exclusively on negative aspects of circumcision. Paul utilizes circumcision as a central metaphor to describe the Judaism which fails to acknowledge Christ. If the new access to God is through faith and spirit, then circumcision represents flesh and human deeds. It is not that the Law is invalid, but the way of the spirit is so far superior as to render it unnecessary. Circumcision for Paul and later Christian writers presents an obstacle for appropriating the Covenant God made with Abraham and all of his biblical descendants. Once the Covenant and its promise of divine protection can be separated from performance of the commandments, Christians can claim that their reading of Hebrew Scriptures is valid.

During the Middle Ages, Jews lived with Christian theology and its political results. In order to provide continuity in their minority status, they developed a literary response to Christian arguments. Once again, circumcision became an important focus. Rabbis refuted Christian spiritual reading of the Bible. They demonstrated that Jesus followed the commandments during his lifetime. On occasion, they appropriated a Christian argument—that Jews are overtly carnal—and turned it against Christians.

In the commandment of circumcision it is possible to observe the history of Judaism in miniature. Non-Jews are both curious and negative toward circumcision. Their response eventually calls forth a Jewish response which links the Covenant between God and Israel with the Covenant in the flesh.

NOTES

1.   M. Stern, *Greek and Latin Authors on Jews and Judaism,* ed. with introduction, translation and commentary (Jerusalem, 1974), 3 vols., Vol. I pp. 2–4.
2.   M. Whittaker, *Jews and Christians: Graeco-Roman Views,* Cambridge Commentaries on Writings of the Jewish and Christian World: 200 B.C. to A.D. 200 (Cambridge, 1984), pp. 50–52.
3.   Ibid., pp. 65; 81.
4.   *Pro Flacco* 28.66-9. in M. Whittaker, *Jews and Christians,* p. 117.
5.   M. Whittaker, *Jews and Christians,* p. 81.
6.   Ibid., p. 81.
7.   Ibid., p. 82.
8.   Ibid.
9.   Ibid., pp. 22–23; 83.
10.   D. Berger, *The Jewish-Christian Debate in the High Middle Ages: A Critical Edition of the Nizzahon Vetus,* ed. with introduction, translation and commentary (Philadelphia, 1979), pp. 47–48.
11.   Ibid., p. 64.
12.   Ibid., pp. 215–216.
13.   D. Berger, *Jewish-Christian Debate,* 27, 295 (par. 209).
14.   M. Saperstein, *Decoding the Rabbis* (Cambridge, Mass., 1980), pp. 97–98.

Berit Mila and the Origin of Reform Judaism

Sanford Ragins

INTRODUCTION

It is remarkable that the Reform Movement today is so seriously pursuing a project to enhance Jewish ceremonial life by establishing a cadre of *mohalim/ot*. Classical Reform Judaism was marked by a coolness, if not by outright hostility, toward many traditional Jewish rituals, especially those which, like *berit mila,* are so earthy. The American Reform rabbis who adopted the Pittsburgh Platform in 1885 declared:

> We recognize in the Mosaic legislation a system of training the Jewish people for its mission during its national life in Palestine, and today we accept as binding only the moral laws and maintain only such ceremonies as elevate and sanctify our lives, but reject all such as are not adapted to the views and habits of modern civilization.

To say the least, such a declaration is not exactly encouraging to those who wish to celebrate observances like *berit mila.*

The purpose of this chapter is to explain how the Reform Movement first emerged at the beginning of the nineteenth century and why it came to adopt positions on ritual, and other matters, that are so different in tone and content from those we accept today. When the early Reformers are placed into the context of the historical forces at work in their generation, we are likely to have greater understanding of the decisions they made and the transformation they sanctioned. Like all human beings, they were a product of their times. An attempt will be made in the following pages to describe the complex set of forces and counterforces which created the early Reform Movement.

THE RISE OF MODERNITY

Throughout the eighteenth century, important economic, social and political transformations were underway in Western Europe which brought a number of nations into modernity. As these changes in the structure of society unfolded, reshaping the life of millions, there were concomitant modifications in the way people thought and believed. The theme of the hour for many, which found consummate expression and an explosion of energy in the French Revolution of 1789, asserted that rational men should eliminate or curtail those irrational practices which prevent them from functioning as "enlightened" human beings. If that meant restricting the power of the Church and the aristocracy, or even decapitating a monarch, so be it.

To understand this mood better from an example quite close to home, consider the great documents of the American Revolution crafted by Thomas Jefferson, a marvelous exemplar of the Age of Reason. When he wrote "We hold these truths to be self evident. . . ," Jefferson was articulating some of the primary assumptions of his era. If the most important truths we need to live our lives are "self-evident," you do not need divine revelation, the darkness of the supernatural, or a priesthood which controls the sacred texts and rituals. Any human being using his reasoning powers should be able to figure out the fundamentals.

And when Jefferson wrote "they are endowed by their *Creator* with certain inalienable rights" [emphasis added], he was choosing his words carefully. In using the term "Creator," rather than one of the many other words to describe God, Jefferson focused on God's most universalistic aspect. Jefferson's God, and the God of the Age of Reason, transcends specific parochial revelations. A "Creator" is available to all humankind in a way that "Jesus Christ, Lord and Savior" is not.

In short, increasingly throughout the eighteenth century, in vast areas of Western Europe, especially those regions where capitalism was most successful in establishing itself, new patterns of thinking were emerging. They emerged not just among philosophers, but among statesmen and bureaucrats, especially the representatives of the rising middle class, who were coming into power and addressing themselves to the restructuring of society and state. And one of the most pressing tasks they faced was that of dealing with the legacy of the Middle Ages, and especially with the need to eliminate or modify numerous patterns of practice and thinking that were no longer functional. And since the legacy of the Middle Ages was being reexamined on all fronts, it was inevitable that the medieval image of the Jew would also be subjected to scrutiny.

As rational planners trying to restructure their societies, these enlightened statesmen of the Age of Reason had to deal with the Jews and implement changes in the relationship between Jewry and general society. They did not do this out of any special affection or concern for the Jewish People and their welfare but rather as part of their general program to reshape their nations. If the priesthood and aristocracy, indeed even the monarchy, were being restructured, then the Jews in their medieval ghetto could not be ignored. What was to be done with the ghetto? The answer was obvious: it had to go, just as all the irrational and absurd encrustations of the old order had to go.

The thinking of these statesmen and planners went something like this: If you continually conceptualize the Jews as medieval Christians did, and treat them as pariahs or semi-human creatures at the edges of society, then they will indeed be radically different from other people. Jews dress differently, act and believe and think differently, speak a bizarre language and engage in weird religious practices which no one understands because they have been shut out of society for so long.

THE EMANCIPATION BARGAIN

It soon became clear that if the Jews were to be changed so they might become part of modern, enlightened, post-medieval society, then two things must be done.

First, the state would have to have to reshape itself by dropping all or most restrictions on the Jews. Those laws which were binding only on Jews and restricted them as second or third class citizens had to go. There should be no special Jewish taxes or disabilities, and Jews should be "emancipated" so they might do anything in society which their talents allowed them. In a rational state, Jews should be free to run businesses, serve in public offices, be elected to Parliament, and do virtually everything as other citizens could do, restricted only by the limitations of their talents and abilities.

Thus began the great movement known as Jewish Emancipation. Of course none of these changes happened overnight, nor did they take place without a struggle or everywhere in the same way. In some countries, like France, the transformations came rather quickly as result of the Revolution, while in the German speaking lands, it took almost a century and a long political battle after the time of the French Revolution to establish Jewish Emancipation. It must also be borne in mind that what motivated Christian statesmen to work for the emancipation of Jewry was not necessarily good will or a spirit of brotherhood but the deep necessity to create a modern state in which all residues of the Middle Ages would be liquidated.

The second task of the hour, and an essential concomitant to the elimination of Jewish restrictions, was a concerted effort by the Jews of Europe to accommodate to the new state of affairs. As the surrounding state and society changed, and the ghetto walls, physical and legal, were torn down, then the Jew had to change himself in order to merit new opportunities being offered. To cite just one example, in the newly forming states the ability to serve in the militia of one's country was an important token of citizenship, not restricted to the sons of the aristocracy and the traditional officer corps. Hence, if the state was going to drop its barriers and give Jews citizenship, then the Jews had to be prepared to serve in the national army. But how could they do that if they did not speak the language of the country or if they adhered to exotic religious habits which made it impossible for them to eat in the mess hall along with their fellow-soldiers or to bear arms on their Sabbath?

THE JEWISH RESPONSE TO THE EMANCIPATION

In short, at the beginning of the Modern Era, overwhelming pressures were being exerted on the Jewish community of Western Europe by the surrounding culture. For many, especially among the younger generation, these pressures proved to be irresistible. The tug of Emancipation was so attractive and the urge to make accommodations to life outside the ghetto was so strong that it was difficult to refuse the new status being offered. Some Jews did, of course, but that refusal meant a deliberate decision to remain encapsulated in an old way of life. Vast numbers of young, talented Jews in the west were simply unwilling or unable to make such a sacrifice. Hence, in many circles, the opening of the ghetto gates was welcomed enthusiastically. The emancipation bargain was accepted: the State was willing to drop barriers to Jewish participation in society so long as the Jews were willing to change themselves.

Consider in this regard the remarkable translation of the *Torah* created by the Jewish philosopher Moses Mendelssohn in the late eighteenth century (see Illustration 14). The typical page of Mendelssohn's translation has three separate parts. In the upper right hand column he provides the classical Hebrew text, and down below is a new commentary in Hebrew by Mendelssohn explaining the doctrines of traditional Judaism in terms of what was then the most advanced philosophy, the rationalism of the Enlightenment. There is nothing terribly unusual about these two features, traditional text and contemporary commentary; they can be found in numerous editions of the *Torah* published by Jewish scholars in earlier centuries.

But the most striking, indeed revolutionary, feature of the Mendelssohn *Torah* appears in the upper left-hand column. Here, in Hebrew characters, he has provided a translation of the *Torah* into German. At a casual glance, it appears to be Yiddish, but looked at more carefully it is actually the "high" German of the educated classes. Why did Mendelssohn do this?

Mendelssohn was not a Reform Jew nor the founder of the Reform Movement. Personally, in his own life and practice, he remained what would be called today a modern Orthodox Jew. But he was convinced that enlightened Jews like himself had a responsibility to put into the hands of their fellow Jews those tools which would enable accommodation to the new world. Granted the conviction of that century that education was a means of human transformation, what he and his followers were doing made good sense. If ghetto Jews could be taught to speak, read and write good German (or French or English), they could become acceptable citizens, productive members of the commercial classes, soldiers in the army and students in the universities. What better way to reach these rude, Yiddish-speaking Jews than by providing them with a *Torah* translation into German. Like Pygmalion or Liza Doolittle, once the language had been mastered properly, all doors would open.

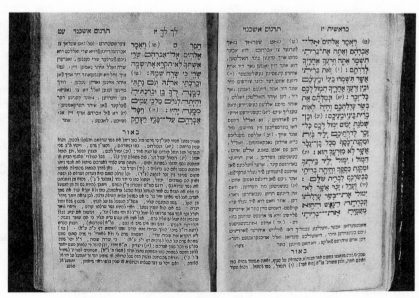

Illustration 14

Translation of the *Torah* by Moses Mendelssohn, late eighteenth century. From the collection of Leo Baeck Temple, Los Angeles. Lelo Carter, photographer.

The Birth of Reform Judaism

Another question immediately arose, however. Once the Emancipation contract had been fulfilled on both sides, once the government had dropped restrictions and the Jews had energetically europeanized themselves, what would become of Judaism, Jewishness, and especially Jewish religious practice? The Reform Movement was created in the struggle to answer that question.

It must be borne in mind that although early Reform did preside over the revision of massive areas of Jewish tradition and sanction the abandonment of whole sectors of practice, this was not done by people who hated Judaism or were embarrassed by being Jewish. In some cases, "self-hatred" was a factor, but for the most part, the new attitude toward tradition which crystallized in Reform was the result of the explosion into Jewish life of a set of extremely powerful social, intellectual, political and economic forces which are still with us. Reform Judaism emerged as part of an age of revolutions. Beginning with England in the seventeenth century, virtually every European society was reshaped by these revolutionary forces so that by the time of the last of these revolutions in Russia at the end of the first World War, the nature of life on the entire continent had been reshaped for all who lived there. It would have been impossible for the Jews, individually or collectively, to have resisted those forces.

During the Napoleonic Era, the Jews living in areas under French occupation were liberated from the ghetto. Indeed Napoleon's armies frequently made a special point of destroying the gates of the ghettos physically because they were a powerful symbol of one of the most irrational features of the old order. In 1810, in one of these areas under Napoleonic control, Israel Jacobson, an enlightened layperson, established his own Jewish house of worship, planned a ceremony of dedication, invited Gentiles to come to the ceremony, and gave a major speech in German.

Dedication Address of the First Reform Temple in 1810[1]

It has been left to the tolerance of our days to bring about and to make possible that which only a little while ago would have appeared impossible. In building this edifice, it has not been my intent to bring about a complete religious unification of all religions. One accomplishes nothing at all if one desires everything or too much at one time. What is needed is gradual and slow development as is demonstrated by nature itself, when it brings forth its greater spiritual and physical accomplishments. Any divergence from this wise procedure of our common mother Nature which human stubbornness or frivolity might suggest, would only be followed by failures or even by the very opposite of that which was desired. What I had in mind when I first thought about building this temple was your religious education, my Israelite brothers, your customs, your worship, etc. Be it far from me that I should have any secret intention to undermine the pillars of your faith, to diminish our old and honored principles through the glitter of new opinions, or that, because of some hidden vanity, I should become a traitor to both our religion and you. You know my faithful adherence to the faith of my fathers. I need not protest it. My actions will witness for me more than my words. But if I do seek here for some rapprochement between you and our Christian neighbors, I would ask more for your gratitude and honest help than for your criticism or even opposition. For your true and progressive enlightenment depends upon this rapprochement. On it depends the education of your spirit for true religiosity and, at the same time also, your future greater political welfare. Who would dare to deny that our service is sickly because of many useless things, that in part it has degenerated into a thoughtless recitation of prayers and formula it, that it kills devotion more than encourages it, and that it limits our religious principles to that fund of knowledge which for centuries has remained in our treasure houses without increase and without ennoblement. On all sides, enlightenment opens up new areas for development. Why should we alone remain behind?

Let us be honest, my brothers. Our ritual is still weighted down with religious customs which must be rightfully offensive to reason as well as to our Christian friends. It desecrates the holiness of our religion and dishonors the reasonable man to place too great a value upon such customs; and on the other hand, he is greatly honored if he can increasingly encourage himself and his friends to realize their dispensability. Our ecclesiastical office, the Israelite Consistory, is willing to help us, is greatly concerned with the improvement of our synagogues and schools, spreads more correct principles abroad, and will, without partisanship, do the best for us even if at the moment we cannot see the flowers or these efforts.

And you, my highly honored other friends, who in name and in some aspects are different from my faith, I hope I have the full agreement of your sympathetic hearts in the principles I have set forth of the intent of this temple building, and of the hope for a happier future for my compatriots. There is nothing in this intent that in any way contradicts the principles of pure religion, of the demands of general morality, of reason, or of your own humanitarian attitude. I trust, therefore, that you will be far from receiving my brothers coldly. I trust that you will not reject them, as did your forebears only too often, but rather, that you will accept them with love into the circle of your society and business; that you will solicitously stretch out your hand to us in that rapprochement which I have sketched in its ideological outline, and for the sake of which partially I have dedicated this temple.

One important detail of these festivities should be given special attention: during the ceremony, an organ was played. It must be recalled that while the ritual of the ancient Temple in Jerusalem was accompanied with abundant instrumental music, for centuries a very different practice had obtained and no instrumental music was allowed in the synagogue as part of regular worship. It was believed that at the End of Time, when the Messiah had arrived, the Jewish People had been regathered from exile into the Promised Land and the Temple in Jerusalem had been rebuilt, all kinds of musical instruments would again be played along with the sacrificial cult. Hence, until Jacobson's action, the *refusal* to use musical instruments in Jewish worship was a potent symbol of commitment to the traditional Messianism of rabbinic Judaism.

And by the same token, Jacobson's overt use of the organ was a powerful symbol of the *rejection* of that belief. By using musical instruments, Jacobson asserted a message to his fellow Jews and to the non-Jewish world: This is our home, now and forever, and we do not expect nor long for a return to Palestine. Hamburg (or Berlin or London or Cincinnati) is our Jerusalem. And if something in the ways of our ancestors contradicts this declaration of at-homeness or undermines our will to live as a permanent part of this society, then those traditions must be abandoned or nullified. Hence the organ, the use of the term "Temple" instead of Synagogue, prayers in the vernacular, and changes in the prayerbook . . . and so on. A whole array of transformations, excisions and revisions was called forth by Jacobson and those who came after him as the Reform

Movement took hold in Western Europe and, in due time, in the New World. All this was done not willfully or casually, but in order to fashion a new form of Judaism which might be viable in the unprecedented circumstances of modernity.

How far might one go with these changes and still preserve Judaism and Jewishness? Some self-conscious assimilators were interested in total disappearance of Jews and Judaism, and more than a few liberal German Christians who defended Jewish emancipation also entertained the hope that before long all Jews would become fully europeanized. But we must remember that the Reform Movement was created not by assimilationist Jews or by non-Jews, but by those modernized members of the Jewish community who believed, with Mendelssohn, that the process of Jewish integration into European society could be accomplished without abandoning Judaism. They believed that even while becoming part of the general culture, Jewish identity and Judaism could be reshaped and then preserved.

How could this happen? In only one manner: the Jew would become a full member of society and be like his Christian neighbor in every way save religion. Anything that seemed to mark the Jew as more than a member of a religious group had to be abandoned, be it a specific form of dress or a unique language. Some of the most radical Reformers even argued that the celebration of the Sabbath ought be moved to Sunday. For the most part, however, more moderate modes of accommodation obtained.

To see where this process eventually led, we shall consider a fascinating organization which was founded in Berlin in 1893. Created by the acculturated Jewish community to deal with the new anti-Semitic movements of the 1880s and 1890s, it was called *Die Central-Verein deutscher Staatsbuerger juedischen Glaubens,* the Central Organization of German Citizens of the Jewish Faith. To the question "What does it mean to be a modern Jew in Germany?," the bold answer was given: "We are like all other Germans in every way, except we happen to have a particular religious tradition. We are German citizens of the Jewish faith."

THE KERNEL AND THE HUSK

To articulate and justify what they were trying to accomplish, the Reformers invoked a very interesting metaphor. They asserted that traditional Judaism was like a seed which has two separable parts, a husk and a kernel. The husk is a protective shell around the living essence of the kernel. That shell is extremely important, because under certain harsh circumstances and inhospitable environments, the living core might be endangered or destroyed were it not protected. But there comes a time when, in order for healthy development to take place, the husk has to be shucked. Once the living kernel begins to sprout, the protective husk has to be thrown aside and discarded because it is no longer necessary and is, in truth, a barrier to new growth and vitality.

What did the Reformers identify as the protective husk that had once served an important purpose but was now discardable? Their answer was Medieval Judaism as a whole, and, some added, the *Talmud* in particular. In this connection, a whole new concept of Jewish history was asserted. It was argued that there were three major periods in Jewish history. The first, the Biblical Period, had been a time of great creativity, vitality and dynamism. The second was the period of the *Talmud* during which, because of destruction of national independence and the persecution visited upon the Jews by the surrounding society, the rabbis created a complex shell of restrictive laws and customs to protect the essence of Classical Judaism from the dangers posed by a hostile outside world. This husk had to be added not because it was required by the nature of Judaism but because of the hostile restrictions and harsh persecutions to which the Jews were subjected during the Middle Ages.

But in the third and last period of Jewish history which is now dawning, the protections of the second era are no longer necessary and are, in fact, dysfunctional. Since the external environment is no longer hostile to Jews and Judaism, it was argued, is it not time to remove those protective barriers which are no longer needed? Once these outmoded practices and rules are abandoned or modified, the vitality of Judaism will reassert itself as in the first period in antiquity. Hence these early Reformers argued with conviction and vigorously moved toward their fundamental affirmation that the essential Judaism of the centuries was alive and well in the emancipated societies in which they were privileged to live in the nineteenth century.

CONCLUSION

Many decades and much history have swept by since the Reform Movement was founded. There have been world wars of unbelievable destructiveness. The once free Jewries of Central Europe and their sister communities to the east have been ravaged by the horrors of Nazism and Stalinism. Israel has become an independent state, and the American Jewish community has grown to unprecedented strength under conditions of full emancipation, social, political and economic, which surpass the wildest dreams of the Jews who first abandoned the ghettoes two centuries ago.

If, under new circumstances, we in the Reform Movement bring new life and imagination to aspects of our tradition which our founders ignored or disvalued, we do so in fulfillment, not betrayal, of their legacy. They first taught that Judaism is never static or fixed, but a dynamic and living tradition which must always be responsive to change. By training our own Reform *mohalim/ot* to serve Jewry, we preserve and extend the achievements of our predecessors.

NOTE

1. Quoted from Gunther Plaut, *The Rise of Reform Judaism* (New York, 1963–65), pp. 29–31.

Berit Mila Within the History of the Reform Movement

Michael A. Meyer

INTRODUCTION

Unlike more traditional forms of Judaism, Reform has not made considerations of Jewish Law paramount. While *halacha* has usually been one factor to be taken into account, the Reform Movement has differed in giving attention, as well, to subjective considerations. Meaningfulness to the individual in the present has been its criterion no less than the imperative to carry on ancestral practices.

Religious significance for the individual is determined by many factors, some intellectual, some emotional. A particular custom may fall into disrespect because it is found to be irreconcilable with a contemporary scientific or moral view of the world. Or it may come under attack because it assaults newly acquired aesthetic sensibilities. By the same token, a discarded custom, viewed with disdain in one intellectual and aesthetic context, may again find favor generations later in a changed climate of thought and feeling. In general, it has been true of the Reform Movement that during the nineteenth and early twentieth centuries, in Europe and America, it reacted to an ambience hostile to physical and particularizing practices by moving away from ritual and concentrating on a lofty doctrine of God and moral aspirations embracing all humanity. In recent decades, its dominant momentum has been in the opposite direction. Customs once regarded as possessing little subjective meaning have been rediscovered and declared of great religious value; particularity has become newly cherished.

The history of *berit mila* within the Reform Movement well illustrates this general pattern. While it was never officially rejected by the Movement, a few individual Reformers were ready to abandon it. Others found it problematic either as such or in the way in which it was carried out. Even though it continued to be generally practiced as an operation, it lost its meaningfulness as a religious rite. Only recently have Reform Jews sought to make circumcision once more into *berit mila*.

How and why Reform attitudes shifted on the question of *berit mila* is the subject of this chapter.[1]

THE GREAT FRANKFURT *Berit Mila* CONTROVERSY

In the premodern Jewish community, there was no question that every healthy son would be circumcised. This was the case for two reasons. First, no Jew doubted that circumcision was God's will, since it was one of the commandments believed to have been handed down on Mount Sinai. Second, even had an individual father chosen not to circumcise his son, such failure would have resulted in exclusion from a Jewish community that maintained the right to govern itself and exercise coercion upon its members.

However, by the fifth decade of the nineteenth century, not only were there some German Jews who questioned the literal nature of the Sinaitic revelation, but the Jewish community had been transformed from a legally autonomous entity free of government interference in its internal religious affairs into a community that could not exercise coercion upon its members and that was subject to government supervision in matters that the state regarded as important for its own interests.

The issue first arose in Frankfurt am Main in the year 1842. There a group of radical laymen, mostly intellectuals and professionals, formed a society that called itself "The Friends of Reform."[2] In their initial program (which they later suppressed), they declared their belief that circumcision was "not binding as a religious act or a symbol." They tried to justify that position by arguing that since circumcision went back beyond Moses to Abraham, it was not determinative of specifically Jewish status. They also noted that, unlike other laws, it was not repeated in Deuteronomy, practiced neither by Moses himself on his own son nor by the

Israelites generally during their desert wanderings, and that there was no equivalent for girls. Quite correctly they pointed out that birth by a Jewish mother, not circumcision, was the halachic test of whether the child was a Jew.

Not long thereafter the Frankfurt Health Department, exercising the broadening preogative of governments, issued a regulation intended to assure maximum medical safety in the performance of circumcision. What made the government action controversial and launched the first major debate on circumcision in modern Jewish history was simply one clause in the regulation allowing for the possibility that some Jews might not want to circumcise their sons at all. This regulation, the department said, applied to local Jews "insofar as they want to let their children be circumcised." And, in fact, there were soon some Jewish fathers who refused to have their sons undergo the operation. How should the community regard these fathers and their sons? Were they nonetheless to be considered members of the community or not? The issue had quickly become a practical one with real consequences.

Before we trace the course of the controversy, we need to ask why some Jews at this time (and later) should have chosen to reject circumcision. At least three factors seem to have played a role. First, there was the medical consideration. The operation certainly was not free of danger. Some physicians counseled against it. Moreover, the *mohalim* who performed the *mila* were sometimes incompetent and stories of disasters or near disasters were widespread. A number of German states tried to deal with the latter problems by insisting that a physician be present or that the *mohel* pass a relevant medical examination. Especially subject to attack in this regard was the practice of *metsitsa* (sucking the wound), which was widely regarded as a source of infection. Second, circumcision was a physical act on the private male member, while religion was to concern itself with more elevated and edifying matters. Reform Judaism was Prophetic Judaism, and had not Jeremiah (as well as Deuteronomy) spoken of circumcising hearts, a notion that could be given universal moral significance? Circumcision in various forms was practiced by primitive tribes. How could it properly be the mark of a higher faith? And the third reason: *berit mila* set the Jewish man apart from his fellows. Circumcision was not commonly practiced among Christians in Germany. For a father to have his son circumcised meant to commit him to a particular Jewish identity. Those Jews who contemplated (not unhappily) the possibility that their sons might one day choose to intermarry or convert to the dominant faith realized that imposing circumcision on their progeny would be a lasting reminder of their Jewish origins.

The Orthodox rabbi of Frankfurt tried, without avail, to obtain rulings from the city government which would exclude both the guilty father and the innocent son from the Jewish community. But in this instance, the authorities did not want to interfere in what they regarded as not just a specific religious issue but the broader one of individual freedom of conscience. It was on this basis that the great Jewish champion of liberalism in Germany, Gabriel Riesser, defended the right of Jews, if they wished, to omit circumcision without thereby losing their status as members of the community. In fact, those rabbis who came to the defense of the Frankfurt radicals on the issue of circumcision did so not because they failed to appreciate the religious importance of the rite, but because they refused to exclude from the community either fathers who had sinned by omitting the act or sons who had not been circumcised.

To be sure, the leading German Reformer, Rabbi Abraham Geiger, possessed a distinct aversion to *berit mila* as such. In a private letter, he admitted that to his mind circumcision was "a barbaric, bloody act, which fills the father with anxiety and puts the new mother into a state of morbid tension." He looked forward to the time when a new ceremony for both boys and girls would drive out *berit mila* just as confirmation had replaced the tomfoolery of *bar mitzvah*. Such a ceremony had in fact been proposed and outlined in an anonymously published pamphlet commissioned by the Frankfurt radicals. The author called it "The Sanctification of the Eighth Day." Its chief purpose was to give a Hebrew name and to welcome each child, regardless of sex, into the covenant.[3] Not until more than a century later would that same task of creating a ceremony equivalent to circumcision for girls be taken up again.

Most Reform rabbis, however, joined their more traditional colleagues in vigorously defending *berit mila* even to the point of sanctions where it was omitted. Recognizing that birth was determinative of Jewish status and objecting to anything approaching excommunication, they nonetheless insisted that *berit mila* was not merely one ceremony among others, but a central institution of Judaism which should not be allowed to fall into disuse.

RABBINICAL CONFERENCES AND SYNODS

When the German Reform rabbis met for the first time as a rabbinical assembly in 1844, circumcision was still too controversial an issue even to discuss. When the radical Rabbi Mendel Hess proposed a seemingly balanced resolution expressing "most painful regret" because some coreligionists were not observing "such an important and generally regarded as sacred commandment," but also protesting against coercion and exclusion of the uncircumcised, the chairman noted that this matter was currently arousing such passion that it would be best just to pass over it. The assembled rabbis unanimously agreed. They also failed to act on requests to speak out against *metsitsa* and for the binding obligation of *berit mila*. All they could agree on was that each rabbi should keep a register of circumcisions in his community.

At the next conference a year later, the rabbis were still not ready to take a stand. When a physician in Berlin complained to the members of the conference that his practice had taught him how the operation often led to later instances of venereal diseases and impotence, the rabbis discussed the delicate matter in closed session before replying that other physicians did not share his view, that Jewish couples were known to be fruitful, and that most governmental authorities were intervening to prevent incompetence in performing the operation. But they also noted that they were not as yet prepared to pass a resolution on the subject.

Once again at the third—and last—conference in 1846, the rabbis avoided the issue. This time, however, they did take a stand on some specifics. A Jewish physician reported that on account of apparent hemophilia on both sides of the family his first son had never fully recovered from circumcision and his second son had bled to death. What should he do if his wife bore a third son, he asked the assembly. Would it be all right to omit circumcision and simply give his son a Hebrew name in the synagogue? The assembly replied by easing the talmudic law that stipulates two sons must die before the operation may be suspended. One death, it declared, was sufficient. The conference also decided upon a series of regulations that would make the rite safer and more hygienic, including the omission of *metsitsa*. But still the Reform Movement had taken no stand on *berit mila* as such.

It was not until a quarter century later, at synods comprised of laity as well as rabbis, that the European Reform Movement finally took a general stand. In the meantime, the number of uncircumcised Jewish children had grown. One of the Austrian delegates reported that many parents were declaring: "Our children shall continue to be Jews, but we shall not let them be circumcised." In 1866, no fewer than sixty-six Jewish physicians had sent a memorandum to the community council in Vienna opposing the continued practice of circumcision. The local rabbis differed in what to do about this situation. Yet everyone was concerned because the matter had grave social consequences. Would a rabbi marry a Jewish woman to an uncircumcised man? Meeting in Augsburg in 1871, the second synod finally gave an answer. Unanimously it resolved:

> While the synod assumes that the highly important meaningfulness of circumcision in Judaism is beyond any doubt, it nonetheless declares that a boy born to a Jewish mother, and for whatever reason not circumcised, is in accordance with the established norms recognized as binding in Judaism . . . to be regarded as a Jew and treated as such in all matters of ritual practice.

By then, American Reform rabbis had already come to a similar conclusion.

Berit Mila IN AMERICAN REFORM

In nineteenth-century America, as in Europe, circumcision was an operation limited almost entirely to Jews. In 1870, the rate in the general population is estimated to have been five to eight percent.[4] And there, too, medical opinion on the operation was decidedly split.[5] When the American Reform rabbis gathered for the first time in Philadelphia in 1869, circumcision was on their agenda. Although Moses Mielziner, later to become the first professor of *Talmud* at the Hebrew Union College, abstained for fear that the proposed statement could be misinterpreted to mean circumcision was not obligatory, the rest of the rabbis agreed upon this resolution.

> The male child of a Jewish mother, no less than the female child, is to be considered as a member of the Jewish community by descent, even if uncircumcised—in accord with a basic principle of Judaism which has never been questioned.[6]

The more divisive issue in Philadelphia was whether to require that male proselytes undergo circumcision. Indeed, *milat geirim,* an issue not discussed collectively in Germany, became the central issue in the United States. Isaac Mayer Wise of Cincinnati, the most important figure in nineteenth-century American Reform, raised the question in Philadelphia. Wise believed that bringing converts into Judaism was part of what the early Reformers called the "Jewish mission" and that the agony of adult circumcision was discouraging to potential Jews. However, not all Reform rabbis shared Wise's desire for "outreach." His most significant rival, David Einhorn, stated in Philadelphia that he favored keeping circumcision for male converts since by the acceptance of proselytes "many impure elements were brought into Judaism" and the requirement of circumcision fortunately helped keep them out. Wise's suggestion was not acted upon.

In succeeding years, however, individual Reform rabbis did admit uncircumcised male converts into Judaism. Not long after the Central Conference of American Rabbis was formed in 1889, this issue was therefore taken up at great length. In 1892, the Reform rabbis reached a decision, never rescinded, which stated in part that rabbis should fully accept "into the sacred Covenant of Israel . . . any honorable and intelligent person, who desires such affiliation without any initiatory rite, ceremony or observance whatever." They went on to stipulate what such a convert must affirm, but no physical act was required.[7]

After that, the American Reform Movement did not much trouble itself about circumcision. As the operation became more and more common among Gentiles and medical opposition was banished to the fringe, Reform Jews had their sons circumcised like everyone else, however, circumcision was not usually *berit mila*. The medical procedure was adopted, but the ceremony was mostly neglected.

It was not until the return to tradition in American Reform was well underway following World War Two, and religious particularism had gained new appeal in the wake of the Holocaust and the creation of the State of Israel, that Reform Jewish parents began increasingly to rediscover *berit mila*. For them, as for other Jews, it assumed new importance as symbolic of the deep desire that the next generation remain Jewish. Until recently, their observance usually consisted of asking a rabbi to do the ritual in the presence of the physician. Ever since the *Minister's Hand Book* of 1917, a Reform version of the ceremony had been available. In 1977, however, a new ritual appeared in *Gates of the House: The New Union Home Prayerbook* (pp. 111—113). Not only did it refer to "parent" rather than the earlier "father" and include a good deal more Hebrew, it also assumed that a *mohel* would be performing the operation.[8]

Two years later, in its *Gates of Mitzvah: A Guide to the Jewish Life Cycle,* the CCAR for the first time put itself strongly on record in favor of *berit mila*, declaring: "It is a *mitzvah* to bring a male child into the covenant through the rite of circumcision," and adding that "circumcision alone, without the appropriate prayers, does not constitute entrance into the Covenant." The operation, whenever possible, was to be performed by a person "specially trained, both religiously and medically, in this procedure, a *mohel.*" Recognizing the claims of egalitarianism, *Gates of Mitzvah* noted that a suitable ceremony should also mark the entry of newly born girls into the Covenant. And, indeed, versions of such a ceremony soon began to multiply.[9]

THE MOST RECENT DEVELOPMENTS

The last decade has been marked by trends both favorable and unfavorable to the practice of *berit mila* in Reform Judaism. To begin with the negative: after a long period during which routine circumcision was almost without exception supported by the medical community, it has in recent years once again come under severe attack, this time for allegedly unfavorable psychological as well as medical effects. A number of books (some perhaps with antisemitic motivations) have taken the operation to task and some have gained a good deal of public attention.[10] In 1975, the American Academy of Pediatrics ad hoc Task Force on Circumcision declared that "there is no absolute medical indication for routine circumcision of the newborn"[11] (see Appendix B). In some places, medical insurance ceased to pay for circumcision. It now seems that medical circumcision may become noticeably less common among Gentiles, removing the environmental support for it among Jews and leaving only the religious reason. Reform Jews who had heretofore favored circumcision of their sons more on medical or social than on religious grounds may lose their principal justification.

Other factors may also play some role in what appears to be a gradual shift in opinion. Increasingly, there are young people whose "respect for nature" (the values of natural childbirth or vegetarianism may be factors) is violated by what is regarded as traumatic and mutilating. Jewish Feminism finds itself unable to compensate fully for circumcision with alternative ceremonies for girls. But whatever the motives may be, an increasing number of Reform Jewish parents, including some very Jewishly committed ones, now express hesitation about circumcising their sons.[12] It remains to be seen whether this trend will continue.

The most significant indication of the counter trend is the recent program to train and certify Reform *mohalim/ot*.[13] Prompted by coincident interest in New York and California, it resulted in the first course for training Reform Jewish physicians to become *mohalim/ot*, taught by the faculty of Hebrew Union College, Los Angeles in 1984, and in the creation of a Reform *Berit Mila* Board. Sixteen physicians and one nurse participated in the first course; seven of them were women. While Reform Jews had increasingly approached traditional *mohalim*, they had often encountered unpleasantness ranging from outright refusal where the Jewish status of the infant was in question, to disrespect for Reform Judaism displayed during the ceremony. Not surprisingly, once Reform *mohalim/ot* made their appearance, the Orthodox, for a variety of stated and unstated reasons, denied them recognition.

Despite the powerful current influences working against circumcision, it seems that, at least in the short run, *berit mila* will continue to enjoy its recently attained and unprecedented status in American Reform Judaism. The delight in life-cycle events and the desire to emphasize particularizing and tangible Jewish experiences seem to be continuing unabated. For many Reform Jews, *berit mila*, once a source of concern and controversy, has become a ritual of profound significance.

NOTES

1. The most comprehensive treatment of *berit mila* is the recent HUC-JIR rabbinical thesis by Bradd H. Boxman entitled "The Significance of *Berit Mila* in Reform Judaism" (Cincinnati, 1986). David Philipson, in his *The Reform Movement in Judaism* 3rd ed., (New York, 1967), discusses all but the most recent developments. A selection of early source material can be found in W. Gunther Plaut, ed., *The Rise of Reform Judaism* (New York, 1963), pp. 206–211. While I have used the original sources, I have limited references in these notes to texts available in English.

2. Michael A. Meyer, "Alienated Intellectuals in the Camp of Religious Reform: The Frankfurt Reformfreunde, 1842–1845," *Association for Jewish Studies Review*, 6 (1981): pp. 61–86; Robert Liberles, *Religious Conflict in Social Context: The Resurgence of Orthodox Judaism in Frankfurt am Main, 1838–1877* (Westport, CT, 1985), pp. 52–61.

3. For an English translation, see Michael A. Meyer, "The First Identical Ceremony for Giving a Hebrew Name to Girls and Boys," *Journal of Reform Judaism*, Winter 1985, pp. 84–87.

4. See the figures in Edward Wallerstein, *Circumcision: An American Health Fallacy* (New York, 1980), pp. 214–217.

5. A. B. Arnold, writing in the *New York Medical Journal* for February 13, 1886, declared: "I am induced to place indiscriminate circumcision in the category of those aberrations that are intended to surpass nature. Thus, the women of China cripple their feet; the Ottentot female elongates her nymphae; some savage tribes compress the skulls of their children, etc." (p. 22). On the other hand, a prominent physician in San Diego, favored the practice, noting its benefits for "better physical, mental, and moral health, as well as . . . the many dangers and disadvantages that follow the uncircumcised." P. O. Remondino, *History of Circumcision from the Earliest Times to the Present* (Philadelphia & London, 1891), iv.

6. The proceedings of the Philadelphia conference, held in German, are translated in Sefton D. Temkin, *The New World of Reform* (Bridgeport, CT, 1974). The discussion of circumcision is on pages 71–73.

7. *Central Conference of American Rabbis Year Book*, 3 (1892 meeting): p. 36. Yet, interestingly enough, in the CCAR *Minister's Handbook* (1917), the prospective convert is specifically asked: Do you agree to have male children circumcised?

8. The *Rabbi's Manual* of 1928 took an intermediate position, in a note mentioning the possibility of using either a surgeon or a *mohel*.

9. One is contained in *Gates of the House*, pp. 114–117.

10. An early example is a section in Bruno Bettelheim, *Symbolic Wounds*, first published in 1954 and revised in 1962. Bettelheim examined circumcision from a critical psychoanalytic perspective. The more recent crop includes: Nicholas Carter, *Routine Circumcision: The Tragic Myth* (London, 1979); Wallerstein, *op. cit.;* and Rosemary Romberg, *Circumcision: The Painful Dilemma* (South Hadley, MA, 1985)—the last with a bibliography of 490 items.

11. In Wallerstein, *op. cit.* 218. The statement was later endorsed by the Executive Board of the American College of Obstetricians and Gynecologists.

12. See, for example, Barbara Cohn, "A Mother's Ambivalence," *Sh'ma*,

February 5, 1892.
13.   Lewis Barth, "Introducing the Reform Mohel," *Reform Judaism,* Fall 1984, pp. 18–19, 32.

The Concept of the Covenant in Reform Judaism

Eugene B. Borowitz

Jews commonly use the term *berit* in two main ways. In particular, it refers to the rite of circumcision; on a more abstract level, it signifies the central affirmation of Jewish belief: that there is a pact between God and the People of Israel. We cannot properly hope to understand the one without exploring the other and this chapter is devoted to the far-ranging faith, traditional and modern, which ritual circumcision embodies and projects.

The very first time we hear of circumcision in the *Torah*, (Genesis 17:10ff.), it is intimately connected with God's promises to Abraham for his descendants and to Abraham's corollary obligations. The first of these to be specified is circumcision: "Thus shall My Covenant be marked in your flesh as an everlasting pact" (Gen. 17:13). It is no wonder then that the rite of surgically removing the foreskin eventually came to be called *berit*. Yet that identification of ceremony and belief often confuses people about the role of circumcision in Judaism and thus about the nature of our religion. In the overall understanding of traditional Jewish Law, one need not be circumcised to be a Jew, that is to participate fully in the Covenant. Medically exempt males are fully kosher Jews; so are women, a matter on which the *Torah* is quite explicit in its Deuteronomic version:

You stand this day, all of you, before Adonai your God, your chief-
tains, your elders and your officials, all the men of Israel, your children, your wives, even the stranger within your camp . . . to enter
into the *berit* of Adonai your God, [the *berit*] which Adonai your
God is concluding with you this day . . .   (Deut. 29:9ff.)

The term *berit* is also closely associated with other rites, most
notably that of keeping Shabbat, which is called a "sign" of the
Covenant (Exod. 31:16-17). Most frequently, however, the Bible
uses the term in speaking of the Ark in which the two tablets of the
Covenant were kept, the tablets Moses received on Mount Sinai
from God. For that is the larger sense of *berit*, the one which lies
between every other usage of covenant in our tradition: our God
calls human beings into partnership, initially all humankind, as with
Noah and his children, (Gen. 9:8ff.), but later, climactically, all the
People of Israel.

Even traditionally, the concept of a pact between God and people
is most astonishing. The God who is the only God of the universe
and thus transcends it in every way nonetheless is understood to
become involved with people. They are known to be frail, perverse
or even malevolent. Yet they are created in God's image and, whatever else that might mean, are therefore capable as no other
creatures are of being called into alliance with God. More, God has
purposes for people and commits these responsibilities into human
hands. Were that not surprising enough, God then resolutely refuses
to infringe on the human freedom to do or not do what God has
commanded. To be sure, God remains free to respond to human sinfulness as to human merit, a matter of no small weight in human
accountability, but, despite their inequality in status and power,
there were two active partners to the agreement. This was the heart
of biblical Jewish faith.

In that unconscious way social groups have of making certain
terms central to their ethos, the Hebrews somehow settled on the
word *berit* to describe their fundamental religious intuition. As is
typical of religious symbols, the original use of the term *berit*
occurred in everyday life, in this case in the legal realm. In Hebrew
jurisprudence, it signified a contract between two parties, whether
the ordinary one of commerce or the more exalted one between one
king and another. The critical features of ancient contracts are quite
familiar to us: two parties are involved; each party takes on certain

responsibilities to the other; these undertakings are entered into with considerable solemnity; and violating them brings serious consequences. To our biblical forebears this model of human relationships seemed the best symbolic expression they could find to represent what they knew to be their tie to God.

Berit was not the only term for relationship that suggested itself to the biblical authors. They occasionally speak of God in a domineering role, as that of an owner to his beast (Isa.1:3) or to his slave ("servant" is too euphemistic a translation of *eved;* Isa. 41:8ff.). This is mitigated in the more frequent use, certainly among the prophets, of the marriage motif, though one needs to keep in mind the male-dominated, Near Eastern marriage which the authors have in mind. It is even more loving and tender when God is described as Father or as Mother concerned with a child. Yet as evocative as were all these other ways of speaking of God's relationship to the People of Israel, none can be said to have become as encompassing as was the legal metaphor of Covenant. (It should be noted, too, that the potential limits of this one relationship, *berit,* were then compensated for by utilizing many other images and, in later Jewish literature, by amplifying them. By extension, the second commandment of the Decalogue warns us that no symbol, no matter how supernal its apparent genius, will ever be great enough to speak to God fully.)

We may conjecture that *berit* was so appealing a term because it conveyed another critical aspect of Jewish faith: that God gave us specific instruction *(torah)* as to how we were to live to carry out our partnership with God. It is, indeed, one of the distinguishing characteristics of Judaism that it claims to possess God's verbal instructions, the story and exhortation as well as the laws and counsel—so to speak, the stipulations of the contract—that are to guide us in fulfilling our awesome role. From this belief derived the Jewish passion for knowledge and the sanctity of study, as well as the activist approach to serving God in community which so runs through biblical teaching.

In sum, Jewish faith has classically centered about the notion of a contract which God, no less, had entered into with the People of Israel, one prefigured in Canaan but properly formalized at Sinai and renewed on numerous occasions thereafter. To live by the Jewish religion meant to abide by the many evolving stipulations of the contract, one of the earliest of which was the circumcision of males.

Put in such bald legal terms, it is difficult for modern Jews to gain a good sense of the living religiosity which characterized our fore-bears. Most of us, from personal experience as well as by Christian apologetic, tend to find law in general and contracts in particular essentially oppressive. Idealistically, we like to think that if people really understand each other, they don't need written agreements, certainly not in anything so personal as religion ought to be. I shall say something more about that later. Here I only want to say some-thing about understanding the centrality of this legal metaphor in traditional Judaism: it never came close to wiping out the personal side of Jewish religiosity. Think, for example, of how the people's acquiescence is needed for the contract to be made at Sinai, and how again and again the prophets strive to bring the people back, not only to religious obedience, but to spiritual understanding. They are so much real partners to the pact that they can even argue with God about God's conduct as a Covenant partner, though, to be sure, this happens only at exceptional moments. And, if more personal evi-dence is required, one can simply turn to the Book of Psalms. Better than anything else I know, it conveys a rich sense of the ennobled inner life of the individual Jew in good times and in bad.

Our central Jewish motif arises from a legal basis to do justice to our belief that the service of God is mandated, with a social as well as a personal dimension and activism; it is not centrally personal and thus easily oriented to the inner life and relatively passive about the world. So when Jews left the ghetto and could no longer affirm a law mandated in detail by God, they nonetheless retained the notion of Covenant, affirming its religious vision while giving it new con-tent.

The modern Jewish thinkers who have suggested how Reform Jews might reinterpret the notion of the Covenant agree on one prin-ciple: our sense of reality demands that we give greater weight to the human partner in the *berit* than did our tradition. That is to say, we believe that we serve God best by being true to our minds and consciences even where, in significant matters, they clash with our heritage. Reform Judaism itself is a result of such trust in the Jewish People's continuing capacity to meet radically new challenges; Zion-ism is another such development, though a secular one. Both move-ments insisted on a human activism that was not acceptable in clas-sic Judaism, particularly as it had evolved in the centuries immedi-ately preceding Jewish modernization.

By taking some liberties, we may say that our modern thinkers have interpreted *berit* less as contract than as what moderns call "a personal relationship." Where the classic notion of *berit* had seen the relationship between God and the People of Israel stipulated in considerable contractual detail—their marriage contract, if you will—modern thinkers stressed what God and Israel meant to one another, thus giving the human partner considerable room to specify the duties that result from this relationship.

This subtle shift of emphasis has many ramifications. Thus, a proper Jewish act would now be judged not simply in terms of what our sages had ruled concerning it—though we might find that still persuasive—but whether the act contributed, as best we can understand it, to our ongoing Jewish relationship with God. Driving to the synagogue for Shabbat services is clearly forbidden in the traditional understanding of the Covenant-contract. Yet attending Shabbat services, *even* if that entails driving on Shabbat, seems to most modern Jews to be a proper way of enhancing the Covenant-relationship. This shift of standards for Jewish practice remains the major basis of argument among Jews in modern times. While we liberal Jews consider this to be a true understanding of how Jews ought to serve God today, only after many generations of Jewish experience with this new emphasis will our People be able to judge whether we have truly acted "for the sake of Heaven."

Most modern Jews, alas, do not also want to hear about the obligations which arise from this new sense of Covenant. They are delighted that Reform teaches that they are entitled to reject our tradition when it conflicts with modernity and they happily chuck whatever does not come easily or pleasantly. Having been granted Jewish autonomy so that they might be more responsible, they mostly use their freedom to avoid duty. One might call that primal Reform Jewish sin: abusing religious freedom by taking it casually. We will know you care by what, in fact, you do; a relationship that does not have a significant effect on one's life is not much of a relationship. One cannot hope to do little or nothing as a Jew and still claim to have a significant relationship with God as part of the Jewish People.

Modern Jewish thinkers have gone on to specify just where Jews today ought to place major religious emphasis in building their sort of Covenant. Since they stress the human aspects of religion, much of their thought has dealt with the personal relationships which ought to characterize contemporary Jewishness.

The primary level on which this has been worked out has been in an insistence on our Jewish Covenant with all humankind, a relationship which lays upon us the responsibility to be ethical to all human beings. That seems so obvious to most modern Jews that they cannot imagine it was not always a central part of Jewish teaching and practice. To be sure, there always was an implicit mandate for universal ethical obligation in our tradition. But social circumstances made responsibility for humankind as a whole a minor part of active Jewish duty. In biblical times, non-Jews were idolaters, hence involvement with them might mean the loss of the one people dedicated to God. Once Christianity and then Islam had established themselves, they segregated and oppressed Jews, keeping them from full citizenship as long as their countries were intertwined with religion. Only where secular, i.e., non-religious, states emerged could Jews become equals and only then, a matter of less than two centuries ago in Europe, could the issue of Jewish duty to non-Jews become anything other than a highly theoretical topic.

When Jews were permitted to live among non-Jews as equals, they had little difficulty embracing the notion that all humankind was one. The Jewish tradition had said the same thing religiously in its vision of human origins. It told of a single progenitive couple for all people and unequivocally said that all human beings, unconditionally, were created in God's image. One God implied one humankind and the duty to create God's rule on earth meant doing good to and with all other human beings.

The very essence of the Jewish religion, it was now suggested, was ethical responsibility. Jews were now to live out their ancient, ever-new Covenant mainly by how they conducted themselves in the general flow of human life, the matrix in which they primarily lived. The extraordinary Jewish contribution to every contemporary cause for human betterment has its roots in this concept. Indeed, it has affected Jews so powerfully that Jews who have given up the religious notion of the Covenant have regularly sought secular causes in which they could, as they thought, more effectively achieve their ethical ends.

One somewhat technical aspect of this universal ethical stress in the modern understanding of the Covenant deserves special attention. Jewish thinkers have been particularly attracted to ethics in the sense in which the philosopher Immanuel Kant used the term. He insisted that a rational mind necessarily manifests itself in an ethical (as well as in a scientific and an esthetic) mode. Since the hallmark of rationality is its effort to create and operate by rule rather than arbitrarily, rational ethics are characterized not by mood or by quality but by their lawfulness. His disciples thus took the ethical implications of being rational most seriously and they spoke of ethics as moral law. That allowed Jewish thinkers to say our religion is the most rational of religions for we are a religion which emphasizes law and the heart of our law, they asserted, is being ethical. Suddenly, modern reason and Jewish being had come together in a most attractive way. And this understanding of our Covenant with all humankind still has a powerful place in our modern Jewish self-understanding.

What other thinkers found missing in this view—for all its human appeal—was a satisfactory sense of our continuing Covenant with all other Jews; that is, with the Jewish People as an entity of its own. The trouble with making the Covenant with all humankind primary is that it may seem to supersede what had been the basic community of the Covenant, the Jewish People. And there have been and are many splendid Jewish humanitarians who have had energy for every troubled people in the world—except their own. Even logically, this exaggerated universalism is ethically odd; surely loving my neighbors cannot mean that I may not give special, indeed priority attention to my own family. And, almost literally, that is what "the Children of Israel" means. We are, to give that phrase literal effect, Jacob's kids. We are also a community united by a glorious history, a rich heritage, an ongoing way of life (in all its diversity), and a common fate as far as our enemies are concerned. On many human levels, then, our Covenant must not slight our bonds to other Jews.

This motif has even been made the most basic understanding of modern Jewishness by those who point to social groups as the source of the most significant human creativity. Our cultures give us our language, our values, our way of living and approaching life. Through our civilization, structured in institutions, empowered by values, transmitted formally by rite and informally by the family and other human networks, we attain our true humanity. The Jewish People need have no apology for desiring to maintain its distinctive folk culture, considering how richly human it has been—and that includes its incomparable concern with ethical action, now extended to reach out to all humankind. But, like every such folk life, it lives by continual creativity and development. Today, in a democratic age, it will benefit most by a pluralism which will happily embrace its diverse cultural experimentation.

For such thinkers, a Jew is primarily one who actively maintains Covenant with all other Jews, avidly participating in their cultural creativity though free to reappropriate the Jewish heritage in quite individual fashion.

One major manifestation of this sense of folk covenant has been the close sense of identification Jews the world over have with the State of Israel. At its simplest, that is an extension of the notion that Jews have a particular responsibility for other Jews who are in trouble. Surely the State of Israel originally awakened widespread Jewish passion as a haven for refugees and a home in which they might be rehabilitated. But the ties have grown far beyond that so that Jews everywhere somehow look upon the State of Israel as "their" state, in an ethnic rather than a political sense, and personally identify with its accomplishments. Over the decades of its existence, the many human triumphs of the State of Israel have awakened extraordinary Jewish pride—and so, it must be said, have its occasional failures awakened great Jewish concern and soul-searching. We would not care so if we were not so involved.

These impressive human extensions of the Covenant might easily so capture our imagination that we permit it to remain almost entirely a human matter. That is, we become so fully occupied with what we must do that we have little or no concern for our erstwhile dominant Covenant partner, God. Some decades back, in the heyday of Jewish satisfaction with what human beings could accomplish on their own, that seemed like a reasonable strategy. The more people learned, the more they could do to transform all human existence.

History has not dealt kindly with the notion that people, so to speak, could take God's place, that we and our resources are adequate to all the challenges which face us personally and humankind generally. As we have reached greater humility about our powers, we have made more room for God in our lives. In psychodynamic terms, having been through our developmental phases of separation and individuation, we are now ready for reconciliation.

This cultural movement has brought us to realize a fear we have in affirming God's role in the Covenant: won't letting God back in our lives mean we must become Orthodox? Surely that is what many

Christian fundamentalists and Jewish "returnees" seem to think. Since modernity causes us such malaise, they argue, its antidote is to return fully to tradition, often with emphasis on its anti-modern aspects. Yet that belittles what we have quite properly learned in modern times, that to be a person in the full sense of the term means to have substantial self-determination. Covenant needs to be interpreted in a way that enables us to keep our activist modern sense of human dignity while recognizing that we exercise it in terms of our relationship with God.

The response to this fear has been to recognize the substantial difference between a deep personal relationship and one which is only acquaintanceship. All of us know some people whom we manage to get through to on a deep level and, because of that, with whom we know we have special relationship. Doctors regularly encounter this phenomenon; with some patients you just hit it off, for reasons that aren't at all clear. Then you really become "their doctor" in a way that, for all your friendliness, you aren't with other people. The same sort of qualitative difference distinguishes "just friends" from "good friends"—and, most of all, from those whom we truly love. The binding, life-affecting relationship we call "Love" here becomes our model for the Covenant as a relationship.

This view asks us to envision the Covenant as the Jewish People's long-lasting love affair with God, one that has survived and been strengthened by its many fights and reconciliations, its intimacies and its duties, its inspiration and its unfathomability. As in every deep human relationship, it is sometimes overwhelmingly certain and other times troublingly shaky. And, so too, it needs to be worked at regularly though one can never quite know what will bring it alive just now—and then something quite trivial occurs which makes one realize how real it is and how much it means to us. One key to such relationships is that each partner participates in it in full integrity; neither one is master, neither one is slave, both can make their demands, each partner saying, if necessary, a painful but self-respecting "No." The moments of genuine love, whether in agreement or loving dissent, are our greatest human experiences. They are one contemporary model for understanding what we mean by Covenant.

These three interpretations of the Covenant converge in our contemporary idea of the family. We want it, in some primary sense, to communicate a high sense of human ethics and by its day-to-day give-and-take exemplify what we believe. We also want it to be a living continuation of all that the Jewish People has creatively stood for over the centuries, transmitting as much by its spirit as by its education and ritual the high human sense of what it is to be a Jew and a human being. But, most of all, we want it to touch and reflect the deepest reality that is in us and the mature love that ennobles human individuality and enables us to transcend ourselves.

Liberal Jews believe that the old contract-terms our People has lived by still often give rich expression to our ethical-Jewish-loving relationship with God. So we happily embrace them in historical, communal, personal continuity of the Covenant—and then not infrequently discover that doing them leads us to need deeper understandings of the *berit,* ones we are unlikely ever to have known without our tradition. Sometimes, however, that is not the case and then we feel religiously obligated to move beyond the old and honored patterns. Proudly and loyally, we seek to create our own, new modes of living our contemporary sense of Covenant loyalty— the kiss after Shabbat services is my favorite example. We continue to work at deepening and strengthening our way of Covenant living. It is not an easy task to bring together a dynamic sense of Jewish responsibility and a modern sensibility which itself is in considerable flux. But when a child is born, we know that by a circumcision or a baby-naming we happily, responsibly want to welcome a child into the Covenant relationship/relationships we embrace—looking forward in hope to all that this new person will now do to carry on our Jewish vision until humankind reaches the Messianic Time.

Circumcision in Early
Halacha: Mishna and *Talmud*

Bernard M. Zlotowitz

INTRODUCTION

Circumcision ranks as one of the foremost commandments of the *Torah* and one of the most crucial for the preservation of Judaism. In the Talmudic Age (second through seventh centuries, C.E.), great emphasis was laid on its significance as a sign of the Covenant. The rabbis considered it so important that even Yom Kippur and the Sabbath could be overridden in order to adhere to the biblical injunction of circumcising on the eighth day. Only the child's health and welfare superseded circumcision *bizemano* (at its appointed time), on the required eighth day.

Ritual circumcision in the *Talmud* is defined, refined and extremely technical in contradistinction to its occurrence in the Bible, where only a simple statement is made regarding circumcision: "And in the eighth day the flesh of his foreskin shall be circumcised" (Lev. 12:3).

MOST IMPORTANT RABBINIC LAWS ON CIRCUMCISION: DESCRIPTION, TIME, HEALTH OF CHILD

In the period of the *Mishna* (70 C.E.–200 C.E.), the foreskin was to be cut off and *peri-a* and *metsitsa* were required: in other words, tearing and sucking (the wound). If enough of the foreskin was not removed and *peri-a* was not done, the male had to be recircumcised.

The *Mishna* reads:

> These shreds [of the foreskin, if they remain] render the circumcision invalid: flesh that covers the greater part of the corona (such a one [if a priest] may not eat of heave-offering);[1] if he waxes fat [and the corona is covered anew] this must be set aright for appearance's sake. If one is circumcised without having the inner lining torn, it is as though he had not been circumcised (mShab. 19:6).[2]

The whole day is valid for circumcision (not the night: Shab. 133b). However, the zealous do it as early as possible in order to be like Abraham who performed his religious duties early in the morning: "and Abraham rose early in the morning" (Gen. 22:3; Pes. 4a). Thus, one should model himself after Abraham and do the *mitzvah* as soon as possible.

A child may never be circumcised before the eighth day[3] and never after the twelfth day (m'Ar. 2:2). This is elaborated in another tractate:

> A child can be circumcised on the eighth, ninth, tenth, eleventh or twelfth day, but never earlier and never later. How is this?[4] The rule is that it shall be done on the eighth day; but if the child was born at twilight, the child is circumcised on the ninth day; and if at twilight on the eve of Sabbath, the child is circumcised on the tenth day; if a Festival-day falls after the Sabbath, the child is circumcised on the eleventh day; and if the two Festival-days of the New Year fall after the Sabbath, the child is circumcised on the twelfth day. If a child is sick, it is not circumcised until it becomes well. (mShab. 19:5).

Thus, if a child is sick, he may not be circumcised on the eighth day[5] and the circumcision is postponed until the child recovers (Shab. 137a).

What constitutes a sick child? According to the *Gemara:*

> If an infant is too red, so that the blood is not yet absorbed in him (into his limbs, but it is still on the under-surface of the skin, this makes circumcision dangerous), we must wait until his blood is absorbed and then circumcise him. If he is green so that he is deficient in blood, we must wait until he is full-blooded and then circumcise him (Shab. 134a; cf. Hul. 47b).

However, if the child has a leprosy spot on the tip of the foreskin, the child may be circumcised because the positive law of circumcision overrides the prohibition against removing the tokens of ritual uncleanness (mNeg. 7:5; cf. mNeg. 7:4; and mNed. 3:11), whether it is done at the proper time or not (Shab. 132b; see Yeb. 35b). On the other hand, the child himself may not even have been sick but had brothers who died from circumcision. The question arises if such a child may be circumcised because of the possibility that it may prove fatal to him, too. There is a disagreement among the rabbis as to how many children had to die before circumcision was to be avoided. Abaye is of the opinion that if it is two children, then the third may not be circumcised. Rabbi Jochanan is of the opinion that if three die then the fourth cannot be circumcised. The children need not be from the same mother either; if the mother's sisters' children died from their circumcisions, then the circumcision is not permitted. When Rabbi Jochanan rendered his opinion setting the number at three, Abaye got so angry that he scolded them: "See, you have permitted a forbidden and dangerous act" (Yeb. 64b; see also Hul. 47b). Incidentally, Jews who have not been circumcised because of these reasons are still considered good Jews (Hul. 4b, 5a).

There are also times when it is considered detrimental to circumcise a child as a result of natural events such as the prevalence of the South Wind, which was thought to bring unwholesome weather and affect health. To buttress this view, the Gemara stated that the Children of Israel were not circumcised in the desert "because of the fatigue of the journey" (Yeb. 71b).

Berit Mila ON THE SABBATH

By far, the preponderance of discussion on circumcision in the *Talmud* centers on *berit mila*, the act of circumcision, on the Sabbath. The Sabbath, after Yom Kippur, is the most sacred day in the Jewish calendar. No work is permitted on that day. Yet if the eighth day of birth falls on a Sabbath, the child must be circumcised because circumcision overrides the Sabbath. The verses "Thou shalt keep My Covenant" (Gen. 17:9), repeated at Sinai, and, "And in the eighth day (*u-va-yom*) the flesh of his foreskin shall be circumcised" (Lev. 12:3), were used for the purpose of permitting circumcision on the Sabbath—by interpreting "on the day" (*u-va-yom*), as "even on the Sabbath" (San.59b).[6]

The rationale behind permitting circumcision to override the Sabbath is the talmudic principle that a positive commandment overrides a negative one (Bez. 8b). Thus, in the preparation of a *berit,* everything may be done even though it violates the Sabbath: "R. Jose says. . . And they may perform on the Sabbath all things that are needful for circumcision" (mShab. 18:3; cf. mNed. 3:11), such as excision, tearing, sucking (the wound) putting on the bandage and cummin (mShab. 19:2).[7] Rabbi Eliezer in his community went so far as to permit the cutting of wood on the Sabbath to make charcoal, in order to forge the circumcision knife (Shab. 130a; Hul. 116a), his reasoning being that "On the day" (Lev. 12:3) implies circumcision and its preliminaries may be performed even on the Sabbath. Rabbi Akiva forbade the work of preparation on the Sabbath in his community on the basis of a law he promulgated "that any labor which may be performed on the Sabbath eve does not supersede the Sabbath" (Shab. 133a; Yeb. 14a; mPes. 6:2 and mMen. 11:3). Rabbi Eliezer permitted openly carrying the circumcision knife on the Sabbath if it had not been brought prior to the Sabbath. And if it was in time of danger (for example, when circumcision wasn't permitted by the government) he could cover it up in the presence of witnesses[8]: (mShab. 19:1). Rabbi Isaac cites an interesting occurrence in support of Rabbi Eliezer:

> There was one town in Palestine where they followed Rabbi Eliezer (in respect of circumcision), and they died there at the (proper) time (never prematurely). Moreover, the wicked State (Rome?) once promulgated a decree against Israel concerning circumcision (forbidding it), yet did not decree (it) against the town (Shab. 130a).

However, Raba totally disagrees with this view and claims that a knife may not be carried on the Sabbath under any circumstances, notwithstanding that the failure to circumcise involves the dire penalty of *karet,* in other words, untimely death at the hands of Heaven (Gen. 17:14; Pes. 92a).

Bathing the child on the Sabbath before and after the circumcision under prescribed conditions is permitted.

They may wash the child either before or after the circumcision and sprinkle it by means of the hand, but not by means of a vessel. R. Eleazar b. Azariah says: They wash the child[9] on the third day if this falls on a Sabbath, for it is written, "And it came to pass on the third day when they were sore."[10] They may not profane the Sabbath for the sake of a child about which there is doubt[11] or that is androgynous'[12] but R. Judah permits it for one that is androgynous (Shab. 19:3).

However, there are rabbis that limit the extent of the violations permitted on the Sabbath. Basic essentials such as those things that can be done before the Sabbath are not permitted to be done on the Sabbath. For example, if warm water that was prepared before the Sabbath was spilled, one may not carry warm water from another house if there is no *eiruv*. However, an exception is made if a Gentile was asked to carry the water, though there is a prohibition against asking a non-Jew to do something when a Jew himself is not permitted to do it ('Eruv. 67b and 68a). Rabbah holds a similar view that one may not heat water on the Sabbath for a circumcision but must prepare it the previous day (Pes. 69a). Beit Shammai didn't permit the carrying of the infant to the synagogue (where the circumcision was performed) but Beit Hillel disagreed (Bez. 1:5). Furthermore,

If this [cummin] had not been pounded up on the eve of the Sabbath a man may chew it with his teeth and then apply it. If the wine and oil had not been mixed on the eve of the Sabbath each may be applied by itself. They may not newly make the special bandage [on the Sabbath] but a rag may be wrapped around the member. If this had not been prepared on the eve of the Sabbath one may bring it wrapped around his finger even from another courtyard (mShab. 19:2).

Though the recognized general principle in the *Gemara* is that circumcision supersedes the Sabbath, in regard to the *tumtum,* a hermaphrodite (one whose sexual organs are underdeveloped or concealed), a birth by cesarean section, a Gentile woman who gives birth and converts the following day, a child who has two foreskins, or a child who is born circumcised, the question of whether a circumcision may take place on the eighth day if that day is the Sabbath is subject to debate. Opinion is divided except concerning the *tumtum.* A *tumtum* is not circumcised on the eighth day if it falls on the Sabbath, "for Scripture said, 'If a woman be delivered, and bear a man-child . . . and in the eighth day [the flesh of his foreskin] shall be circumcised.'"[13] Since he must be a male at the time of his birth, which he wasn't, the Sabbath is not overridden (B.B. 127a).

Therefore, regarding the hermaphrodite, the rabbis claim that such a case doesn't override the Sabbath. Rabbi Judah disagrees and claims that if it is not done, the penalty is *karet* (Shab. 134b and 135a). A child born by cesarean birth or one that has two foreskins or two membra is the subject of a difference of opinion between Rabbi Huna and Rabbi Hiyya ben Rab.

> One maintains, we desecrate the Sabbath for them; whilst the other holds, we do not desecrate the Sabbath for them. Thus they differ only concerning the desecration of the Sabbath for them, but we certainly circumcise them on the eight day?—One is dependent on the other (Shab. 135b).

The circumcision of a child born circumcised does not supersede the Sabbath. However, Beit Shammai maintains: One must cause a few drops of the Covenant blood to flow from him and the Sabbath is desecrated. Beit Hillel holds the opposite view and the Sabbath is not to be desecrated (Shab. 135a).[14]

When there is a doubt as to whether it is the eighth day,[15] the Sabbath may not be desecrated, i.e., in the case of a child born at twilight (on Friday, and it is not known whether it was Friday or Saturday). Also, if it is unknown whether the fetus is seven or eight months old, there is a question whether or not the Sabbath may be desecrated. If it was definitely seven months, the Sabbath may be desecrated. If the fetus is eight months old, the Sabbath may not be desecrated (Shab. 134b, 135a).

When there is a doubt whether the child will live, he may be circumcised on the Sabbath if it is the eighth day. However, the Sabbath is not to be violated for the preliminary preparations (Shab. 135b, 136a).

Where a man unwittingly circumcised a child on the Sabbath when it was not the eighth day but the seventh day, it is not a circumcision but merely inflicting a wound which makes the circumciser culpable (mShab. 19:4; cf. Pes. 72a).[16]

The same penalty is meted out if the circumciser comes at

twilight on the Sabbath and was warned that he wouldn't have time to finish the *berit* but nevertheless goes ahead and does it but doesn't have time to trim the membrane and the shreds remain. This circumcision is invalid and is considered to be a wound (Shab. 133b).

Since circumcision overrides the Sabbath as discussed above, it certainly supersedes the festivals, even allowing things to be done that are prohibited on the Sabbath. For example, cummin may be crushed and wine and oil may be beaten up together (Shab. 134a). However, where there is a doubt whether it is the eighth day, circumcision doesn't override the festival. For example, if a child was born at twilight, there is a doubt as to the correct day for circumcision, and the child is circumcised on the ninth day, but if the ninth is a festival, it is postponed to the tenth day (Shab. 135a and Hul. 84b).

LEGAL RESTRICTIONS ON UNCIRCUMCISED JEWS

Invalid circumcisions (e.g., shreds of the corona) prohibit the eating of *terumah,* the Paschal lamb, holy food and tithe (Yeb. 74a). Such an uncircumcised child may not be anointed with the oil of *terumah* (Yeb. 71a; see Shab. 86a). An uncircumcised male may not eat the Paschal lamb for he could have circumcised himself as late as the eve of Passover and thereby fulfilled the requirement of eating the Paschal lamb. For the sin of not partaking of the Paschal lamb he incurs the penalty of *karet* (Pes. 69a).

If a Paschal lamb was slaughtered for those uncircumcised men who, because their brothers died as a result of circumcision, were not circumcised, they may not eat of it, and in fact, the sacrifice is disqualified (Pes. 60a, 61b; see also 62b and 63a; cf. 96a).[17] However, these males are not subject to the penalty of *karet.*

Even if a man is himself circumcised, if any of his sons or slaves are eligible for circumcision but remain uncircumcised (see Ex. 12:44, 48), he may not eat of the Paschal lamb (Yeb. 70b).

If a child is born circumcised, according to Rabbi Akiva, he may not eat of the Paschal lamb unless blood was drawn, whereas Rabbi Eliezer holds the opposite view (Yeb. 71a).

Of course, exceptions are made. Such is the case of a child who had pain in his eyes, and, therefore, the circumcision was postponed. If he recovered on the eve of Passover, he may eat of the Paschal lamb. Other exceptions are the case where the parents of the child are in prison; whereas they normally have an obligation to circumcise their son, in this case they are unable, due to their imprisonment; and in the case of a *tumtum* (Yeb. 71b); in either case, he may eat of the Paschal lamb.

RABBINIC RULES REGARDING THE CIRCUMCISER

Who is obligated to circumcise? According to the *Talmud*, first the father; if he doesn't do it, then the *beit din;* and failing that, the man himself. The mother is not obligated since it says " 'And Abraham circumcised his son. . . as God had commanded him'—him, but not her" (Kid. 29a; cf. 30b).

Who may circumcise? An Israelite or a heathen physician who is a recognized expert (Men. 42a and 'A.Z. 26b, 27a). There is even a disagreement in the *Talmud* concerning whether a Gentile who performs circumcisions is permitted to do so for Jews and, if he is permitted, if he may recite a blessing (Men. 42a).

The question of whether a woman may circumcise is also subject to debate even though the Bible clearly states that Zipporah circumcised her son. In order to deny women that right, the *Talmud* reinterprets the biblical text "So Zipporah took a flint"[18] (Exod. 4:25), to read "she caused to be taken"; and "she cut off" to read "and she caused it to be cut off" by either asking another man or her husband, Moses ('A.Z. 27a).

Scholars were encouraged to be *mohalim*. In fact, " . . . Rab Judah said in the name of Rab, 'a scholar must learn three things, viz.: writing, ritual slaughtering and circumcision'" (Hul. 9a). And if he himself wasn't a *mohel*, then he should not live in a town where there is no *mohel* (Sanh. 17b).

BLESSINGS AT A *Berit Mila*

The blessing to be recited by the *mohel* is talmudically established:

He who circumcises must recite . . . "who hast sanctified us with Thy commandments, and has commanded us concerning circumcision" (Shab. 136b).

Note should be taken that two opposing views are put forward concerning when the blessing should be recited—before or after the circumcision—and regarding the proper wording to be recited by the *mohel*. With regard to the former, it is to be recited before the circumcision on the basis of the principle that "for all precepts a benediction is recited prior to [*ober*] their being performed" (Pes. 7b).[19] With regard to the latter, the question arises whether the circumciser is to say "concerning circumcision" *(al ha-mila)* or "to circumcise" *(la mol)*. If he says "to circumcise" it implies that it is the circumciser who is obligated to circumcise when, in fact, the obligation is the father's. Therefore, the blessing to be recited by the *mohel* is "concerning circumcision." However, if the father circumcises, he must say "to circumcise" (Pes. 7b).

CIRCUMCISION OF PROSELYTES AND SLAVES

One becomes a proselyte only after he is both circumcised[20] and immersed (Yeb. 46a, 'A.Z. 59a).[21] If he were merely circumcised, he is not permitted to eat of the Paschal lamb (Yeb. 71a) because he is still considered a Gentile ('A.Z. 59a). Three men are required to be present at the conversion, i.e., at the conversion and immersion, since "law has been written in this case" (Yeb. 46b)—by which it is meant that no point of law can be authoritatively decided by a *beit din* of less than three men. So here too with regard to a proselyte, a *beit din* is required consisting of at least three men.[22]

There is a dispute among Tannaim whether a circumcision in special cases may take place at night; for example, in the case of a *mashuk* (a circumcised person whose prepuce has been drawn forward to cover the corona), a proselyte (who had previously been circumcised with no religious motive), or for a child whose *berit* had been postponed. (It already has been established that circumcision in its proper time has to be during the daytime on the basis of "and in the day" [Lev. 12:3; Yeb. 72b].) Some Tannaim confine it to daytime. However, Rabbi Eleazar ben Simon says: "if not at the proper time they may be circumcised both by day and by night" (Yeb. 72b).

Incidentally, one should not confuse a *ger toshav* who is a Gentile with a proselyte. A *ger toshav* is a Gentile who takes upon himself, in the presence of three *chaverim,* not to worship idols. If a *ger toshav* said he would undergo circumcision but "allows twelve months to pass without becoming circumcised, [he] is to be regarded as an heretic among idolaters" ('A.Z. 68a).

Slaves owned by Jews had to be circumcised (Shab. 135b). Failure to do so prohibited a man from partaking of the Paschal Lamb, a grievous sin (Yeb. 70b). A slave bought on the eve of the Sabbath may not be circumcised on the Sabbath (slaves were generally circumcised soon after purchase) for only on the eighth day of a child's birth may circumcision override the Sabbath *(mila bizemano)* (Shab. 135b).

A concern is raised in the *Talmud* whether children of female slaves who had been circumcised but not immersed render wine *nesek* (an Orthodox Jew is not permitted to drink wine handled by a non-Jew. Hence the concern of the status of such children). The Gemara concludes that the wine is not *nesek* since children do not understand the nature of an idol. However, adults in such a situation do render wine *nesek* since they know the significance of idolatry ('A.Z. 57a).

IMPORTANCE OF CIRCUMCISION: *Halacha* and *Aggadah*

In the hierarchy of Jewish values and *mitzvot,* circumcision overrides the Sabbath and Yom Kippur. It also takes precedence over attending the burial of a near relative (Meg. 3b, see also Sanh. 34a and b) and even takes precedence over disposing of *hametz* before Passover (mPes. 3:7).

For those who fail to fulfill the *mitzvah* of circumcision, even Yom Kippur does not procure atonement (Yoma 85b). In fact, extirpation, i.e., *karet,* "cutting off," is the lot of such an individual (mKer. 1:1). If someone nullifies "the Covenant of Abraham our father" (stretches the foreskin to disguise circumcision), he has no share in the World to Come (mAb. 3:12). Here the phrase "Covenant of Abraham our father" is interpreted by some to mean circumcision, though others interpret it to mean *Torah.*

Once circumcised, a Jew is eligible to enter the World to Come (Sanh. 110b). Circumcision is cause for rejoicing. By and large, Jews accept the *mitzvah* from its very inception with great joy, which accounts for its perpetuation—unlike those *mitzvot* which were accepted hesitantly, hence not always practiced, like *te-filin,* and are not universally observed today. Jews were ready to die for circumcision but not for *te-filin* (Shab. 130a).

Curiously, knowing the importance and necessity of circumcision, as well as its centrality as a covenantal ritual, one can still discern a strong appeal to the Jewish People to maintain it and preserve it. In other words, at certain times in history, there seems to have been the need for a strong polemic to convince the Jews of its necessity and distinctiveness. In different periods of Jewish history, there were times when the Jews were ashamed of it and some even went through the painful process of epispasm; i.e., putting the foreskin back on. On the other hand, they were willing to be martyred when kings issued decrees forbidding the practice of circumcision.

So important and crucial was the sign of circumcision that in times of danger, if some Jews practiced epispasm, when the danger passed they had to go through recircumcision even though Rabbi Judah objected that they should not because it could prove fatal. The *Gemara* cites a powerful example to refute his position: "Surely many were circumcised (i.e., recircumcised) in the days of Ben Koziba and yet [lived and] gave birth to sons and daughters" (Yeb. 72a).[23] According to the *Aggada,*, the practice of epispasm was so heinous that had it not occurred, the Temple may not have been destroyed (Men. 53b). Even the pleadings of Abraham could not reverse the decision.[24]

Those that observe the *mitzvah* of circumcision were thought to be especially blessed and virtuous, assuring the continuity of the Jewish People. David composed a Psalm in praise of circumcision (Men. 43b). It was deemed so sacred that Jews were willing to be martyred for the sake of circumcision. "Rabbi Joshua ben Levi said (the verse, 'yea, for thy sake, we are killed all day long') can be applied to circumcision" (Git. 57b). Rabbi Tanchum was thrown into the arena when in a debate with the Roman Emperor over circumcision, he bested him. The animals, however, did not eat him (Sanh. 39a).[25]

One rabbi outwitted the Romans and had a decree against circumcision rescinded. When the Roman Government passed a decree against circumcision, Rabbi Reuben, son of Istroboli, cut his hair in the Roman fashion and joined the Romans.

He asked them: "If one has an enemy, what does he wish him, . . . to be weak or healthy?"
They answered "weak."
He said to them: "Then let their children be circumcised at the age of eight days and they will be weak."

They said: "He speaketh rightly," and it was annulled (Me'il. 17a).

Another account in the *Gemara* explains how the rabbis had a decree against circumcision lifted by going to a Roman matron whose advice they sought and followed, resulting in the withdrawal of the harsh decree (R.H. 19a; c.f. Ta'an. 18a).[26]

In an unusual incident, a non-Jew, who defended the Jews against the anti-Semitic Caesar and was ordered to be burned alive, circumcised himself on the way to the furnace. After he was martyred, a *bat-kol,* a heavenly voice, then exclaimed: "'Ketiah ben Shalom is destined for (eternal) life in the World to Come!' The rabbi (on hearing of it) wept, saying: 'One may acquire eternity in a single hour, another may acquire it after many years!'" ('A.Z. 10b).

The reward granted to Abraham for circumcising himself was that he was able to control his lust and not be led to sin (Ned. 32b) and was called perfect only by virtue of circumcision (Ned. 32a).[27] In contradistinction, there is the aforementioned example of Achan, whose act of epispasm led to lust and sinfulness.

With all of Moses' virtues and meritorious deeds, they did not stand him in good stead when he exhibited "apathy towards circumcision" according to Rabbi Joshua benKarha (Ned. 31b). On the other hand, Jethro, Moses' father-in-law, circumcised himself (Sanh. 94a).

Above all, circumcision was viewed with special joy by the rabbis of the Talmudic Period. In interpreting Esther 8:16, "the Jews have gladness, joy and honor," the rabbis declared that the word "joy" is to be understood to mean circumcision (Meg. 16b). This joyous event takes place on the eighth day based on the verse: "And on the eighth day shall the flesh of his foreskin be circumcised" (Lev. 12:3).

NOTES

(Translations of the *Mishna* throughout this chapter are from Herbert Danby. The *Mishnah*. Oxford, 1933. Translations of the *Gemara* in general use as a basis the translation of the *Talmud* by the Soncino Press).

1. Danby: "he is not qualified to serve as a priest. Compare Bekh. 7:5."
2. Samuel maintains that unless it is fully visible, he must be recircumcised; whereas the *Baraitha* teaches that only when it is quite invisible is recircumcision required (Shab. 137b). "These are the shreds which render the circumcision invalid: flesh which covers the greater part of the corona, (a priest having been so circumcised) is not permitted to eat *terumah;* (another opinion states) "Flesh which covers the greater part of the height of the corona (i.e., even if only on a minor portion of the circumference)" (Yeb. 47b).
3. In the case of circumcision any hour of the eighth day is acceptable (except the night). But if a child becomes ill, one must wait until the child recovers, "For Samuel said that a child who recovered from a fever must be allowed a period of convalescence of full seven days." Yeb. 71a and b. For example, if he recovered in the afternoon then a full seven days must be counted and on the eighth in the afternoon the *berit* takes place.
4. Danby: "The principle is, that if the ceremony is not done on the eighth day itself it does not override a Sabbath or Festival-day."
5. A child fit for circumcision makes his mother ritually unclean (Lev. 12:2; Nid. 24b).
6. This command was applied to Abraham and his decendants through Isaac—excluding Ishmael and Esau—on the basis of "For in Isaac shall thy seed be called" (Gen. 21:12), which excludes Ishmael. And by taking the preposition "in" of "in Isaac" it was confined to Isaac, "but not all Isaac" (San. 59b) and therefore, by extension, to Jacob and through him to his descendants.
7. Danby: "See *J. E.,* IV. 92ff." It is understood that these allowances are applicable on the Sabbath only if there is no doubt that it is the eighth day. Otherwise, no violation of the Sabbath is permitted.
8. One witness besides the *mohel* is sufficient (Shab. 130a).
9. Danby: "see Shab. 9:3".
10. Because the effects of the circumcision, and therefore its power to override the Sabbath endures to the third day—cf. Shab. 19:3 and 134b. A debate ensued whether bathing is meant literally. The *Gemara* concludes that the whole body may be washed and not just the member (Shab. 134b).
11. Danby: "whether it is an eight or nine months old child, and it is in doubt whether it can live."
12. Danby: "Of double sex. See Bikk. 1:5, 4:1 ff."
13. Danby: "Lev. XII:2-3, from which is derived the suspension of the Sabbath laws in favor of circumcision on the eighth day (v. Shab. 131b)."
14. It should be understood that in these discussions, the status of the ritual cleanness of the mother is a basic fact here.
15. Birth is reckoned when the fetus puts its head out of the ante-chamber and later withdraws it. It is considered born as of that moment (Nid. 42b).
16. "If a man had two children, one of which was to be circumcised on the day

after the Shabbath (the eighth day, Lev. 12:3) and the other was to be circumcised on the Sabbath, and he forgot and circumcised on the Sabbath the one that was to be circumcised after the Sabbath, he is culpable; if one was to be circumcised on the eve of Sabbath and the other on the Sabbath, and he forgot and circumcised on the Sabbath the one that was to be circumcised on the eve of Sabbath, R. Eliezer declares him liable to a sin-offering, but R. Joshua declares him exempt." (Shab. 19:4).

17. The same being true for a priest in similar circumstances, who, incidentally, is also disqualified from eating *terumah* (Yeb. 70a, see also 99b).

18. By the time of the *Talmud*, metal was common (Hullin 116a). However, a reed *(halum)* was prohibited for there was danger of splinters breaking away from the reed and penetrating the penis (Hul. 16b).

19. There are exceptions. For example, in the case of *mikveh*, where the blessing is recited afterwards.

20. If a proselyte converts, though already born circumcised, Beit Shammai contends that a few drops of blood have to be drawn. Whereas, Beit Hillel says it is not necessary (Shab. 135a).

21. According to Rabbi, not only is circumcision and immersion required, but so is the sprinkling of blood (i.e., offering sacrifices, cf. Exod. 24:5 ff). However, the latter is set aside since there are no longer sacrifices (Kerithoth 9a).

22. For the blessings on the circumcision of a proselyte: "The person performing the circumcision for a proselyte says: 'Blessed art Thou, 0 Lord our God, King of the universe, Who hast sanctified us with Thy commandments and hast commanded us concerning circumcision.' He who pronounces the benediction recites, '. . . Who hast sanctified us with Thy commandments and has commanded us to circumcise proselytes and to cause the drops of the blood of the Covenant to flow from them, since but for the blood of the Covenant heaven and earth would not endure, as it is said, If not my Covenant by day and by night, I had not appointed the ordinances of heaven and earth (Jer. 33:2S). Blessed art Thou, 0 Lord, Who makest the Covenant' (Shab. 137b)." See Soncino trans., p. 693, note 1.

23. Ben Koziba, also known as Bar Kochba, the leader of the Judean revolt against Rome in 132 C.E., according to a footnote in the Soncino *Talmud*, "In the course of the persecution that preceded the revolt, many had their prepuces forcibly drawn in order to obliterate the sign of the Abrahamic covenant, and when liberation came, they were again circumcised."

24. Rabbi Isaac said, 'At the time of the destruction of the Temple, the Holy One, Blessed be He, found Abraham standing at the Temple. Said He, *'What hath my beloved to do in My house?'* (Jer. 11:15). Abraham replied, 'I have come concerning the fate of my children.' Said He, 'Thy children sinned and have gone into exile . . . he pleaded, 'Thou shouldst have remembered unto them the Covenant of circumcision.' And He replied, 'The hallowed flesh is passed from thee' (Jer. 11:15); (i.e., they attempted to hide their circumcision.' " (Men.53b)

25. "The Emperor proposed to R. Tanhum, 'Come, let us all be one people.' 'Very well,' he answered, 'but we who are circumcised cannot possibly become like you; do ye become circumcised and be like us.' The Emperor replied: 'You have spoken well; nevertheless, anyone who gets the better of the king [in debate] must be thrown into the *vivarium.'* So they threw him in, but he was not eaten" (Sanh. 39a).

26. The Jews were able to get this decree annulled in an interesting vignette that they relate: "On the twenty-eight (of Adar) came glad tidings to the Jews that they should not abandon the practice of the Law. For the Government [of Rome] had

issued a decree that they should not study the *Torah* and that they should not circumcise their sons and that they should profane the Sabbath. What did Judah b.
Shammu'a and his colleagues do? They went and consulted a certain matron whom
all Roman notables used to visit. She said to them: 'Go and make proclamation [of
your sorrows] at night time.' They went and proclaimed at night, crying, 'Alas, in
heaven's name, are we not your brothers, are we not the sons of one father and are
we not the sons of one mother? Why are we different from every nation and tongue
that you issue such harsh decrees against us?' The decrees were thereupon annulled,
and that day was declared a fast day."

27.   There are different versions as to Rabbi's attitude to the high regard and value
of circumcision. According to Rabbi, Abraham is called perfect only by virtue of
circumcision. Another version of his teachings is that circumcision counterbalances
all of the precepts of the *Torah*. Another version is: "Great is circumcision, since
but for it heaven and earth would not endure: as it is written [*Thus saith the Lord*]
But for my covenant by day and night (this is taken to mean circumcision), *I would
not have annointed the ordinances of heaven and earth* (Jer. 33:25). However,
Rabbi Eleazer takes this verse to mean *Torah*. (Ned.32a).

Berit Mila Issues in Modern Orthodoxy and Reform Judaism

Mordecai Finley

INTRODUCTION

There are many ways that Reform Jews find meaning in the observance of ritual circumcision. Some see *berit mila* as the ancient sign of the Covenant, others as a way to establish Jewish identity for a boy. The meaning of the observance to be discussed in this paper is perhaps the weakest for the Reform Jew: *berit mila* as a legal requirement, a *mitzvah*, a commandment. Not that we Reform Jews don't have or don't talk about *mitzvot;* we do, but our notion of *mitzvah* is a much attenuated one compared to the traditional notion. For the Jew living in an halachic world, a *mitzvah* is a commandment from God and the Jew is commanded and obligated to perform it.

An examination of the differing attitudes toward *mitzvot* would serve well as a guide to the differences between the various streams of religious Judaism, and would especially serve to distinguish Orthodoxy from Reform. For the Orthodox, the *Torah* and the legal system which grows out of it, *halacha,* are both incontrovertibly authoritative. *Torah* is understood to be direct and divine revelation, and the rabbis (and in the modern period, only Orthodox rabbis) are the sole authoritative interpreters of *Torah* and *halacha*. A *mitzvah*, then, whether found in the *Torah*, in the Oral Law tradition derived therefrom, or simply enacted by rabbis who had such authority, is required action. One may find the *mitzvah* meaningful or not, tasteful or not, enjoyable or not, but *halacha* as understood by the rabbinic tradition must be fulfilled and the *mitzvot* must be observed. The Reform approach, certainly still very much being formed, begins in the rejection of the notion that the *Torah* is direct, divine revelation, that the *halacha* is coterminous with divine will, and that the rabbis (any rabbi) has the moral power to establish authoritatively what *Torah* means or what a Jew is obligated to do before God.

For the orthodox, then, ritual circumcision is a *mitzvah*, a commandment, a legal requirement, which is part of a larger system of commandments. The authoritative status of *berit mila*, like all *mitzvot*, is much less clear for Reform Jews. Let it suffice to say at this point, that while *mitzvot* do not have legal authority within Reform Judaism they have "normative" authority, an authority often presented and discussed, however, within the rhetoric of law. What is the basis of this authority? Simply put, for various reasons, our religion and the path to God which it forms, grasps us in a meaningful and demanding way. To say that *mitzvot* are not legally or halachically authoritative, does not mean that they have no force in our lives, or that we don't feel in some non-legal sense obligated to observe *mitzvot* as part of our relationship with the tradition and with God.

This notion of the normative as opposed to the legal, which characterizes the Reform approach to *halacha*, serves to preserve notions of personal choice and responsibility in religious life. However, when this admittedly ambiguous Reform approach meets up with questions that are already problematic or ambiguous even in the Orthodox world, we find that the notion of choice—a cornerstone of our religious practice—becomes something of a obstacle in developing a methodology by which we can account for the decisions we make. In this chapter, I will address this larger theological and interpretive issue through a discussion of *berit mila*.

THE NATURE OF POST TALMUDIC LEGAL

Literature and the Development of Jewish Law

Halachic literature is based on the *Talmud*, itself comprised of two interwoven sections, the *Mishna* (c. 200 C.E.), and the *Gemara*, which further elucidates, expands on and develops in three ways: commentaries on the *Talmud*, codification or restatements of the law, and responsa. Since the focus of this chapter is the interpretation and application of a specific element in Jewish law, a few more words about the nature of responsa would be appropriate. The closest equivalent in secular law to responsa would be case law, i.e., the study of law as applied in specific cases, as opposed to the study of legal statutes. Typically, a question of Jewish law not answerable by reference to a code would be addressed to an halachic authority. This authority would examine authoritative statutory texts, the *Talmud* and its commentaries, the legal codes, as well as prior case law, and arrive at some decision by applying his reading of the law to the case at hand. It should be noted that just as the *Talmud* is full of controversy and legal contradiction, so too is the responsa literature.

The wide diversity of opinion which we find in Jewish case law should give us pause. The legal and normative activity of the *Talmud* reflects a time of jurisprudential fluidity and pluralism. The codes, however, reflect the desire to decide the law *(pisuk halacha)*, while at the same time preserving, through the accompanying commentaries, the history of the inherent tension in Jewish law. If the great codes, Maimonides' *Mishneh Torah*, Jacob ben Asher's *Arba Turim*, and especially Joseph Karo's *Shulhan Aruch*, state rather clearly what the law should be in a certain case, why then should we find such controversy in responsa literature?

We can answer this question in two ways: historically and jurisprudentially. From a historical perspective, it is perhaps technically incorrect to call the literature of halachic decision-making "codes." The word "code" suggests, in Stephen Passamaneck's words, "a statutory force which renders previous codes inoperative."[1] Passamaneck prefers the word "compendia" to the word "code," because, in the Jewish legal tradition, no statement of law ever completely superceded the authority of that which went before it. In this paper, we shall use the more common locution "code," but with Passamaneck's caveat in mind. The powerful but non-supercessory force of codes creates a unique situation in Jewish law. For example, Karo's *Shulhan Aruch* certainly has immense legal and normative authority.

Nevertheless an individual rabbi presented with a legal question not clearly covered in Karo's code may ground his response in talmudic, early post-talmudic and other responsa literature, or in responsa post-dating Karo's work. One could even countenance a clash of law, where only a trained legal scholar could make the right decision, halachically speaking. (Breaking the Sabbath to preserve life, for example. That which precisely constitutes preserving life is something that no law could could exhaustively define). As Ronald Dworkin, in his book *Taking Rights Seriously,* might state, in "hard" cases,[2] the law code is more a tool than a final arbiter; the human judge becomes the arbiter of which side of the law to uphold, or of whether new sides are to be discovered. Would a traditional rabbi come right out and say that Karo's code is insufficient on some issue? *Rarely.*

This leads us to our second point in accounting for the diversity in responsa literature, the jurisprudential aspect. An uncritical view of legal adjudication looks something like this: A judge or rabbi has a case presented before him. He looks in the statutes/codes and previously adjudicated law to find precedent. He makes a reading of the established law, applies those texts which fit the current case the best, and according to this fit, decides the case. There are several premises in this view, including the notion that the case before him and the law itself have some clear, unequivocal, objective reading, and that the fit between the case and the law is clear and compelling. The idea that any judge in any hard case simply applies the law is philosophically and jurisprudentially unsound.

A better way to describe adjudication would be first to see law not as the reflection of the will or mores of society, but rather reflective of the enormous tensions which inhere in any jurisprudentially active culture. In other words—and this is certainly borne out in the study of *Talmud*—any legal stand which is favored involves a legal stand denied. In the Jewish tradition, as previously mentioned, no legal code is supersessory. Minority opinions and their rejection are recorded, admittedly, so that they will not be reintroduced at a later date. But we find evidence in responsa literature that opinions rejected in one case, find greater legal standing in another. There are times when some later legal decisor may make use of previously rejected law if he feels that current circumstances differ enough. We recall that the reading of circumstances, in hard cases, are never purely objective; the will and vision of the judge is read into them as well. Therefore, if a legal decisor finds some ruling in the *Shulhan Aruch,* for example, to be inadequate to the present circumstances, he may have the resources of a vast expanse of legal tradition to find ground for a legal stand.

The same consideration concerning ambiguity in legal tradition holds true when we consider the meaning of individual statutes. Just as no hard case has an objective reading, and no fit is compelling, and even if we remember that every statute implies a minority or (heretofore) unadopted view, we should recall that no statute has an unequivocal meaning or "reading." Often a statute when adopted seems clear and straightforward. However, when new historical or even intellectual circumstances arise, just what those words mean becomes a matter of intense debate.

Theories of Juridical Meaning and Jewish Law

Theories of juridical meaning abound. We may look at the author's intentions, the meaning of the words in their context, the multiple meanings that the words might possibly bear, and so forth. The philosophical endeavor which works to find meaning through theories of meaning is usually referred to as "hermeneutics." However, there is no established or authoritative methodology for finding meaning, in the larger sense, in Jewish legal hermeneutics. We are not speaking here directly of the hermeneutical rules for the interpretation of *Torah*. But even there, the existence of a rule doesn't mean that there is not disagreement on how any individual rule is to be used or applied. Our interest here, however, is with larger philosophical questions. The hermeneutical question, "What does a statute mean?" can be extrapolated to theories of law, society, or meaning in general. Can we say that Jewish law has a central concern, is it trying to establish something, and should we interpret law according to that final vision? And if so, how do we preconstruct that final vision? Or is Jewish law reflective of the ultimately unknowable mind of God, and must we must interpret the best we can, with faith that words will give up their meaning to the authentically faithful? Or is law simply the will of those who make it up at any one time, and its meaning resides in its authority? These larger hermeneutical issues are not matters of luxurious intellectual play—a legal decisor's theory of meaning, law and society will greatly inform his or her decision making, consciously or not.

The above remarks may be applied to the reading of a legal case as well. How one describes what the case is has great implications for how a case may be decided. Theories of knowledge tell us that the world "out there," especially the cultural, moral world, is socially constructed, and even the empiric, material world is held together by intentionality. When we arrive, then, at the problem of "fit," applying the law to the case, we see that the juridical order is created as much as or more than it is being lived, according to— especially in hard cases—when the ambiguity described above is powerful.

In the face of all this ambiguity, how does a judge operate? We would argue that a judge does carry with him theories of law and theories of society. He understands that his decisions have both implications for the integrity of the law and social consequences, if the two are in fact separable. In other words, a judge has a sense of how the case should be resolved, how the law should work. This is not to say that he knows what he will decide regardless of what the law says, but rather that he too, has received his training and intellectual grounding in the legal/linguistic world which is now his to create and carry on. A judge too, then, embodies its tensions and controversies, its ambiguities, ambivalences, and possibilities for partiality.

When we turn to the rabbi who needs to go beyond the *Shulhan Aruch,* then, we see that his way out is not to call some aspect of Jewish law inadequate, but rather to deeply inquire what the law means or can mean, or even should mean. The traditionalist who feels that some aspect of the *Shulhan Aruch* does not countenance the social and legal reality in which he lives, has limited options. He cannot call for new, creative legislation, as it were. But he does have the option of reinterpretation, and in hard cases, this option is quite powerful. We must recall, in this context, that the task of any judge is to uphold the authority of the legal tradition even as he molds it to apply to new circumstances. The interpretive method, while certainly conservative and cumbersome, can operate in both a conserving and ameliorative way.

What then gives validity to a specific response to a tough legal question? A study of responsa shows legitimacy is a function of an interplay between methodology and consequences. Methodology itself is based on notions of what the legitimate sources of authority are, and what the legitimate jurisprudential methods are. If one refers to the appropriate sources, and argues them in the appropriate way, and does not come up with an answer that offends the sensibilities of the wider community, then one's responsum tends to be considered valid. The problem in hard cases, though, is that what the sources are and what they say, and how to argue them, and what the consequences should be, are themselves often at issue. The kind of ambiguity which defines "hard cases" is exacerbated in Reform Judaism because the authoritative nature of those texts which have normative force for us is deeply in question. While questions of sources, method, and legitimacy are found in any jurisprudential enterprise, for Reform Jews they are especially acute.

LEGAL PROBLEMS RELATING TO *Berit Mila*

The questions of the meanings of statutes and theories of law and society, and personal identity are precisely those which form the legal problems of the issue of *berit mila*. The statute is fairly clear. The *halacha* tells us that it is the father's duty to have his son circumcised (*Shulhan Aruch, Yoreh Deah,* 260.1). We ask: Does this son have to be Jewish? And if so, who is a Jew? This later question is, of course, one of the thorniest and most hotly debated issues of Jewish law in the current era—but the way both questions are argued and resolved will have an impact on the work of a *mohel/et*. The *mohel/et* must have some sense of who is eligible to receive a Jewish, religious circumcision, and who is not. The *mohel/et*, therefore, must have in mind some theory of Jewish law, and some theory of Jewish identity in order to know how to handle a hard case. Consider the following not-too-unlikely scenarios confronting the Reform *mohel/et* on the telephone:

1. A Jewish father affiliated with a Reform synagogue, a non-Jewish mother who practices a religion other than Judaism.
2. Jewish parents who are both Jews for Jesus.
3. A Jewish father and a non-Jewish mother, neither of whom practice or affiliate with any religion, want a circumcision for their child in case he wants to "go Jewish" at a later date.
4. Two non-Jewish parents, both in conversion classes, want their child "already Jewish."
5. An affiliated Jewish man and a non-Jewish woman, not married to each other.
6. A Jewish mother and non-Jewish father who practices another faith. They intend to raise the child in the father's faith, but she

wants circumcision "so he'll have something Jewish."

How might we respond to these various situations? The remainder of this paper will be devoted to outlining some of the ways the questions of circumcision and Jewish identity have been addressed in the modern period.

Let us first address the less difficult issue of circumcision of a non-Jewish child. In the *Shulhan Aruch, Yoreh Deah* 266.13, we find that a Jew who has a son born to him of a non-Jewish woman is not permitted to have the circumcision performed on the Sabbath. The reasoning would be that only a *mitzvah* can possibly override another *mitzvah* and there is no *mitzvah* in circumcision of the non-Jew. Therefore, the *mitzvah* and medical operation of *berit mila* which normally overrides the Sabbath, does not in this case. However, we see that there is no prohibition in circumcising a non-Jewish child, according to the *halacha* as presented in the *Shulhan Aruch*. The question concerns whether we should do it.

By the mid-nineteenth century, the most common answer was no. We see this response typified in a controversy which occurred in New Orleans in 1864. Rabbi Bernard Illowy had ruled that sons of Jewish fathers and Gentile mothers should not be circumcised lest the children be mistakenly identified as Jews. Illowy had the support of leading Orthodox rabbis in Europe for his stance, with one notable exception. Rabbi Zvi Hirsch Kalischer, a leading Orthodox thinker and halachist, held in favor of the practice of circumcising non-Jewish children in general, and children of Jewish fathers in particular. Kalischer felt that *Torah* was intended for all humanity, and limited to the Israelites because of the condition of the nations of the world when God decided to give the *Torah* to human beings.

Therefore, anything that can be done to enable or encourage a non-Jew to accept *Torah* should be done. The prospect of facing circumcision as an adult is certainly an obstacle, Kalischer felt, and therefore circumcision of a non-Jewish infant is advisable. Furthermore, Kalischer felt that the offspring of a Jewish father was to be considered "holy seed," and to circumcise the child would be to enable him to convert that much more quickly as an adult, thus rejoining the holiness of the seed to the purity of *Torah*. The father would be performing a *mitzvah* by facilitating his son's future conversion, and Kalischer felt that the perhaps religiously baneful influence of the mother should not be taken into account, but that we should rather do all we could to bring the child into the faith.

Kalischer countenanced the idea of performing a circumcision on a child who remained non-Jewish. Later Orthodox decisors decided that circumcison of a non-Jewish child by a *mohel* should only take place on the premise that the circumcision was part of a conversion process, and must be completed with ritual immersion. When circumcision of a non-Jewish infant was permitted, then, it was with the understanding that the change of status was already taking place.

Reform responsa concur in this understanding. Rabbi Solomon Freehof, the great *posek* (legal decisor) of North American Reform Jewry, was asked whether a rabbi should consent to be present at a *berit* of a child with a non-Jewish mother. He responded, ". . . the rabbi should certainly participate in the *berit mila*, but only if the parents will agree to raise the child as a Jew and give it a Jewish education."[3] Raising the child as a Jew and giving the child a Jewish education is, of course, tantamount to conversion in Reform Judaism, so on this issue the stance of Reform is like that of the Orthodox; circumcision only with conversion. Karo's lack of prohibition in the *Shulhan Aruch* is largely not taken advantage of, and Kalischer's stand on circumcision with no commitment on the part of the parents to raise the child Jewishly is not advised at the institutional level. There seems to be a somewhat broad consensus, then, that circumcision should only be performed on Jews or those undergoing conversion.

THE PROBLEM: "WHO IS A JEW?"

At this point we reach the more difficult of the two questions raised above, namely, "Who is a Jew?" A Jew has traditionally been defined as one born of a Jewish mother, or one who has converted to Judaism. The question of "Who is a Jew?" is more often-than-not raised around that of the validity of non-Orthodox conversions. For male converts, Orthodoxy requires *berit mila*, circumcision, *mikveh,* immersion in the ritual bath, and the proselyte's appearance before a *beit din* which will ascertain that the proselyte intends to fulfill the commandments incumbent upon him. The non-Orthodox understanding of the fulfillment of commandments differs from the Orthodox to the point that the latter do not feel that this basic requirement of accepting the responsibility to perform *mitzvot* has been fulfilled in any non-Orthodox conversion. In fact, it is possible to cite many modern responsa which show that in their own conversions, the Orthodox are often less than punctilious in demanding the acceptance of and commitment to practice of Orthodox *halacha*. However, this occasional permissiveness may obtain only in Orthodox conversions, because the Orthodox feel that only their *beit din* has the authority to decide when to push this point or not. As to the legitimacy of non-Orthodox conversions, the Orthodox approach is unanimously negative, although in some Orthodox circles, there seems to be some softening on this point.

Until very recently, all streams of Judaism concurred that a Jew is one born of a Jewish mother, or one who converted to Judaism. Reform Judaism tacitly considered conversion to be effected, at least in the case of mixed marriage, by events so routine as enrolling a child in religious school, or by the child's undergoing *bar/bat mitzvah* or confirmation. However, in March of 1983, the Central Conference of American Rabbis decided to change this longstanding policy and considered children born of Jewish fathers and non-Jewish mothers to be under the presumption of Jewishness at birth, and not needing to undergo any conversion process. The *berit mila*, then, of a child born of a Jewish father and non-Jewish mother would not, in Kalischer's terms, afford the child an easier entrance into Judaism later in life. Nor would it be the *mila* of conversion as has been accepted by all movements. Rather, it would be the regular religious *berit mila* performed on all Jewish males. The practical consequence is clear: a rabbi need not be present to conduct a conversion ceremony at the circumcision of a child of a non-Jewish mother and Jewish father. The child is already Jewish.

If the Reform Movement had remained committed to the position that circumcision was part of the conversion process, a great and often bitter debate might have been avoided. In many ways, the debate is an opportunity for revived polemics. This paper is not the place for an in-depth analysis of the issue; however, a broad-brushed portrayal of the debate is important for understanding both what is at stake and the effects of the Patrilineal Descent Resolution on the work of the Reform *mohel/et*.

First, we should consider the larger rubric under which this discussion takes place. Clearly, we have moved away from the question of the circumcision of a non-Jewish child, to the question of "Who is a Jew?" In other words, the consensus has been first, that one circumcises for conversion, and second, that a child of a non-

Jewish woman is not Jewish until converted. While the Orthodox do not recognize Reform conversion and therefore the Jewish status of Reform converts, there was, up until recently, formal agreement as to what defined one as a Jew. With the CCAR's Patrilineal Descent Resolution (actually something of a misnomer, see below, p. 188), this agreement concerning personal status, the determination of whether one is a Jew or not, breaks down.

In Jewish law, the jurisprudence of personal status is called *"ishut,"* or "personhood." Before directly discussing the so-called patrilineal descent issue, it might be helpful to briefly outline the importance of personhood in Jewish law.

A person's status, as defined by Jewish law, determines such crucial issues as availability (in an halachic sense) for marriage, inheritance, burial, and so on. According to traditional Jewish law, a marriage between a Jew and non-Jew is not considered a marriage. Inheritance in Jewish law only obtains for Jews; a man's non-Jewish issue has no inheritance rights. Other examples of the critical nature of the question of personhood could be adduced here, but, in short, what we find is a characteristic rabbinic concern for boundaries and categories, a concern which grows right out of biblical and rabbinic religion. The laws of personhood, then, are a part of the halachic concern with categorizing the moral world and observing the distinctions.

It should be noted here that one of the earliest theological and interpretive shifts made by Reform Judaism during its inception in the early nineteenth century was the movement away from ceremonial and ritual law toward an emphasis on ethical and moral life. Reform Judaism was born at a time which was perhaps the height of liberal political and philosophic thought, one of the tenets of which is the near apotheosis of the individual. The individual has rights against the State, the individual contracts his obligations rationally and willfully, the individual chooses and forms his own identity and place in the moral world. All human beings are, philosophically at least, born equal and endowed with inalienable rights.

The political and philosophical pillars of liberalism in many ways run against the grain of Rabbinic Judaism. One severe cut against this grain is the notion of personal status. Reform Judaism has deleted the categories of the *mamzeir* (see Glossary) and *kohen* (priest), among others, from its theological lexicon, and all prohibitions or distinctions connected thereto. The question of patrilineal descent is raised in this context. Why is it that only a Jewish mother should be the determining factor in natal religion? If we are truly an egalitarian movement, how can we countenance such a blatantly sexist notion? Furthermore, the Reform approach, in focusing on the individual human condition rather than abstract categories, questions the morality of denying Jewish status to children born of only one Jewish parent, the father, who clearly desires this child to be considered Jewish, *ab initio*.

We see, then, that the decision on the patrilineal descent issue is a step toward the removal of all restrictive personhood categories from Jewish life, and a step toward making Judaism a voluntaristic, creedal/communal commitment. This notion is borne out in the text of the Resolution, which is brief enough to be cited here:

> The Central Conference of American Rabbis declares that the child of one Jewish parent is under the presumption of Jewish descent. This presumption of the status of the offspring of any mixed marriage is to be established through appropriate and timely public and formal acts of identification with the Jewish faith and people. The performance of these *mitzvot* serves to commit those who participate in them, both parent and child, to Jewish life.

We note two very interesting shifts here. First, only one Jewish parent is needed for the presumption of Jewish descent. Secondly, a child of any mixed marriage, whether the mother or father is Jewish, claims his or her Judaism through some public act. The automatic Jewish status of a child in a mixed marriage born to a Jewish mother is rescinded, and the presumption is provided to the child born of a Jewish father. Both of these shifts point to a moving away from traditional rabbinic categorizations to a more voluntaristic process of religious identification.

We may see, then, why "patrilineal descent" is something of a misnomer; what is really being advocated is non-lineal descent (patrilineality is a new variable which disestablishes matrilineality). In addition to non-lineality, the insufficiency of any lineality is being asserted; any mixed marriage offspring must take some act or have an act taken for him or her for the attainment of Jewish status.

The criticism against the Reform acceptance of patrilineal descent as a determinant of Jewish identity has been vocal even in the Reform camp, and more often than not, bitter in the Orthodox camp. The criticism is largely against Reform's presumed cavalier attitude toward Jewish law; it has been argued that the Reform jurisprudential hermeneutic has been: "when the law doesn't fit reality, change the law." The Reform response to this criticism is twofold. First, the Orthodox critique is actually rather disingenuous, since Orthodoxy doesn't recognize any Reform activity in the laws of personhood. Even if Reform rabbis reverted to require traditional conversion for patrilineal babies, the Orthodox would not accept those conversions. The second response is based on a justification for changing law. Many liberal scholars have pointed out that matrilineality and conversion are themselves rabbinic inventions rooted in historical conditions; they were created to solve thorny legal questions. Reform rabbis, then, are simply operating as jurists have always acted: updating the law to meet new conditions.

A larger criticism of Reform's acceptance of patrilineal descent concerns a seeming lack of concern about the effects of this decision on the Jewish community. It is argued that the decision came at a particularly inauspicious time. There is afoot in certain camps of the Orthodox world a certain softening of the polemic against Reform Judaism. The image of the Reform rabbi getting up in the morning and trying to figure out what new havoc he or she could wreak on Jewish law has given way to one which sees Reform rabbis as serious scholars and dedicated Jews. The opportunities for the different camps working together has certainly never been greater, and many question the wisdom of the resolution, especially since it is perceived that Reform's requirements and process of conversion are certainly not strict. It is undeniable that Reform Judaism philosophically prefers a more voluntaristic and non-lineal attitude toward personal status. The question arises whether such an attitude is of such dogmatic and theological importance (or, in other words, such an important sociolgocial need), that it be pressed to the exclusion of other Jewish communal concerns.

To summarize, what we see in the early twentieth century was a certain consensus among American Jews concerning Jewish personhood and *berit mila*; a Jew was one born of a Jewish mother or one who converted to Judaism, and circumcision of non-Jews was necessary only for conversion. In the last quarter of the century, Reform Judaism has greatly altered this definition and broken the consensus by the so-called Patrilineal Descent Report. The authority of the resolution and its theological significance are still being discussed.

If the resolution on patrilinial descent had solved all of the problems of Jewish identity, then much of the foregoing in this chapter would have been refuted. Unfortunately, perhaps, very little has been solved, and the ambiguity of Jewish legal decision-making still exists. If we return to the cases mentioned above, we still may ask: How should the *mohel/et* act in these circumstances?

It would seem that the decision to or not to circumcise, in hard cases, rests partly on the *mohel/et*'s understanding of the ritual itself. Does it signify or symbolize? Is it declaratory, promissory or performative? These questions pierce to the very heart of legal thinking. Does the law simply reflect the will of the group, or does the group engage in legal thinking so that its laws will most closely approximate the divine or natural law? Or is law transformative of ourselves and the cosmos?

These questions have not been, and perhaps are not to be answered with any finality. Rather, any time a Jewish clergyperson is brought face-to-face not with theoretical questions alone but with human beings struggling with abstract concepts of personal status, he or she finds him/herself contemplating some of the deepest issues of legal philosophy. And a decision must be made, and action taken.

For example, in ritually circumcising a child of a Jewish father and practicing Christian mother, one might sense that the act of *mila* on the part of the father through the agency of the *mohel/et* serves to establish identity for a child whose status is not only ambiguous, but contended. Here, *berit mila* might be seen to be performatory, for example, it performs action, changes the moral world. In the case of the "Messianic Jews," where the parents are of Jewish descent, but practice a version of Christianity, is the performative power of *berit mila* emasculated to the point where, if done, it would be akin to *bracha l'vatala* (a prayer said for nothing)—or worse? In other words, must there be Jewish *kavana* (religious intentionality) on the part of at least one of the parents, for the ritual to be performed?

If *berit mila* were *only* significatory, in other words, signifying which boys were Jewish, then some of these deeper issues would not be raised; the question would always default to a question of "Who is a Jew?" But it seems that the obverse might have some truth to it as well; Jewish boys are those on whom a *mohel/et* performs a *berit*. *Berit mila,* then, may have effective, transformative power as well. Perhaps we do have an indeterminate status in

Jewish personhood; aside from those born-Jews, and those born non-Jews, we have those whom we have to claim. The tensions that the *mohel/et* faces, then, are the tensions of a juridicial/normative system at work. He or she must have a sense of what *berit mila* means, what it does, what its powers are, what its limits are.

More than anything, we have tried to show here that in hard cases we are perforce, definitionally, thrown back to a thorough reevaluation of what the normative system means, what its vision is, and how its rules effectuate that vision. Defining that vision, taming the rules, establishing the meaning is not something which is accomplished, but rather is discovered on the horizon toward which we lead our religious lives. Our laws and rules and definitions perhaps frame our questions for us, perhaps lead us to the edge, but *mohalim/ot,* like all *klei kodesh,* at times will have to take the final steps themselves. Our prayer is that our decisions and actions, the work of our hands, conform to God's will, and that God will establish the work of our hands.

NOTES

1. Stephen M. Passamaneck, "A Handbook of Post-Talmudic Halachic Literature," unpublished student handbook (Hebrew Union College-Jewish Institute of Religion, Los Angeles: 1965); p. 8.
2. Ronald Dworkin, *Taking Rights Seriously,* see especially Chapter 4, "Hard Cases," (Cambridge, MA., 1977), p. 81ff.
3. See Solomon Freehof, *Modern Reform Responsa,* (New York, 1971), pp. 165–169.

Medical Issues and *Berit Mila*

Thomas Goldenberg

The other chapters in this book discuss the social and religious ramifications of *berit mila*. This chapter approaches *berit mila* from the point of view of the physician, who must strike a balance between a background of medical training and opinion and that of religious observance.

This chapter opens with a discussion of the debate over the medical advantages of circumcision, including the medical reasons for delay or avoidance of *berit mila*. Operative methods will be considered, including instruments used, as well as preoperative, operative and postoperative techniques. How the physician *mohel/et* fulfills the religious commandment is then discussed. Finally, the chapter focuses on the psychology of both the child and the physician during circumcision.

MEDICAL BACKGROUND OF CIRCUMCISION

Circumcision has been the source of medical debate for many years.[1-8] Prior to the 1970s, it was generally considered a medical benefit, even a necessity, for the newborn to undergo routine circumcision. The main motivation for this opinion was that circumcision was assumed to reduce the chances of various health problems associated with the presence of the prepuce, or foreskin.

There is evidence that circumcised males have a lower incidence of urinary tract infections,[9-11] and that circumcision offers almost

Appreciation is extended to Dr. Stan Stead for his contribution to this article.

Illustration 15

Circumcision Set, rosewood with brass inlaid case, London, England, 1821. Makers: John and Henry Lias. From the collection of the Temple Judea Museum of Kenesseth Israel, Elkins Park, Pennsylvania, (C1.55), Harry Finberg, photographer.

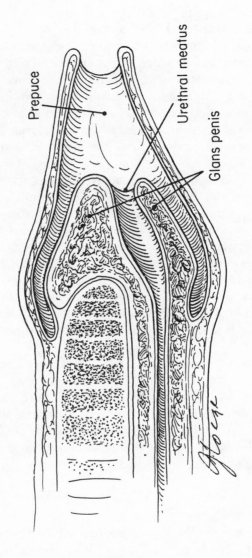

Ilustration 16

Side view of infant penis. Gwynne M. Gloege, artist.

complete protection against penile carcinoma.[12] In addition, uncircumcised males are twice as likely to have gonorrhea or genital
herpes, and five times as likely to have candidiasis or syphilis.[13]

The circumcised male is also protected from various medical
problems associated with the foreskin.[14] Such problems include
balanitis, or glandular inflammation; posthitis, or preputial
inflammation; balanoposthitis, a combination of balanitis and posthitis; phimosis, or unretractable prepuce; and foreskin adhesions,
which are skin bridges from the outer preputial remnant to the
denuded area of the glans.

In 1975, the American Academy of Pediatrics Ad Hoc Task Force
on Circumcision published a report on the efficacy and necessity of
elective circumcision.[15] The report stated that circumcision does
prevent carcinoma of the penis, but also states that proper hygiene
of the uncircumcised penis would equally prevent carcinoma. The
Task Force said that there was no evidence that noncircumcision
results in increased cervical cancer in female sexual partners, noting
that while the rate of cervical cancer is very low in Israel, where
there is a high concentration of circumcised males, the rate of cervical cancer is also low in Finland, where most males are not circumcised.

The main thrust of the Ad Hoc Task Force's report was that there
was no absolute medical indication for routine circumcision of the
newborn male. Even with this report, circumcision to this day
remains that most prevalent surgery performed by physicians in the
United States. A new report by the American Academy of Pediatrics
Ad Hoc Task Force on Circumcision is anticipated to be more
favorable to the medical advantages to routine circumcision.

THE CHILD'S HEALTH

It is important that the infant be evaluated prior to the *berit mila*
ceremony, because there are various medical conditions that can
delay the *berit mila* ceremony in the interest of the child's
health.[16,17]

Jaundice, or hyperbilirubinemia, is common in newborns. Jaundice is an excess of bilirubin in the blood that often results in the
deposition of bile pigment in the skin, which is observed clinically
by skin yellowing. A very mild case of jaundice may not cause a
delay in circumcision; however, jaundice on the eighth day of life

may be significant, and the physician should carefully evaluate the infant as to whether the *berit mila* ceremony should be postponed.

Prematurity is a critical area in the preoperative evaluation of the neonate, because performing any elective surgery on a premature infant is usually medically contraindicated. While size and weight are important factors, a physician's evaluation of the neonate's immune response, stress response and overall health and strength is crucial in the decision of when to perform circumcision.

Anatomic anomalies often require a preoperative decision. The more common anomalies include hypospadias and other variations of the location of the ureteral opening. It is vital that the surgeon performing the circumcision have a extensive understanding of normal and abnormal penile anatomy, so that anomalies can be identified and that the decision to continue with the circumcision can be made.

INSTRUMENTS

The instruments used for circumcision have evolved through the ages. The initial flint stone employed by Abraham has been improved upon with the use of metals and surgical steel. With the advent of metals, a scalpel or knife was utilized and the ancient shield was developed (see Illustration 17). While a simple knife or scalpel and shield will produce a safe and successful circumcision, many contemporary *mohalim/ot* and most physicians use a modern-day surgical clamp. A circumcision clamp has a two-fold function: 1) it protects the glans from injury during the surgical procedure, as did the ancient shield, and 2) its clamping effect provides hemostasis, the surgical reduction of blood flow, during and after the surgical procedure.

Many types of modern surgical clamps are used for the neonatal circumcision. A partial list would include the Leff clamp, the prepu-tome, the Kantor clamp, the Maryan clamp, the Tibone clamp, the Nutech clamp, the Mogen clamp, the Glans Guard, the Circumstat and the Gomco clamp. All these surgical clamps protect the glans and provide some degree of hemostasis. The decision as to which clamp to use depends on the comfort and technique of the operator.

In my experience, I have used the Mogen clamp, which has several attributes that make it an appropriate clamp for the *berit mila* ceremony. The Mogen clamp is small, lightweight and easily

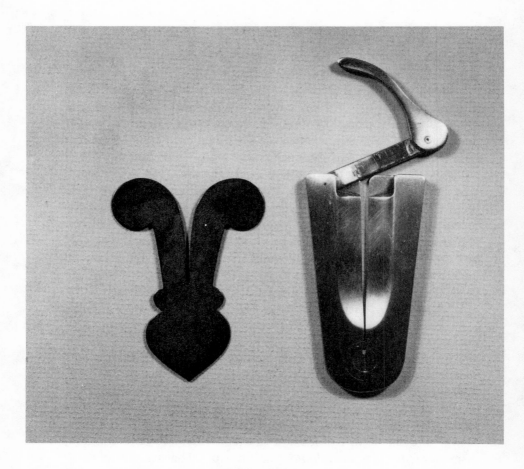

Illustration 17

Circumcision Shield, Germany? 19th C.? From the collection of the Hebrew
Union College Skirball Museum, (15.21), Lelo Carter, photographer.
Modern Mogen Clamp, 20th C. Manufactured by Mogen Circumcision
Instruments, Ltd. Lelo Carter, photographer.

handled. It is easily and quickly used, and provides adequate hemostasis. The clamp, however, does not provide complete hemostasis, therefore allowing for the requisite drop of blood. In performing the *berit mila* ceremony, it is in the interest of the child that the surgical procedure be done as quickly and as effortlessly as possible; the Mogen clamp promotes this aim (see Illustration 17).

TECHNIQUES OF CIRCUMCISION

The technique of *berit mila* is dependent upon the types of instruments used, the positioning of the child, and the choice of postoperative care. Regarding instruments, the *mohel/et* should be extremely familiar with the clamps to be used, so that the procedure can be done swiftly, carefully and accurately. In addition to care and accuracy, it is very important that the appropriate amount of foreskin is removed to avoid any undue risk of infection or other complications.

As with any surgical procedure, instruments must be clean and sterile. Many different types of autoclaves are available and there are many different materials for wrapping instruments; the important issue is that the instruments be sterile and conveniently wrapped so that they may be quickly prepared and laid out prior to the *berit mila* ceremony.

All physicians performing the *berit mila* ceremony should have available emergency materials in order to achieve hemostasis in a difficult or complicated circumcision. Materials needed to control hemorrhage include hemostat, needle holder and suture. Additionally, a cauterizing solution should be available; silver nitrate is easy to use, although it has the disadvantage of leaving the tissue with a blackened color which can be somewhat disturbing to a parent. An alternative is a dilute solution of adrenalin, or epinephrine, which provides excellent hemostasis when applied in a liquid form with a gauze and which does not discolor the tissue. However, care should be taken when using topical epinephrine, since it can result in marked cardiovascular distress or heart failure.[17-19]

Sterile drapes are used to isolate the penis for cleanliness and to avoid any potential postoperative infection. Gauze in various sizes is used both in cleaning the surgical area and in the postoperative wrapping of the penis. In addition, salves such as vaseline are used postoperatively to dress the wound.

The method of positioning the child for the *berit mila* must be considered prior to the ceremony, since the baby must be held securely so that a safe circumcision may be performed. The traditional *mohel* will have the *sandak* hold the baby on his lap—sometimes held free-hand, and sometimes assisted with a cloth wrapping to hold the baby still. Many modern *mohalim/ot* will use a board (e.g., Circumstraint), which has velcro straps to hold the baby in place. The board may be held on the *sandak's* lap, or may be placed on a table.

There are various techniques of circumcision, and many variations of techniques. While all cannot be described here in detail, a general summary of the Gomco technique[8] follows:

A cut is made in the foreskin, exposing the glans. A circular metal cap is applied between the glans and the foreskin. The foreskin and glans are pulled through a hole at the end of a rectangular flat plate, which compresses the foreskin against the inner metal cap. Pressure is applied the foreskin, rendering it ischemic, and a scalpel is then used to remove the ischemic foreskin.

Postoperative care is based on keeping the wound area clean and dry. The usual dressing of gauze and vaseline is adequate for protection in the early healing period until the area has completely healed and re-epithelialized. It should be noted that, while the complication rate of circumcision is quite low, some complications can result not from the surgical procedure itself, but rather from the postoperative care and the wrapping of the glans penis. The glans penis should not be wrapped too tightly, and any wrapping should be removed within the first twenty-four hours.

Two complications can occur if the wrapping around the glans penis is not removed within that time period. First, if the wrapping is left tightly in place for too long a time, necrosis of the glans penis can occur. Second, if improperly placed, the wrapping may become adherent to the wound area, the removal of which may also remove the blood clots that have formed in achieving hemostasis. As a result, this may cause renewed hemorrhage, which would require either a suture or other hemostatic technique.

Following the *berit mila*, the *mohel/et* should have a safe and easy-to-follow program of postoperative care, with careful instructions to the parents so that it can be carried out without unnecessary complications.

FULFILLMENT OF THE RELIGIOUS COMMANDMENT

While it is important that, in the performance of the *berit mila* ceremony, the *mohel/et* use modern surgical techniques meant to promote safe hemostasis and to prevent infection, it is still possible to carry out the religious requirements defined as *peri-a, mila* and *metsitsa,* the three steps of the traditional circumcision. *Peri-a,* the tearing or separating of the membrane, is usually performed with a surgical probe or a hemostat. The actual *mila,* or cutting off of the foreskin, is performed after the placement of the clamp, with a scalpel or knife used to cut and remove the foreskin. The final step is the *metsitsa,* which involves the sucking of a drop of blood from the wound.

Metsitsa has provoked some controversy. Many traditional *mohalim* actually use their mouths to suck the blood from the wound. Most modern trained physicians find this practice difficult to reconcile with aseptic technique. However, various compromises have been devised which satisfy this commandment. In one technique, a glass pipette is used to draw out a drop of blood from the wound. In another, a syringe with the plunger removed is used, with the drop of blood then aspirated by mouth. A third technique is to aspirate a drop of blood via a cotton gauze. Reform Judaism, however, has no requirement of *metsitsa,* actual or symbolic. Each individual *mohel/et* will need to make a personal decision with regard to this last aspect of the traditional ritual.

The timing of the *berit mila* ceremony is important in fulfilling the *mitzvah.* There are many pressures in our modern world to perform this ceremony at times other that the eighth day for convenience of family and relatives. Therefore, the *mohel/et* should emphasize to the family that the timing of the *berit mila* is biblically and traditionally significant, and that all efforts should be made to adhere to it strictly. While, as previously noted, in the interests of the child's health the procedure may be delayed, *berit mila* should not be performed earlier than the eighth day for any reason.

THE PSYCHOLOGY OF *Berit Mila*

1. Psychology of the Child

Circumcision is obviously a very stressful event for an infant, and various studies have attempted to quantitate this stress in an attempt to prove the validity of using regional or local anesthesia.[20-24] Dorsal penile nerve block has been shown to minimize pain and "behavioral disruptions,"[24] and infants receiving lidocaine in this manner were found to be more attentive to stimuli following circumcision.[21] However, there is no way to make the actual surgical procedure painless, as even the infiltration of local anesthetic causes a certain degree of pain and discomfort.

While many physicians performing the circumcision in the hospital use an anesthetic, most of the traditional *mohalim* do not use any in the performance of *berit mila*. It is my own belief that a local anesthetic is unnecessary, and that performing the procedure in a swift manner minimizes any adverse psychological impact on the child.

There has always been a concern for the comfort and psychological well-being of the baby during the *berit mila* ceremony. I believe that the measure of the infant's comfort is largely a function of time, and that the amount of crying and obvious displeasure on the part of the baby is directly proportional to the amount of time held in a restricted position. The more swiftly the *berit mila* is performed, the better the baby will tolerate the procedure.

2.   Psychology of the *Mohel/et*

The traditional *mohel* comes to the practice of *berit mila* with a background of tradition and with experience in officiating at religious ceremonies. Most physicians, however, come to the performance of this *mitzvah* from a background of performing surgical procedures in typical medical settings. While a physician may have performed hundreds of circumcisions under routine and comforting medical settings, sudden placement in a crowded room without the usual quiet of the operating area places the physician in a somewhat foreign environment.

It is often quite stressful for the beginning *mohel/et* to perform a religious ceremony containing a surgical procedure, generally in the presence of a community of family or friends, in a home or some other non-medical setting. Therefore, significant mental discipline is required to perform this procedure in a calm and dignified manner under these new and different conditions.

Many physicians may have some discomfort when other people

compare them to traditional *mohalim*. During the performance of the *berit mila* ceremony, many family members may be present who are accustomed to traditional (Orthodox) *mohalim*, and who feel free in commenting and making comparisons, especially regarding the *mohel/et's* ability to recite the Hebrew prayers or to perform the surgical procedure quickly. The physician coming to the practice of *berit mila* must develop an attitude of competence and confidence which can only come from disciplined study, commitment and experience.

When a physician decides to take up the practice of *berit mila*, he/she takes on a new role. The new *mohel/et* must realize that he/she is not functioning merely as a physician performing a surgical procedure. Rather, the role of a physician becomes one of a religious officiant, not only performing an important *mitzvah*, but also helping to guide the family through this particular religious event. In the instance of a first-born child, for example, this may be the first step in the religious life of a family, and they may turn toward the *mohel/et* for guidance in the development of their religious life.

In this setting, the physician who has become a *mohel/et* has truly become a religious role model. Therefore, the physician should feel confident in his/her understanding of the Jewish ritual of *berit mila*, be aware of the limits of his/her knowledge, and yet feel comfortable in suggesting religious observance.

NOTES

1. Waszak SJ: The historic significance of circumcision. Obstet Gynecol 1978;51(4):499–501.

2. Grossnan E, Posner NA: Surgical circumcision of neonates: a history of its development. Obstet Gynecol 1981;58(2):241–6.

3. Slaby AR, Drizd T: Circumcision in the United States. Am J Public Health 1985;75(8):878–880.

4. Wallerstein E: Circumcision: An American Health Fallacy. New York, Springer, 1980.

5. Wallerstein E: Circumcision. The uniquely American medical enigma. Urol Clin North Am 1985;12(1):123–32.

6. Wiswell TE: Do you favor . . . .routine neonatal circumcision? Yes. Postgrad Med 1988;84(5):98–104.

7. Metcalf T: Do you favor . . . routine neonatal circumcision? No. Postgrad Med 1988;84(5):9–108.

8. Gibbons MB: Circumcision. The controversy continues. Pediatr Nurs 1984;10(2):103–9.

9. Wiswell TE et al: Decreased incidence of urinary tract infections in circumcised male infants. Pediatrics 1985;75(5):901–3.

10. Wiswell TE, Roscelli JD: Corroborative evidence for the decreased incidence of urinary tract infections in circumcised male infants. Pediatrics 1986;78(1):96–9.

11. Roberts JA: Does circumcision prevent urinary tract infection. J Urol 1986;135(5):911–2.

12. Boczko S, Freed S: Penile carcinoma in circumcised males. NY State J Med 1979;79(12):1903–4.

13. Parker SW et al: Circumcision and sexually transmitted disease. Med J Aust 1983;2(6):288–90.

14. Herzog LW, Alvarez SR: The frequency of foreskin problems in uncircumcised children. Am J Dis Child 1986;140(3):254–6.

15. Thompson HC et al: Report of the Ad Hoc Task Force on Circumcision. Pediatrics 1975;56(4):610–1.

16. Redman JF: Rare penile anomalies presenting with complications of circumcision. Urology 1988;32(2):130–2.

17. Kaplan GW: Complications of circumcision. Urol Clin North Am 1983;10(3):543–9.

18. Beaton J et al: Circumcision complication reaction to treatment of local hemorrhage with topical epinephrine in high concentration. Clin Pediatr 1976;17:285–6.

19. Mor A et al: Tachycardia and heart failure after ritual circumcision. Arch Dis Child 1987;62(1):80–1.

20. Williamson PS, Williamson ML: Physiologic stress reduction by a local anesthetic during newborn circumcision. Pediatrics 1983;71(1):36–4.

21. Dixon SD et al: Behavioral effects of circumcision with and without anesthesia. J Dev Behav Pediatr 1984;5(5):246–50.

22. Rawlins DJ et al: The effect of circumcision on transcutaneous PO_2 in term infants. Am J Dis Child 198D;134(7):676–8.

23. Kirya C, Werthmann MW: Neonatal circumcision and penile dorsal nerve block: a painless procedure. J. Pediatr 1978;92(6):998–1000.

24. Holve RL: Regional anesthesia during newborn circumcision. Clin Pediatr 1983;22(12):813–8.

Appendices

Appendix A

CCAR Report on Patrilineal Descent

Following is the final text of the Report of the Committee on Patrilineal Descent on the Status of Children on Mixed Marriages as adopted by the Central Conference of American Rabbis on March 15, 1983:[1]

The purpose of this document is to establish the Jewish status of the children of mixed marriages in the Reform Jewish community of North America.

One of the most pressing human issues for the North American Jewish community is mixed marriages with all its attendant implications. For our purposes, mixed marriage is defined as a union between a Jew and non-Jew. A non-Jew who joins the Jewish people through conversion is recognized as a Jew in every respect. We deal here only with the Jewish identity of children born of a union in which one parent is Jewish and the other parent is non-Jewish.

This issue arises from the social forces set in motion by the Enlightenment and the Emancipation. They are the roots of our current struggle with mixed marriage. "Social change so drastic and far reaching could not but affect on several levels the psychology of being Jewish . . . The result of Emanicipation was to make Jewish identity a private commitment rather than a legal status, leaving a complex mix of destiny and choice" (Robert Seltzer, *Jewish People, Jewish Thought,* p. 541). Since the Napoleonic Assembly of Notables of 1806, the Jewish community has struggled with the tension between modernity and tradition. This tension is now a major challenge, and it is within this specific context that the Reform

Movement chooses to respond. Wherever there is ground to do so, our response seeks to establish Jewish identity of the children of mixed marriages.

According to the *halacha* as interpreted by traditional Jews over many centuries, the offspring of a Jewish mother and non-Jewish father is recognized as a Jew, while the offspring of a non-Jewish mother and a Jewish father is considered a non-Jew. To become a Jew, the child of a non-Jewish mother and a Jewish father must undergo conversion.

As a Reform community, the process of determining an appropriate response has taken us to an examination of the tradition, our own earlier responses, and the most current considerations. In doing so, we seek to be sensitive to the human dimensions of this issue.

Both the biblical and the rabbinical traditions take for granted that ordinarily the paternal line is decisive in the tracing of descent within the Jewish people. The biblical genealogies in Genesis and elsewhere in the Bible attest to this point. In intertribal marriage in ancient Israel, paternal descent was decisive. Numbers 1:2, etc., says: "By their families, by their fathers' houses" *(lemishpechotam leveit avotam),* which for the Rabbis means, "The line [literally: 'family'] of the father is recognized; the line of the mother is not" *(Mishpachat av keruya mishpacha; mishpachat em einah keruva mishpacha;* Bava Batra 109b, Yevamot 54b; cf. *Yad,* Nachalot 1.6)

In the rabbinic tradition, this tradition remains in force. The offspring of a male *kohen* who marries a Levite or Israelite is considered a *kohen,* and the child of an Israelite who marries a *kohenet* is an Israelite. Thus: *yichus,* lineage, regards the male line as absolutely dominant. This ruling is stated succinctly in Mishna Kiddushin 3.12 that when *kiddushin* (marriage) is licit and no transgression *(ein avera)* is involved, the line follows the father. Furthermore, the most important parental responsibility to teach *Torah* rested with the father (Kiddushin 29a; cf. *Shulchan Aruch,* Yoreh De-a 245.1).

When, in the tradition, the marriage was considered not to be licit, the child of that marriage followed the status of the mother (Mishna Kiddushin 3.12, *havalad kemotah).* The decision of our ancestors thus to link the child inseparably to the mother, which makes the child of a Jewish mother Jewish and the child of a non-Jewish mother non-Jewish, regardless of the father, was based upon the fact that the woman with her child had no recourse but to return to her own people. A Jewish woman could not marry a non-Jewish man (cf. *Shulchan Aruch,* Even Ha-ezer 4.19, *la tafsei kiddushin*). A Jewish man could not marry a non-Jewish woman. The only recourse in rabbinic law for the woman in either case was to return to her own community and people.

Since Emancipation, Jews have faced the problem of mixed marriage and the status of the offspring of mixed marriage. The Reform Movement responded to the issue. In 1947, the CCAR adopted a proposal made by the Committee on Mixed Marriage and Intermarriage:

> With regard to infants, the declaration of the parents to raise them as Jews shall be deemed sufficient for conversion. This could apply, for example, to adopted children. This decision is in line with the traditional procedure in which, according to the *Talmud,* the parents bring young children (the *Talmud* speaks of children earlier than the age of three) to be converted, and the *Talmud* comments that although an infant cannot give its consent, it is permissible to benefit somebody without his consent (or presence). On the same page the *Talmud* also speaks of a father bringing his children for conversion, and says that the children will be satisfied with the action of their father. If the parents therefore will make a declaration to the rabbi that it is their intention to raise the child as a Jew, the child may, for the sake of impressive formality, be recorded in the Cradle-Roll of the religious school and thus be considered converted.

> Children of religious school age should likewise not be required to undergo a special ceremony of conversion but should receive instruction as regular students in the school. The ceremony of Confirmation at the end of the school course shall be considered in lieu of a conversion ceremony.

> Children older than confirmation age should not be converted without their own consent. The talmudic law likewise gives the child who is converted in infancy by the court the right to reject the conversion when it becomes of religious school age. Therefore the child above religious school age, if he or she consents sincerely to conversion, should receive regular instruction for that purpose and be converted in the regular conversion ceremony (*CCAR Yearbook,* Vol. 57).

This issue was again addressed in the 1961 edition of the *Rabbi's Manual:*

Jewish law recognizes a person as Jewish if his mother was Jewish, even though the father was not a Jew. One born of such mixed percentage may be admitted to membership in the synagogue and enter into a marital relationship with a Jew, provided he has not been reared in or formally admitted into some other faith. The child of a Jewish father and non-Jewish mother, according to traditional law, is a Gentile; such a person would have to be formally converted in order to marry a Jew or become a synagogue member.

Reform Judaism, however, accepts such a child as Jewish without a formal conversion, if he attends a Jewish school and follows a course of studies leading to Confirmation. Such procedure is regarded as sufficient evidence that the parents and the child himself intend that he shall live as a Jew (*Rabbi's Manual,* p. 112).

We face today an unprecedented situation due to the changed conditions in which decisions concerning the status of the child of a mixed marriage are to be made.

There are tens of thousands of mixed marriages. In a vast majority of these cases the non-Jewish extended family is a functioning part of the child's world, and may be decisive in shaping the life of the child. It can no longer be assumed a priori, therefore, that the child of a Jewish mother will be Jewish any more than that the child of a non-Jewish mother will not be.

This leads us to the conclusion that the same requirements must be applied to establish the status of a child of a mixed marriage, regardless of whether the mother or the father is Jewish.

Therefore:

The Central Conference of American Rabbis declares that the child of one Jewish parent is under the presumption of Jewish descent. This presumption of the Jewish status of the offspring of any mixed marriage is to be established through appropriate and timely public and formal acts of identification with the Jewish faith and people. The performance of these *mitsvot* serves to commit those who participate in them, both parent and child, to Jewish life.

Depending on circumstances,[2] *mitsvot* leading toward a positive and exclusive Jewish identity will include entry into the covenant, acquisition of a Hebrew name, *Torah* study, *bar/bat mitsva* and *kabbalat Torah* (Confirmation).[3] For those beyond childhood claiming

Jewish identity, other public acts or declarations may be added or substituted after consultation with their rabbi.

NOTES

1. *Central Conference of American Rabbis Yearbook,* XCIII, 1983 Convention, (New York, 1984), pp. 157–160.
2. According to the age of setting, parents should consult a rabbi to determine the specific *mitzvot* which are necessary.
3. A full description of these and other *mitzvot* can be found in *Sha-arei Mitzvah.*

Appendix B

Joint statement of 1983 by the American Academy of Pediatrics and the American College of Obstetrics and Gynecologists Regarding Circumcision.

"Circumcision.   There is no absolute medical indication for the routine circumcision of the newborn. The procedure of daily stretching of the foreskin is probably not necessary, as many foreskins do not completely retract until the child is three years of age. When parents desire the procedure, circumcision should be performed after the first 12–24 hours of the neonatal period. Circumcision should not be performed during the stabilization period after birth."

Appendix C

Faculty for the *berit mila* courses (1984–1989) include:

Los Angeles
Isa Aron, Ph.D.
Lewis M. Barth, Rabbi, Ph.D.
Stanley F. Chyet, Rabbi, Ph.D.
William Cutter, Rabbi, Ph.D.
David Ellenson, Rabbi, Ph.D.
Mordecai Finley, M.A.H.L.
Stanley Gevirtz, Ph.D.
Thomas Goldenberg, M.D.
Stuart Kelman, Rabbi, Ph.D.
Richard N. Levy, Rabbi, M.A.H.L.
Norman Mirsky, Rabbi, Ph.D.
Stephen Passamaneck, Rabbi, Ph.D.
Bruce Phillips, Ph.D.
Sanford Ragins, Rabbi, Ph.D.
Michael Signer, Rabbi, Ph.D.
Michael Zeldin, Ph.D.

New York
Eugene B. Borowitz, Rabbi, D.H.L., Ed.D.
Gary Bretton-Granatoor, Rabbi, M.A.H.L.
Martin A. Cohen, Rabbi, Ph.D.
Lawrence A. Hoffman, Rabbi, Ph.D.
Miriam Shapero, Rabbi, M.A.H.L.
S. David Sperling, Rabbi, Ph.D.
Marjorie Yudkin, Rabbi, M.A.H.L.
Bernard M. Zlotowitz, Rabbi, D.H.L.

Boston
Terry Bard, Rabbi, M.A.H.L.
Henry Kapholz, M.D.
Bernard Mehlman, Rabbi, D.H.L.
Paul J. Menitoff, Rabbi, M.A.H.L.
Marsha Slotnick, M.A.

Rifat Sonsino, Rabbi, Ph.D.
Donald Splansky, Rabbi, Ph.D.
Henry Zoob, Rabbi, M.A.H.L

Seattle
Stephen Chentow, M.D.
Jeffrey Glickman, Rabbi, M.A.H.L.
Norman Hirsh, Rabbi, M.A.H.L.
James Mirel, Rabbi, M.A.H.L.
Richard Rosenthal, Rabbi, M.A.H.L.
Earl Starr, Rabbi, M.A.H.L.

Philadelphia
Richard Address, Rabbi, M.A.H.L.
Ronald Kaplan, Rabbi, M.A.H.L.
Richard K. Harkavy, Rabbi, M.A.H.L., J.D.
Judith Maslin, M.A.
Barnett Brickner, Rabbi, M.A.H.L.
Susan Harris, Rabbi, M.A.H.L.
Sineon J. Maslin, Rabbi, M.A.H.L., M.A., D.D., D.Min.
David Wortman, Rabbi, M.A.H.L., M.A., M.Phil.
Nina Mizrahi, Rabbi, M.A.H.L.
Arthur P. Nemitoff, Rabbi, M.A.H.L.
Patrice E. Heller, Rabbi, M.A.H.L., M.A., A.B.D.
Mark A. Lebovitz, M.D.

San Francisco
Joseph Asher, Rabbi, D.D.
Rafael Asher, Rabbi, M.A.H.L.
Richard Block, Rabbi, M.A.H.L.
David Cohen, Rabbi, M.A.H.L.
Thomas Goldenberg, M.D.
Morris Hershman, Rabbi, M.A.H.L.
Stuart Kelman, Rabbi, Ph.D.
Robert Kirschner, Rabbi, M.A.H.L., Ph.D.
Arthur J. Kolatch, Rabbi, M.H.L., D.D.
David Meyer, Rabbi, M.A.H.L.
Jacob Milgrom, Rabbi, D.H.L., D.D.
Jo Milgrom, Ph.D.
Gerald Raiskin, Rabbi, M.A.H.L., D.D.
Peter Rubenstein, Rabbi, M.A.H.L.
Marvin Schwab, Rabbi, M.A.H.L.

Albuquerque
Paul Citrin, Rabbi, M.A.H.L.

Appendix D

*Mohalim/ot Certified by the Berit Mila Board of Reform Judaism
as of June, 1989:*

Joseph Adolph, M.D.	Sudbury, MA
Douglas Attig, M.D.	Tacoma, WA
Barbara Bassil, M.D.	Brookline, MA
Stuart Berlin, M.D.	Westlake Village, CA
Sheldon Biback, M.D.	Seattle, WA
Wesley Blank, M.D.	Andover, MA
Richard Brodsky, M.D.	Seattle, WA
Ronald Clavin *, M.D.	Beverly Hills, CA
Deborah Cohen, M.D.	Pasadena, CA
Nancy Cohen, M.D.	Burbank, CA
Marjorie Cramer, M.D.	Brooklyn, NY
Paul Eisman, M.D.	Irvine, CA
Leonard Finn, M.D.	Needham, MA
Richard Fraser, M.D.	Westwood, MA
Stanley Frochtzwajg, M.D.	Ventura, CA
Ilene Gelbaum, C.N.M.	Torrance, CA
Charles Glassman, M.D.	Scarsdale, NY
Wayne Glazier, M.D.	Worcester, MA
Thomas Goldenberg, M.D.	South Lake Tahoe, CA
Alan Green, M.D.	Nashua, NH
Michael Grodin, M.D.	Needham Heights, MA
Philip Herzog, M.D.	Seattle, WA
Stuart Jaffee, M.D.	Worcester, MA
David James, M.D.	Scarsdale, NY
Fred Kogen, M.D.	Santa Monica, CA
Samuel Kunin, M.D.	Tarzana, CA
Sheldon Lavin, M.D.	Encino, CA
Mark Lebovitz, M.D.	Cherry Hill, NJ
Robert Levenson, M.D.	Cambridge, MA
Julie Luks, M.D.	Wausau, WI
Leslie Mackoff, M.D.	Seattle, WA
Michael Medwed, M.D.	Seattle, WA
Jeff Mazlin, M.D.	New York, NY

Barry Meisel, M.D.	*Armonk, NY*
Barrie Paster, M.D.	*Exeter, NH*
Steven Shoham, M.D.	*IL*
Robert Shpall, M.D.	*Covina, CA*
Robert Sloves, M.D.	*Rolling Hills Estate, OA*
Sidney Smith, M.D.	*Los Angeles, CA*
Janet Stein, M.D.	*New York, NY*
Nancy Taylor, M.D.	*Sherman Oaks, CA*
Richard Tischler, M.D.	*Corona Del Mar, CA*
Joel Thurm, M.D.	*Ossining, NY*
Joyce Wallace, M.D.	*New York, NY*
Barbara Zipkin, M.D.	*Santa Monica, CA*

(* deceased)

Contributors

ISA ARON, Ph.D., is Associate Professor of Education, Hebrew Union College-Jewish Institute of Religion, Los Angeles. She has authored numerous articles on the philosophy of education, a variety of issues in Jewish education, moral training and on *havurot*.

LEWIS M. BARTH, Rabbi, Ph.D., Professor of *Midrash* and Related Literature at Hebrew Union College-Jewish Institute of Religion, Los Angeles. He has authored numerous articles and reviews in the field of *Midrash* and is editor of this volume. In addition, he is the Co-chair of the *Berit Mila* Board of Reform Judaisn.

EUGENE B. BOROWITZ, Rabbi, D.H.L., Ed.D., is Professor of Education and Jewish Religious Thought at the New York School of Hebrew Union College-Jewish Institute of Religion. He is the author of ten books and numerous articles on Jewish theology and ethics. In 1970 he founded *Sh'ma, a Journal of Jewish Responsibility,* an interdenominational magazine of Jewish ethics, and as been its editor since its inception.

STANLEY F. CHYET, Rabbi, Ph.D., is Professor of Jewish History at Hebrew Union College-Jewish Institute of Religion, Los Angeles. He has written extensively in the areas of American Jewish history and Modern Hebrew Literature.

WILLIAM CUTTER, Rabbi, Ph.D., is Professor of Education and Hebrew Language and Literature at Hebrew Union College-Jewish Institute of Religion, Los Angeles. He was founding director of the Rhea Hirsch School of Education, and currently teaches in its Graduate Programs as well as in the Rabbinic School of the College. He has written extensively on the relationship of modern literature to the field of education and on the area of literary theory as applied to Modern Hebrew Literature.

DAVID ELLENSON, Rabbi, Ph.D., is Professor of Jewish Religious Thought at Hebrew Union College-Jewish Institute of Religion, Los Angeles. He has written over forty articles and reviews for a variety of Jewish and general academic journals. His forthcoming volume is entitled, *Continuity and Innovation: Rabbi Esriel Hildesheimer and the Creation of a Modern Jewish Orthodoxy.*

MORDECAI FINLEY, M.A.H.L., is completing his doctorate at the

U.S.C. School of Religion, and his rabbinic studies at the Hebrew Union College-Jewish Institute of Religion. Mr. Finley has lectured and taught widely in the Los Angeles area on Jewish spirituality and the Reform view of *halacha*.

STANLEY GEVIRTZ, Ph.D., *zichrono l'veracha,* was Professor of Bible and Ancient Near Eastern Civilization at Hebrew Union College-Jewish Institute of Religion, Los Angeles, and authored *Patterns in the Early Poetry of Israel* (Second Edition 1973), and numerous scholarly studies on the languages and literatures of ancient Israel and its neighbors.

THOMAS A. GOLDENBERG, M.D., CERTIFIED MOHEL, South Lake Tahoe, California. Dr. Goldenberg was a nember of the first class of Reform *mohalim/ot* and has lectured to subsequent classes in Los Angeles, and San Francisco.

GRACE GROSSMAN, M.A., is Curator of the Skirball Museum, Hebrew Union College-Jewish Institute of Religion, Los Angeles. She has worked in the field of Jewish art for twenty years, and has served as Consultant Judaica Curator to the Smithsonian Institution and has catalogued the Judaica in the National Collection.

RICHARD N. LEVY, Rabbi, is Executive Director of Los Angeles Hillel Council and a lecturer on Jewish religious thought at Hebrew Union College-Jewish Institute of Religion, Los Angles. He has edited and translated a High Holyday prayerbook, published by B'nai B'rith Hillel Foundations, entitled *On Wings of Awe,* and most recently, a *haggada* also published by Hillel.

MICHAEL A. MEYER, Ph.D., is Professor of Jewish History at Hebrew Union College-Jewish Institute of Religion, Cincinnati. His history of the Reform Movement, *Response to Modernity,* was published by Oxford University Press in Spring 1988.

NORMAN MIRSKY, Rabbi, Ph. D., is Professor of Contemporary Jewish Studies and Sociology at Hebrew Union College-Jewish Institute of Religion, Los Angeles. He is the author of *Unorthodox Judaism* and numerous articles on contemporary Jewish life.

BRUCE A. PHILLIPS, Ph.D., is Associate Professor of Jewish Communal Studies in the School of Jewish Communal Service, Hebrew Union College-Jewish Institute of Religion, Los Angeles. He has authored several demographic studies of Jewish communities in the United States.

SANFORD RAGINS, Rabbi, Ph.D., is rabbi of Leo Baeck Temple in Los Angeles. He is the author of *Jewish Responses to Anti-Semitism in Germany, 1870–1914.* A student of European and Jewish history, he is also a lecturer on Jewish history at Hebrew Union College-Jewish Institute of Religion, Los Angeles School.

MICHAEL SIGNER, Rabbi, Ph.D., is Professor of Jewish History at Hebrew Union College-Jewish Institute of Religion, Los Angeles. He is a specialist in medieval biblical exegesis and has authored numerous articles in the area of the Jewish-Christian encounter in the Middle Ages.

BERNARD ZLOTOWITZ, Rabbi, D.H.L., is Regional Director of the New York Federation of Reform Synagogues and is a Lecturer on Rabbinics at Hebrew Union College-Jewish Institute of Religion, New York. He has written extensively on the Septuagint and on issues of Jewish legal and ritual practice.

Glossary

I. Hebrew, Religious and Historical Terms.

acharonim. אַחֲרוֹנִים. Late medieval and early modern rabbinic legal authorities, fifteenth century and after.

alot hashachar. עֲלוֹת הַשַּׁחַר. Sunrise. Period from which *berit mila* is traditionally permissible.

amud hashachar. עַמּוּד הַשַּׁחַר. Dawn. Period from which *berit mila* is traditionally permissible.

androginos. אַנְדְּרוֹגִּינוֹס. Hermaphrodite.

atara. עֲטָרָה. Glans penis. Lit. Crown.

baruch. בָּרוּךְ. The first word of the *beracha* (blessing), usually translated "praised" or "blessed." Describing God, it suggests the spontaneous bending of the knee (*beireich,* בֶּרֶךְ) in submission to God's awesome presence. It is related to the word *barakah* in other Semitic languages which means "power."

be-damayich chay-yi. בְּדָמַיִךְ חֲיִי. "In your blood (literally, in your bloods) you shall live," a quotation from Ezekiel 16:6, and found in the final blessing of the traditional *berit mila* service. The plural refers to Israel's two great acts of shedding blood, the lamb on the doorpost before the Exodus and *berit mila.* The verse suggests the life-giving properties of the blood shed at the *berit mila,* and symbolically reminds the Jew that out of the blood shed through our many sufferings has also come the faith that has ensured our survival.

bein hashemashot. בֵּין הַשְּׁמָשׁוֹת. Twilight. An inexact period of time between day and night. *Bein hashemashot* is an important concept for determining a child's eighth day. See *shemini*

beit din. בֵּית דִּין. Rabbinical court.

beracha. בְּרָכָה. Blessing (see *Baruch*). A praise of God often evoked by doing a *mitzvah,* such as *mila.* It consists of words that infuse an ordinary act (e.g., eating, seeing a natural phenomenon, doing a circumcision) with a sense of the presence of God.

birkat hamazon. בִּרְכַּת הַמָּזוֹן. Grace after the meal. A special *birkat hamazon* is recited after the *se-udat mitzvah* following the *berit mila.*

birkat kohanim. בִּרְכַּת כֹּהֲנִים. The Priestly Blessing. The words from Numbers 6:24-26 with which God instructed the priests, the *kohanim,* to bless the people: "May Adonai bless you and keep you; may Adonai cause the light of the divine countenance to shine upon you and be gracious to you; may Adonai raise up the divine countenance upon you and grant you peace." Used to conclude the *berit mila* service in *Gates of the House.*

berit mila. בְּרִית מִילָה. The Covenant of Circumcision. Biblical source: Genesis 17.

chituch. חִתּוּךְ. Removal of prepuce. Another term for *mila.*

choleh bechol gufo. חוֹלֶה בְּכָל גוּפוֹ. A medical phrase. Refers to infant who has systemic illness or disease. A primary reason to delay *berit mila.*

chuppa. חֻפָּה. The traditional canopy spread over the bride and groom during the wedding service. In the *berit mila* service, it is a symbol of hope that the baby will grow up to know the joy and fulfillment of marriage.

Codes. פּוֹסְקִים. Medieval systematic compendia of Jewish law. Best known are Maimonides' *Mishne Torah* or *Yad HaChazaka,* Jacob ben Asher's *Arba Turim* and Joseph Karo's *Shulchan Aruch.* See *posekim.*

dam berit. דַּם בְּרִית. Blood of the Covenant. See *hatafat dam berit.*

Decalogue. The Greek, and subsequently English, word for the Ten Commandments (Exodus 20:1-14; Deuteronomy 5:6-18).

eiruv. עֵירוּב. In traditional Judaism, "a symbolic act by which the legal fiction of a community is established, e.g. a) with ref. to Sabbath limits (Jastrow)." Although Jewish law forbids carrying objects on the Sabbath, under certain conditions, the instruments used for a *berit mila* when it is performed on the Sabbath may be carried within the limits established by the *eiruv.* Not an operative category with Reform Judaism.

Elijah. אֵלִיָּהוּ. The prophet traditionally believed to be present at each *berit mila,* as a reward for what the *midrash* believes to be his defense of the practice of *mila* even after the wicked Queen Jezebel had abolished it and sought to kill Elijah because he remonstrated with her and King Ahab. He was rewarded with the privilege of attending every *berit mila* conducted among the Jewish People. As at Pesach when a cup is set aside for him when the door is opened after the meal, he has long been believed to be a symbol of Israel's Messianic hopes, present with the Jewish People at all times until the Messianic Age dawns.

epispasm. A medical operation or cosmetic surgery to simulate the uncircumcised male. Performed during the Hellenistic period so that Jewish athletes would remain inconspicuous when competing in the games. See *mashuch.*

Gemara. גְּמָרָא. An analysis of and commentary on the *Mishna.*Together they comprise the *Talmud.*

gematria. גִּימַטְרִיָא. A technique of rabbinic scriptural interpretation in which meanings are derived through the numerical values of Hebrew letters. Also an important technique of scriptural exegesis in Jewish mysticism.

ger.(m.s), *giyoret* (f.s.), *geirim* (m.p.), *geirot* (f.p.)
גֵּרוֹת, גֵּרִים, גִּיוֹרֶת, גֵּר.
Convert, proselyte, Jew by Choice.

get. גֵּט. A religious divorce document issued by a rabbinical court in accord with traditional Jewish law.

hadlakat neirot. הַדְלָקַת נֵרוֹת. Lighting of Candles. A custom also at *berit mila.*

halacha. הֲלָכָה. Jewish Law.

halacha lemosheh mi-Sinai. הֲלָכָה לְמֹשֶׁה מִסִּינַי. "A law revealed to Moses at Mt. Sinai." The phrase is used in classical rabbinic sources to provide authority for laws or traditions whose origin is unknown, of great antiquity and without scriptural support.

haneits hachama. הָנֵץ הַחַמָּה. First light, crack of dawn. Period from which *berit mila* traditionally may be performed.

hatafat dam berit. הֲטָפַת דַּם בְּרִית. The extraction of a drop of blood from the remnant of the prepuce as a sign of the Covenant. Traditionally required of already circumcised male converts or of children whose circumcision is considered invalid from a religious point of view. Often not required in either case in Reform Judaism.

hidur mitzvah. הִדּוּר מִצְוָה. Beautification of a commandment. Refers to any artistic or visual enhancement associated with the fulfillment of a commandment. Examples include the beautifully carved designs of a *magein* (shield).

imuts yeladim. אִמּוּץ יְלָדִים. Adoption.

izmeil. אִזְמֵל. Knife. Yiddish: *mohel-messer. Mohel's* knife.

Kasher. כָּשֵׁר. Ritually fit, appropriate, suitable, valid, qualified.

kavana. כַּוָּנָה. Proper intention. Refers to a religious attitude or spiritual directedness which is required at the time of the observance of a *mitzvah* or the recitation of specific prayers.

keri-at hashem. קְרִיאַת הַשֵׁם. Naming of the child. Second part of the *berit mila* ceremony, after the circumcision has taken place.

kisei shel Eili̯-yahu. כִּסֵּא שֶׁל אֵלִיָּהוּ. Elijah's Throne or Chair. In Jewish legend, Elijah was believed to be the forerunner of the Messiah. According to tradition (first mentioned in the eighth century *midrash, Pirké d'Rabbi Eliezer*), Elijah is present at every *berit mila*. The *kisei shel Eili̯-yahu* is a place of honor for him. At the beginning of the ceremony the *sankak* places the infant on this chair.

korban. קָרְבָּן. Offering, from the Hebrew root *krv,* meaning "near." The Hebrew word for "sacrifice."

koret. כּוֹרֵת. "Cutting," the verb used in the Bible for making a covenant, related to the ancient practice of rulers cutting up animals as part of the covenant-making rite to suggest their willingness to be cut up if they fail to keep the covenant (see *she-vuah,* below). Perhaps related to the cutting performed in *berit mila.*

kos shel beracha. כּוֹס שֶׁל בְּרָכָה. Cup for Blessing. Contains wine for blessing recited after *berit mila* at the beginning of *se-udat mitzvah.*

kos shel metsitsa. כּוֹס שֶׁל מְצִיצָה. Cup for *metsitsa.*

kvatter. (m.s.), *kvatterin* (f.s.). קוואטערין, קוואטער. Godfather, Godmother. Probably from German, a contraction of Gottvater. Godparents bring the infant to room where *berit mila* takes place. Traditionally, Godparents often accepted responsibility for rearing and educating child in case parents met with misfortune or death.

leil shemurim. לֵיל שִׁמּוּרִים. Watch night. Traditionally, a night of study and prayer at the home of the infant before a *berit mila.*

magein. מָגֵן. Shield, name of the traditional circumcision clamp.

mamzeir. מַמְזֵר. Traditional term to describe the issue of incestuous unions or of a woman whose marriage was not dissolved with a *get,* a religious divorce document issued by a rabbinical court in accord with traditional Jewish law. According to Orthodox Judaism, a *mamzeir* is not permitted to marry a "legitimate" Jew, but may marry another *mamzeir* or a convert. Reform Judaism rejects the concept of *mamzeirut* absolutely and deems it as no longer having any Jewish religious validity whatsoever.

mamzeirut. מַמְזֵרוּת. Category of Jewish law dealing with status and regulations relating to the *mamzeir.*

mashuch. מָשׁוּךְ. One who has undergone epispasm. See *epispasm.*

Matrilineal Descent. The name of the principle in traditional Judaism in which a child is considered a Jew if his or her mother is Jewish. Reform Judaism also recognizes the principle of Patrilineal Descent.

Mechilta. מְכִילְתָּא. A *midrash* to Exodus developing principles of Jewish law out of the biblical text. It includes rabbinic writings thought by many scholars to originate at the end of the second century C.E.

metsitsa. מְצִיצָה. Suction of blood from the circumcision wound. The third of three steps of traditional circumcision. The others are *mila* and *peri-a.* In some Orthodox communities this is still performed by mouth. However, the general practice of traditional *mohalim* is to use a glass pipette. This practice of oral suction is rejected by Reform Judaism.

metsitsa befeh. מְצִיצָה בְּפֶה. The performance of *metsitsa* by mouth.

midrash. מִדְרָשׁ. Classical rabbinic biblical interpretation.

mikveh. מִקְוֶה. Ritual bath.

mila. מִילָה. Circumcision. Traditionally, the removal of the *orla. Mila* is the first of three steps of the traditional circumcision. The others are *peri-a* and *metsitsa.*

mila lesheim geirut. מִילָה לְשֵׁם גֵּרוּת. *Mila* for the sake of conversion. This refers to the practice of circumcision as the first step leading toward conversion. Sometimes an Orthodox *mohel* will officiate only with this stipulation when the mother of an infant is a Gentile or has been converted by a Reform or Conservative rabbi. The term may also apply to the *mila* of a proselyte (a Jew by Choice).

mila docha shabbat ve-yom tov. מִילָה דּוֹחָה שַׁבָּת וְיוֹם טוֹב. The fulfillment of the *mitzvah* of *berit mila* takes precedence over the Sabbath or a festival, i.e., it supercedes the law prohibiting work on those days.

minhag. מִנְהָג. Jewish custom or practice.

minyan. מִנְיָן.   A quorum. Traditionally, ten men constitute a *minyan,* which is required for regular prayer. Reform Judaism and many Conservative Rabbis count both men and women in any *minyan.* A *minyan* is not required for *berit mila.*

mi-she-berach. מִי שֶׁבֵּרֵךְ. Literally, "The One Who Blessed." The beginning words for a prayer in the traditional *berit mila* service asking God's blessing on the newly circumcised child. The term is also used for a blessing for someone called to read from the Torah or a blessing for a person who is ill.

Mishna. מִשְׁנָה. The first post-biblical compilation of Jewish law, attributed to Rabbi Judah HaNasi (Rabbi Judah the Prince). The *Mishna* was compiled in the land of Israel, c. 200 C.E. The commentary on the *Mishna* is called *Gemara,* and the two together comprise the *Talmud.*

mishpara-yim. מִסְפָּרַיִם. Scissors.

mitzvah. מִצְוָה. Religious commandment. Popular meaning: good deed, favor.

mohel.(m.s.), *mohelet* (f.s.), *mohalim* (m.pl.), *mohalot* (f.pl) מוֹהֵל, מוֹהֶלֶת, מוֹהֲלִים, מוֹהֲלוֹת. Ritual circumciser(s).

mohel-messer. מוֹהֵל–מעסער. Yiddish: *mohel's* knife.

na-asheh ve-nishma. נַעֲשֶׂה וְנִשְׁמַע. "We shall do and we shall understand," suggesting Israel's willingness to do the *mitzvot* of God even before they understood them. (Exod. 24:7)

neifel. נֵפֶל. Stillborn.

neirot. נֵרוֹת . Candles. It is customary to light *neirot* in the room where *berit mila* takes place. This adds a festive touch.

nolad mahul. נוֹלַד מָהוּל. Infant who is born circumcised. In fact, refers to infant who appears to have no foreskin. Jewish legend often described great religious personalities such as Abraham, Moses and David as being *nolad mahul.*

onein. אוֹנֵן. A mourner whose close relative has died, but has not yet been buried. Special laws relate to the *onein* if he is the father of an infant or the *mohel* at the time of *berit-mila.* [Note: the *berit* itself is not postponed, but natural sentiments of bereavement suggest that the festivities should be somewhat curtailed.]

or haperi-a. עוֹר הַפְּרִיעָה. Membrane. Tearing the *or haperi-a* is the second step of the traditional *mila.*

orla. עָרְלָה. Prepuce, foreskin.

orla kevusha. עָרְלָה כְּבוּשָׁה. When an infant appears to be *nolad mahul,* it is probable that his prepuce is pressed against the membrane and is not immediately visible.

ot. אוֹת. A sign, like *mila* or Shabbat, of God's Covenant with Israel.

pasul. פָּסוּל. Ritually unfit, disqualified. This religious term applied to a person, animal or thing which is not considered *kasher* for a particular religious act or relationship.

Patrilineal Descent. A principle of Reform and Reconstructionist Judaism in which a child is presumed to be Jewish if either his mother or father is Jewish, and if the child's Jewish identity is confirmed by timely acts of commitment.

peri-a. פְּרִיעָה. Tearing of the membrane. Second of three steps of the traditional circumcision. The others are *mila* and *metsita.*

pidyon haben. פִּדְיוֹן הַבֵּן. Redemption of the first-born son on the thirty-first day after birth. Traditionally, the first-born son was redeemed by the parent who gave five shekels to a *kohen* (priest). The religious background of this act was the view that the first-born son belonged to God and had to be redeemed, that is "repurchased" by the father. A custom abolished in Reform Judaism.

posekim. פּוֹסְקִים. Later (Post-talmudic) rabbinic authories of Jewish law. See Codes.

rishonim. רִאשׁוֹנִים. Early medieval rabbinic legal authorities, prior to the fifteenth century.

sandak. סַנְדָּק. Helper. From Greek: *sundikos* or *sunteknos,* advocate or helper and companion of the child. The *sandak* traditionally assists the *mohel* and holds the infant on a pillow or table during *berit mila.*

sandak sheni. סַנְדָּק שֵׁנִי. Second *sandak.* Holds the infant after he is reclothed following *berit mila.* Also, sometimes referred to as the *omid liverachot* לִבְרכוֹת עוֹמֵד, the one who holds the baby during the part of the *berit* ceremony in which the child is named.

se-udat mitzvah. סְעוּדַת מִצְוָה. Special celebratory meal often held immediately after *berit mila.*

shacharit. שַׁחֲרִית. The morning service.

shaliach. שָׁלִיחַ. Agent. The parents legally designate or appoint the *mohel/et* as their *shaliach* for the actual performance of *mila.*

shalom zachar. שָׁלוֹם זָכָר. "A son [brings] peace [to the world]" (cf. Nidah 31b). A custom observed on the Friday night before *berit mila*. Family and friends gather at the home of the newborn infant to sing songs, study and hear the *Torah* expounded. Also called: *ben zachar.*

she-eilot u-teshuvot. שְׁאֵלוֹת וּתְשׁוּבוֹת. The Responsa Literature. An extensive branch of halachic literature comprised of questions *(she-eilot)* put to rabbinic legal experts and their answers *(teshuvot)*. Much halachic discussion of *berit mila* is found in this vast literature.

shemini. שְׁמִינִי. Eighth. Refers to the eighth day after birth of an infant, on which his *berit mila* is to take place.

sheki-a. שְׁקִיעָה. Sunset. Traditionally, *berit mila* is to take place during the day and not after sunset.

she-vuah. שְׁבוּעָה. Hebrew for oath, from the number seven, *sheva*, שֶׁבַע, implying the willingness of the maker of the oath to be cut up in seven pieces if the oath is not kept. *She-vuah* is a synonym of *berit,* Covenant (see *koret,* above).

siman tov u-mazal tov. סִימָן טוֹב וּמַזָּל טוֹב. Literally, "a good sign and a good constellation," a popular song sung at joyous occasions to express to the participants the hope that the heavens may smile upon them.

talit. טַלִּית. Traditional four-cornered garment worn over the clothes during prayer. Each corner has *tsitsit,* knotted cords reminding the wearer of the 613 mitzvot.

ta-anit. תַּעֲנִית. Fast, fast day. In Reform Judaism, the only fast day commonly observed is Yom Kippur, although some Reform Jews now fast on the Ninth of Ab. Special rules obtain for *berit mila* which occurs on a *ta-anit.*

tachanun. תַּחֲנוּן. Special elegies recited in the traditional liturgy on festivals and fast days, omitted on days when *berit mila* occurs.

tamei.(m.), *temeiah* (f.). טָמֵא, טְמֵאָה. Ritually unclean. See *pasul.*

Talmud. תַּלְמוּד. Major compendia of Jewish Law and lore. Consists of two parts: *Mishna* and *Gemara*. There are two *Talmudim:* the *Bavli* (Babylonian Talmud, compiled c. end sixth century C.E.) and the *Yerushalmi* or *Talmuda deErez Yisra-eil* (Jerusalem, or Palestinian Talmud or Talmud of the Land of Israel, compiled probably c. 425 C.E.).

taryag mitzvot. תרי״ג מִצְווֹת. 613 Commandments. (ת = 400, ר = 200, י = 10, ג = 3). The traditional number of commandments of Classical Judaism.

te-filin. תְּפִלִּין. Phylacteries. Biblical versus wrapped in two wooden boxes, atached to leather straps. One box is wrapped around the arm and the other placed on the forehead in observance of the *mitzvah* to bind the words of the *shema* "as a sign upon your arm and for frontlets between your eyes" (Deut. 6:8).

te-omim. תְּאוֹמִים. Twins. In the case of twins, generally the complete *berit mila* ceremony is recited for each child.

tumtum. טומטום. Refers to a physiological "anomaly where caul, or heavy skin, covers the scrotal area and there are no signs of external genitalia" (Cohen, p. 20).

wimpel. Swaddling clothes of infant. Refers to a custom of German Jews. Clothes used to bundle the child are bound together in one long strip, embroidered or otherwise decorated. The *wimpel* is later used to bind *Torah* on special occasions in that child's life: entry into study of *Torah*, *bar mitzvah*, wedding. The art of decorating *wimpels* has been recently revived in various American Jewish communities.

yarok. יָרוֹק. Green/Yellow. As a visual description of the child, *yarok* is a medical term referring to jaundice.

zeman mila. זְמַן מִילָה. Time specially appointed each child for *mila*, his *shemini*, or day soon thereafter, depending on the health of the infant or time of birth.

II.   English Medical Terms.

anatomy. The structure of the body and the relation of its parts.

asepsis. A condition in which living pathogenic organisms are absent.

balanoposthitis. Inflammation of the glans penis or clitoridis.

balanitis. Information of the glans penis.

bilirubin. A red bile pigment formed during normal and abnormal destruction of red blood cells in the body. Can be especially elevated in a new born, causing jaundice. Bilirubin can be measured quantitatively in the blood serum.

cesarean section. An operation in which an incision is made through the abdominal wall and uterus for extraction of the fetus.

chordee. Downward bowing of the penis as a result of congenital anomaly or urethral infection.

clamp. Generic term used for instrument used to perform modern circumcision. Example: Mogen clamp. Also general instrument of compression utilized to achieve hemostatis, i.e., hemostat.

corona glandis. Rounded proximal (closest to the body) border of glans penis.

corpus cavernosa. One of the two columns of erectile tissue forming the top and sides of the penis.

corpus spongiosum. Column of erectile tissue which forms the under surface of the penis, the distal expansion forms the glans penis.

epispadias. Congenital defect in which the urethra opens on the dorsum (upper surface) of the penis.

gestation. Period of development of the fetus from conception to delivery.

glans. Also glans penis, cap-shaped expansion of the corpus spongiosum at the end of the penis, i.e., the head of the penis.

glans penis. See glans.

hematology. The study of diseases of the blood.

hemophilia. An inherited disorder of the blood marked by a permanent tendency to bleed excessively due to a defect in the coagulating power of the blood.

hemostatis. The arrest of bleeding either by normal mechanisms or surgical means.

hemostat. Small surgical clamp, used to constrict a blood vessel or grasp tissue.

hermaphrodite. Individual with ambiguous appearing genitalia with potentially ovarian and/or testicular tissue.

hypospadias. Congenital defect in which the urethra opens on the under side of the penis.

meatus. The external opening of a canal, used here to refer to the opening of the urethra at the tip of the penis.

microbiology. The science of microorganisms.

pathology. The medical science which deals with the nature, cause and development of abnormal conditions and diseases.

phimosis. Narrowness of the opening of the foreskin, preventing its being drawn back over the glans.

prepuce. A covering of skin, i.e., foreskin.

physiology. The science of the normal vital processes of living organisms.

probe. A smooth elongated surgical instrument utilized in probing and dissection of skin.

smegma. A whitish secretion of sebaceous (sweat) glands that collect under the prepuce of the foreskin of the penis.

sterilization (of instruments). The process by which surgical instruments are rendered free of microorganisms which could potentially cause infection.

urethra. Membranous canal conveying urine from the bladder to the exterior of the body.

Note on Transliteration

The system utilized in this book follows, with some deviation, the system used in the recent liturgical publications of the Central Conference of American Rabbis. See *Gates of Prayer* (New York, 1975), p. 728. As noted there, the system is based on the "Proposed Standard Romanization of Hebrew" prepared for the American National Standards Institute.

The following exceptions should be noted based on common usage in contemporary English: *Torah, mitzvah* and *mitzvot,* rather than *Tora, mitsva* and *mitsvot.* In addition, where Hebrew words in transliteration are quoted from other sources, the original spelling has been preserved, rather than changed to conform to the system used here. Finally, abbreviation and spelling of tractates of the *Mishna, Tosefta* and *Talmud* have been based on usage in the translation published by the Soncino Press, see *Index Volume to the Soncino Talmud* (London, 1952), pp. 1–2.

Vowels and Consonants for Special Notice (see: *Gates of Prayer,* p. 728).

a	as i 'papa' (short) or 'father' (long)
e	as in 'get' or 'the' (sheva)
eh	as in 'get' (used only at the end of a word)
i	as in 'bit' (short) or 'machine' (long)
o	as in 'often'
u	as in 'pull' (short) or 'rule' (long)
ai	as in 'aisle'
oi	as in 'boil'
ei	as in 'veil'
g	as in 'get' (hard)
ch	as in Scottish 'loch' or German 'ach'
ts,tz	as in 'its'

Abbreviations

I. Books of the Bible

Amos	Amos	Jud.	Judges
1 Chron.	Chronicles I	1 Kings	1 Kings
2 Chron.	Chronicles II	2 Kings	2 Kings
Dan.	Daniel	Lam.	Lamentations
Deut.	Deuteronomy	Lev.	Leviticus
Ecc.	Ecclesiastes	Mal.	Malachai
Esth.	Esther	Mic.	Micah
Exod.	Exodus	Nah.	Nahum
Ez.	Ezra	Neh.	Nehemiah
Ezek.	Ezekiel	Num.	Numbers
Gen.	Genesis	Ob.	Obadiah
Hab.	Habakkuk	Prov.	Proverbs
Hag.	Haggai	Ps.	Psalms
Hos.	Hosea	Ruth	Ruth
Isa.	Isaiah	1 Sam.	1 Samuel
Jer.	Jeremiah	2 Sam.	2 Samuel
Job	Job	Cant.	Song of Songs
Joel	Joel	Zech.	Zechariah
Jonah	Jonah	Zep.	Zephaniah
Josh.	Joshua		

II. Tractates of the *Mishna* (m), *Tosefta* (t) and *Talmud*

Ab.	Aboth	B.K.	Baba Kamma
'Az.	'Arakin	B.M.	Baba Mez'ia
'A.Z.	'Abodah Zara	Dem.	Demai
B.B.	Baba Bathra	'Eduy.	'Eduyyoth
Bek.	Bekoroth	'Eruv.	'Erubin
Ber.	Berakoth	Git.	Gittin
Bez.	Bezah	Hag.	Hagigah
Bik.	Bikkurim	Hal.	Hallah

Hor.	Horayoth	'Or.	'Orlah
Hul.	Hullin	Par.	Parah
Kel.	Kelim	Pes.	Pesahim
Ker.	Kerithoth	R.H.	Rosh Hashanah
Ket.	Kethuboth	Sanh.	Sanhedrin
Kid.	Kiddushin	Shab.	Shabbath
Kil.	Kil'ayim	Sheb.	Shebi'ith
Kin.	Kinnin	Shebu.	Shevu'oth
Ma'as.	Ma'asroth	Shek.	Shekalim
M.S.	Ma'aser Sheni	Sot.	Sota
Mak.	Makkoth	Suk.	Sukkah
Maksh.	Makshirin	Ta'an.	Ta'anith
Meg.	Megilla	Tam.	Tamid
Me'il.	Me'ilah	Tem.	Temurah
Men.	Menahoth	Ter.	Terumoth
Mid.	Middoth	Toh.	Tohoroth
Mik.	Mikwa'oth	T.Y.	Tebul Yom
M.K.	Mo'ed Katan	'Uk.	'Ukzin
Naz.	Nazir	Yeb.	Yebamoth
Ned.	Nedarim	Yom.	Yoma
Neg.	Nega'im	Zab.	Zabim
Nid.	Niddah	Zeb.	Zebahim
Oh.	Oholoth		

III.   Midrashic Collections

BR   *Bereshit Rabba*
Mech.   *Mechilta*
PRE   *Pirké de Rabbi Eliezer*

Select Bibliography

GENERAL INTRODUCTIONS AND LITURGIES

"Circumcision," in *Encyclopaedia Judaica,* Jerusalem, Israel, 1971.

Cohen, Rabbi Eugene J. *Guide to Ritual Circumcision and Redemption of the First-Born Son.* New York, 1984.

Harlow, Jules, ed. *A Rabbi's Manual,* pp. 9–12. New York, 1965.

Hertz, Joseph, ed. *Daily Prayer Book,* Service at a Circumcision, pp. 1021–1032. New York, 1955.

Klein, Isaac. *A Guide to Jewish Religious Practice,* Ch. XXIX, Ritual Circumcision, pp. 420–432. New York, 1979.

Kolatch, Alfred J. *The Complete Dictionary of English and Hebrew First Names.* Middle Village, New York, 1984.

Mass, Ronald S. *Berit Milah: a Manual for Jewish Physicians.* Unpublished manuscript, UAHC-CCAR Joint Commission on Jewish Education, New York, 1983.

Rabbi's Manual, rev. ed., pp. 9–13. New York, 1961.

Stern, Chaim, ed. *Gates of the House,* "The Covenant of *Milah,* the Covenant of Life, and Naming a Child," pp. 111–119. New York, 1977.

BIBLICAL PERIOD

I. Biblical references to circumcision:

A. Actual

Gen. 17:9-14	Gen. 21:4
Gen. 34:13-24	Exod. 4:25-26
Exod. 12:43-49	Lev. 12:3
Josh. 5:2-8	Jer. 9:24-25

B. Metaphorical

Exod. 6:12,30	Jer. 4:4
Lev. 19:23-25	

Deut. 10:16

Deut. 30:6

II.   Circumcision in neighboring areas of the Ancient Near East:

A.   Biblical reference: Jer. 9:24-25
B.   Canaanites (?)/Desert People (?)

Pritchard, James B. *The Ancient Near East in Pictures Relating to the Old Testament,* p. 111, No. 332. Princeton, 1954.

C.   Syrians

Braidwood, Robert J. and Braidwood, Linda S. *Excavations in the Plain of Antioch I: The Earlier Assemblages Phases A-J,* pp. 302 f., and Plates 56–59. Chicago, 1960.

D.   Egyptians

Herodotus, Book II, 104 f.

Pritchard, James B. ed. *Ancient Near Eastern Texts Relating to the Old Testament,* p. 326. Princeton, 1955.

Pritchard, James B., ed. *The Ancient Near East in Pictures Relating to the Old Testament,* p. 206, No. 629. Princeton, 1954.

III.   Secondary sources and discussions

de Vaux, Roland. *Ancient Israel: Its Life and Institutions,* pp. 44–48. Translated by John McHugh. London, 1961.

Isaac, Erich. "Circumcision as a Covenant Rite." *Anthropus* 59 (1964): pp. 444–456.

Jonckheere, Frans. "La circoncision des anciens Égyptiens." *Centaurus* 1 (1951): pp. 212–234.

Kosmala, Hans. "The 'Bloody Husband.'" *Vetus Testamentum* 12 (1962): pp. 14–27.

Morgenstern, Julian. *Rites of Birth, Marriage, Death and Kindred Occasions Among the Semites,* chapters IX and X. Cincinnati and Chicago, 1966.

Sasson, Jack M. "Circumcision in the Ancient Near East." *Journal of Biblical Literature* 85 (1966): pp. 473–476.

LATE ANTIQUITY: HELLENISM, NEW TESTAMENT, RABBINIC AND MEDIEVAL PERIODS

1. The ancient world:

Herodotus, *Historiae*, II:104:1-3.
Diodorus, *Bibliotheca Historica*, I:28:1-3.
Petronius, *Satyricon*, 102:13-14.

2. *New Testament:* Romans 3:21-4:25.

Collins, John J. "A Symbol of Otherness: Circumcision and Salvation in the First Century." In *"To See Ourselves as Others See Us": Christians, Jews and "Others" in Late Antiquity*, pp. 163–186. Edited by Jacob Neusner and Ernest S. Frerichs. Chico, 1985.

3. Jewish and Hellenistic material:

Hecht, Richard D. "The Exegetical Contexts of Philo's Interpretation of Circumcision." In *Nourished With Peace: Studies in Hellenistic Judaism in Memory of Samuel Sandmel*, pp. 51–80. Edited by Frederick E. Greenspahn, Earle Hilgert, and Burton L. Mack. Chico, 1984.

Philo of Alexandria, *De Specialibus Legibus*, 1.1-11; *Quaestiones et Solutiones*, Gen. 3:46-53; *De Somniis*, 2:25; *De Migratione Abrahami*, 86-94; *De Agricultura*, 39.

Sandmel, Samuel. *Philo's Place in Judaism: A Study of Conceptions of Abraham in Jewish Literature*, augmented edition, pp. 67–87. New York, 1961.

Smallwood, E. Mary. "The Legislation of Hadrian and Antoninus Pius against Circumcision", *Latomus*, 18 (1959), pp. 334–347.

Smallwood, E. Mary. "Addendum," *Latomus*, 20 (1961), pp. 93–96.

Smallwood, E. Mary. *The Jews under Roman Rule: From Pompey to Diocletian*, pp. 464–473. Leiden, 1976.

4. Rabbinic Sources: *Agada*

Genesis Rabba, Ch. XLVI, Soncino trans., pp. 389–398.

Mishna Shabbat, Ch. 19.

5. Medieval Jewish material, non-halachic. Anti-Christian literature:

Isaac ben Yedaiah, *Commentary on Aggada, Numbers Rabba*, Ch. 12, 8.

Sefer Nizzahon Vetus, Sections 12, 13, and 224, in D. Berger, *The Jewish Christian Debate in the High Middle Ages.* Philadelphia, 1979.

CIRCUMCISION AND JEWISH LAW

I.   Sources

Babylonian Talmud, Kiddushin 29a, Soncino trans., pp. 137–138.

Babylonian Talmud, Shabbat, Ch. 19, ff. 130a–137b.

"Divre Gerut: Guidelines Concerning Proselytism," pamphlet, CCAR. New York, 1983.

Goldin, Hyman. *Hamadrikh, The Rabbis' Guide,* Chapter IV, Laws Concerning Circumcision, pp. 27–32. New York, 1965.

Jacobs, Walter, ed. *American Reform Responsa.* Responsa numbers 54–71, pp. 149–242. New York, 1983.

Maimonides, Moses. *Yad HaHazaka, Hilchot Mila,* various English translations.

"Report of the Committee on Patrilineal Descent on the Status of Children of Mixed Marriages," adopted by the CCAR. New York, 1983.

"Statement of MARAM: CCAR Report on Patrilineal Descent," Israel Council of Progressive Rabbis. Jerusalem, Israel.

II.   Scholarly Literature

Edelheit, Joseph. "Children of Mixed Marriages: A Non-Lineal Approach." *Journal of Reform Judaism,* (Winter, 1983), pp. 34–42.

Ellenson, David. "Accommodation, Resistance, and the Halakhic Process: A Case Study of Two Responsa by Rabbi Marcus Horovitz." In *Jewish Civilization: Essays and Studies in Honor of the 100th Birthday of Mordecai Kaplan,* ed. Ronald Brauner, pp. 83–100. Philadelphia, 1985.

Ellenson, David. "The Development of Orthodox Attitudes to Conversion in the Modern Period." *Conservative Judaism,* Vol. XXXVI:4, pp. 57–73.

Ellenson, David. "Rabbi Z. H. Kalischer and a Halachic Approach to Conversion." *Journal of Reform Judaism,* (Summer, 1981), pp. 50–57.

Ellenson, David. "Representative Orthodox Responsa on Conversion and Intermarriage in the Contemporary Era." *Jewish Social Studies,* (Summer-Fall, 1985), pp. 209–220.

Levine, Robert N., and Ellenson, David. "Jewish Tradition, Contemporary Sensibilities, and Halacha: A Responsum by Rabbi David Zvi Hoffmann." *Journal of Reform Judaism,* (Winter, 1983), pp. 49–56.

COVENANT

Baeck, Leo. *The Essence of Judaism.* New York, 1948.

Borowitz, Eugene. *Choices in Modern Jewish Thought,* pp. 256–289. New York, 1983.

Borowitz, Eugene. "Covenant Theology." *Worldview* (March, 1973), pp. 21–27.

Borowitz, Eugene. *Liberal Judaism,* Part I, Chs. 1,3,7; Part III, Ch. 6; Part IV, Chs. 5,6. New York, 1984.

Buber, Martin. *I and The World.* New York, 1948.

Buber, Martin. *I and Thou.* New York, 1957.

Kaplan, Mordecai. *Judaism as a Civilization.* New York, 1957.

Polish, David. "Covenant-Jewish Universalism and Particularism." *Judaism,* Vol. 34, No. 3, (Summer, 1985), pp. 284–299.

JEWISH IDENTITY, SOCIOLOGY AND DEMOGRAPHICS

Borowitz, Eugene. *The Masks Jews Wear,* Chs. 2,10,11,12. Port Washington, 1980, second edition.

Hertzberg, Authur. "Jewish Identity." *Encyclopaedia Judaica,* Jerusalem, Israel, 1971.

Hochbaum, Jerry. "Who is a Jew: A Sociological Perspective." *Tradition,* (Spring-Summer, 1973), pp. 35–41.

Ellenson, David. "The New Ethnicity, Religious Survival, and Jewish Identity: The Judaisms of our Newest Members." *Journal of Reform Judaism,* (Spring, 1979), pp. 47–60.

Vogel, Manfred H. "Some Reflections on the Question of Jewish Identity." *Journal of Reform Judaism,* (Winter, 1983), pp. 1–13.

Sklare, Marshall and Greenbaum, Joseph. *Jewish Identity on the Suburban Frontier.* New York, 1967; Chicago, 1979, second ed.

MEDICAL SOURCES

Beaton, J. et al. 1976. Circumcision complication reaction to treatment of local hemorrhage with topical epinephrine in high concentration. *Clin Pediatr* 17:285-6.

Boczko, S. and Freed, S. 1979. Penile carinoma in circumcised males. *NY State J Med* 79(12):1903-4.

Dixon, S.D. et al. 1984. Behavioral effects of circumcision with and without anesthesia. *J Dev Behav Pediatr* 5(5):246-50.

Fink, Aaron, J., M.D. 1988. *Circumcision: A Parent's Decision For Life.* Mountain View, California.

Gibbons, M.B. 1984. Circumcision. The controversey continues. *Pediatr Nurs* 10(2):103-9.

Grossman, E. and Posner, N.A. 1981. Surgical circumcision of neonates: a history of its development. *Obstet Gynecol* 58(2):241-6.

Herzog, L.W. and Alvarez, S.R. 1986. The frequency of foreskin problems in uncircumcised children. *Am J Dis Child* 140(3):254-6.

Holve, R.L. 1983. Regional anesthesia during newborn circumcision. *Clin Pediatr.* 22(12):813-8.

Kaplan, G.W. 1983. Complications of circumcision. *Urol Clin North Amer* 10(3):543-9.

Kirya, C. and Werthmann, M.W. 1978. Neonatal circumcision and penile dorsal nerve block: a painless procedure. *J Pediatr* 92(6):998-1000.

Metcalf, T. 1988. Do you favor . . . routine neonatal circumcision? No. *Postgrad Med* 84(5):9-108.

Mor, A. et al. 1987. Tachycardia and heart failure after ritual circumcision. Arch Dis Child 62(1):80-1.

Parker, S.W. et al. 1983. Circumcision and sexuality transmitted disease.*Med J Aust* 2(6):288-90.

Rawlins, D.J. et al. 1980. The effect of circumcision on transcutaneous PO_2 in term infants. *Am J Dis Child* 134(7):676-8.

Redman, J.F. 1988. Rare penile anomalies presenting with complications of circumcision. *Urology* 32(2):130-2.

Roberts, J.A. 1986. Does circumcision prevent urinary tract infection. *J Urol* 135(5):911-2.

Slaby, A.R. and Drizd, T. 1985. Circumcision in the United States. *Am J Public Health* 75(8):878–880.

Thompson, H.C. et al. 1975. Report of the Ad Hoc Task Force on Circumcision. *Pediatrics* 56(4):610–1.

Wallerstein, E. 1980. *Circumcision: An American Health Fallacy.* New York: Springer.

Wallerstein, E. 1985. Circumcision. The uniquely American medical enigma. *Urol Clin North Am* 12(1):123–32.

Waszak, S.J. 1978. The historic significance of circumcision. *Obstet Gynecol* 51(4):499–501.

Wiswell, T. E. 1988. Do you favor . . . routine neonatal circumcision? Yes. *Postgrad Med* 84(5):98–104.

Weiss, Gerald N., M.D. 1985. Neonatal Circumcision. *Southern Medical Journal* 78(10):1198–1200.

Williamson, P.S. and Williamson, M.L. 1983. Physiologic stress reduction by a local anesthetic during newborn circumcision. *Pediatrics* 71(1):36–4.

Wiswell, T.E. et al. 1985. Decreased incidence of urinary tract infections in circumcised male infants. *Pediatrics* 75(5):901–3.

Wiswell, T.E. and Roscelli, J.D. 1986. Cooroborative evidence for the decreased incidence of urinary tract infections in circumcised female infants. *Pediatrics* 78(1):96–9.

PSYCHOLOGY, ANTHROPOLOGY, MYTHOLOGY

Berent, Irving, M.D. "Original Sin: 'I Didn't Mean to Hurt You, Mother'—A Basic Fantasy Epitomized by a Male Homosexual." *Journal of the American Psychoanalytic Association,* Vol. 21, No. 2, (1973), pp. 262–284.

Bolands, Robert P., M.D. "Ritualistic Surgery—Circumcision and Tonsillectomy." *The New England Journal of Medicine,* Vol. 280, No. 11, (March 13, 1969), pp. 591–596, and responses, Vol. 280, pp. 1076–77, Vol. 281, pp. 621–22, Vol. 292, p. 538.

Campbell, Joseph P. *The Hero with a Thousand Faces,* New York, 1949.

Cansever, Gocke. "Psychological effects of Circumcision." *British Journal of Medical Psychology,* Vol. 38, No. 4, (1965), pp. 321–331.

A series of short articles on circumcision in *Sh'ma*, 12/227, (February 5, 1982), pp. 49–55.

Freud, Sigmund. *Moses and Monotheism*. New York, 1955.

Hazaz, H. "The Bridegroom of Blood." In *Yisroel: the First Jewish Omnibus*, revised ed. Edited by J. Leftwich. Translated by I. M. Lask. New York, 1963.

Malev, Milton, M.D. "The Jewish Orthodox Circumcision Ceremony." *Journal of the American Psychoanalytic Association*, Vol. 21, No. 2, (1973), pp. 262–284.

Ozturk, Orhan M. "Ritual Circumcision and Castration Anxiety." *Psychiatry*, Vol. 36, (February, 1973), pp. 49–60.

Schlossman, Howard H., M.D. "Circumcision as Defense: A Study in Psychoanalysis and Religion." *Psychoanalytic Quarterly*, Vol. 35, (1965), pp. 340–356.

Weiss, Charles. "A Worldwide Survey of the Current Practice of Milah (Ritual Circumcision)." *Jewish Social Studies* (Ritual Circumcision)." *Jewish Social Studies*, Vol. 24 (1962), pp. 30–48.

Wrana, Phoebe. "HISTORICAL REVIEW: Circumcision." *Archive of Pediatrics*, Vol. 56, (1938), pp. 385–392.

REFORM JUDAISM

Blau, Joseph L. *Reform Judaism: A Historical Perspective*. New York, 1973.

Borowitz, Eugene. *Reform Judaism Today*. Vols. 1-3. New York, 1978.

Meyer, Michael A. *Response to Modernity: A History of the Reform Movement in Judaism*. New York, 1988.

Plaut, W. Gunther. *The Growth of Reform Judaism*. New York, 1965.

Plaut, W. Gunther. *The Rise of Reform Judaism*. New York, 1963.

Philipson, David. *The Reform Movement in Judaism*. New York, 1967, second edition.

Index